WHY THINGS ARE GOING TO GET

WORSE

AND WHY WE SHOULD BE GLAD

An Inquiry into Wealth, Work and Values

Michael Roscoe

WHY THINGS ARE GOING TO GET

WORSE

AND WHY WE SHOULD BE GLAD

An Inquiry into Wealth, Work and Values

Michael Roscoe

WORLD
CHANGING

Why things are going to get worse...
and why we should be glad
First published in 2014 by
New Internationalist Publications Ltd
The Old Music Hall
106-108 Cowley Road
Oxford OX4 1JE, UK
newint.org

© Michael Roscoe

Aberdeenshire Library Service	
4003145	
Askews & Holts	21-Nov-2016
330.905	£9.99

Design: Ian Nixon
Imprint editor: Chris Brazier
All illustrations are by the author

Printed by T J International Limited, Cornwall, UK
who hold environmental accreditation ISO 14001.

British Library Cataloguing-in-Publication Data
A catalogue record for this book is available from the British Library.

ISBN 978-1-78026-176-8
Library of Congress Cataloging-in-Publication Data
A catalog record for this book is available
from the Library of Congress.

Contents

Preface

This book came about because I wanted to explain to my children why things were getting tougher, why it was that I'd been made redundant for the third time and was having trouble finding work; why a lot of the things we'd taken for granted in our lives would no longer be affordable.

I'd been thinking for some time about the tendency for technology to kill jobs (including mine, after 30 years in journalism) and where this trend might lead, as populations continue to grow. I'd also been thinking about the conflicting needs of the economy and the environment – how our economic system depends on growth, but that same growth is bad for the earth.

It seemed obvious that, sooner or later, we would have to confront these dilemmas and change the way we lived. But it was equally obvious that we weren't going to give up our easy lifestyles, not voluntarily anyway. We are only human, after all.

And then one day I was reading a United Nations report about this very subject – an attempt to resolve the growth-versus-environment issue – when I saw a chart that, according to the authors, showed how world growth had begun to 'decouple' from natural-resource depletion. The authors thought this a hopeful sign, though they couldn't explain why it was happening.

The real reason for this apparent decoupling seemed clear to me however, because it indicated something I'd been expecting, and unfortunately it wasn't the hopeful sign the report's authors had been looking for. What it was showing, I reckoned, was the failure of the economic system that had made the West wealthy.

In this book I investigate the reasons for this failure and try to explain what's really gone wrong with the global economy, why we haven't seen the worst yet, and why, despite all the hardship and tough years to come, we should be glad that the boom times are over and we are forced to confront the real issues – issues that were bound to blow up anyway, one way or another.

Introduction

In the last few years, following the financial crash of 2008, economic problems have taken over from terrorism and war as the biggest threat to our Western way of life. For the first time in over half a century, the majority of Europeans and North Americans are getting poorer – not just a bit of belt-tightening due to a cyclical recession, but a real decline in earnings. And it's going to get worse, especially in Europe.

Much has been said about the financial crash, the folly and greed of bankers, sub-prime loans and the Eurozone crisis, but these are all symptoms rather than causes, and very little has been said about the causes. It's almost as if most economists and politicians have lost sight of certain fundamental truths about life, as if these truths fly below everyone's radar – too simple and too obvious to register in the sophisticated, high-tech world in which we live.

By the end of the 20th century we had become accustomed to the idea that the world was on a continuous path to ever-greater prosperity and, even though it might make a few dips along the way, and although not everyone might be very far along it yet, the path would keep rising. Anyone who questioned how long it could do so was considered a bit cranky, dismissed as an eco-warrior or tree-hugger.

The general consensus was that free-market capitalism was the best system to ensure this prosperity, that it would always provide jobs for those willing to work and that economic growth was not only a necessary part of the system, but desirable in itself. This system had gradually taken over the world, was considered superior to other economic systems because it appeared to work where others had failed – it ruled by default. And, as long as it appeared to work, even supposedly communist governments such as China's seemed happy to embrace it.

But free-market capitalism has one slight problem in its purest form – the form we've been heading towards for some decades now. Like any greedy animal, human or otherwise, its need for continuous growth will inevitably lead to its own destruction. It must literally consume itself to death, not just because it will eventually run out of resources – that is a potential problem, certainly – but before that happens there is another major failing that will kill the growth, and therefore kill the system. The process has already begun.

This self-destructive tendency of free-market capitalism just happens to be our best hope regarding the long-term survival of civilization, but in the meantime we will have to endure a period of considerable hardship, because the inevitable result of the system's failure is mass unemployment.

Why should free-market capitalism lead to mass unemployment? Because the growth on which the system depends is reliant on the ever-increasing productivity of industry, a process that's been going on for centuries and which new technology seems capable of delivering, and even accelerating, for the foreseeable future.

In the past, workers who lost their jobs in agriculture found work in the new manufacturing industries and, when these industries in turn shed workers, as they have been doing over the last 30 years or more, jobs were created in the booming service sector. Not always enough jobs, perhaps, but in the post-War boom the economies of the West had become wealthy enough to ensure that the unemployed received a payment while they looked for other work, successfully or otherwise.

Now, however, we appear to have arrived at that point where ever-increasing productivity reaches its logical conclusion: there is no longer enough work to go round. The service sector cannot create more jobs, because services are dependent on the wealth created by manufacturing, which itself is dependent on the natural wealth of the earth. And the public sector can no longer take up the slack because governments have overburdened themselves with debt – debt that will kill any prospect of real growth for many years to come, while making us all poorer in the process, as the inevitable inflation takes hold.

The seeds for this self-destruction of the system were sown in 1971, when the US government severed the link between the dollar and gold, but the effect of this move was masked for three decades by the steady growth in Western economies, fuelled by international oil money and the US-led boom in technology – the same technology that now plays a major part in the system's demise. The final growth spurt came as the 20th century neared its end, powered this time by the huge expansion of the financial sector, a non-productive 'industry' that feeds off the accumulated wealth of real industry, like a giant parasite whose life-blood is credit.

Apart from those directly affected, hardly anyone seemed worried about the decline of jobs in the wealth-creating sectors of the economy. Some even thought we'd entered a post-industrial age where wealth could be conjured out of nothing. And as long as the good times were rolling, who cared? So what if the boom times of the last decades were fuelled by debt, or if finance had ballooned into a major sector of the economy by trading in nothing more than bets and promises? Hardly anyone questioned what gave money its value and how this value could be assured when there was no longer anything to measure it against; when, in fact, as with the financial sector as a whole, the value of money since 1971 has been based on nothing more than trust.

But as we are about to discover, trust and promises can be broken – *will* be broken. The system itself is broken, and in this book I endeavor to explain why, even to show why in graphic form.

It was thanks to graphs – and to one chart in particular – that the truth about wealth and values first hit me, enabled me to see clearly what had until then been only a vague idea in the back of my mind. So I use charts to illustrate my reasoning, to cut through the fog of economic jargon and show what's going on at ground level, where, whatever great heights technology might reach, the foundations of the economy still rest.

If there is one fundamental truth that sums up the problem, it is this: real wealth creation requires real work, and real work must involve the transformation of nature's raw materials into something of value to us humans. There is no other way to create wealth. I have a feeling that, beneath all the financial wizardry and the complexity of the global marketplace, this simple truth has been lost.

In the opening chapters I explain in more detail the points touched on above, and in subsequent chapters I delve more deeply into the reasons why we find ourselves at this critical stage in the development of civilization. My aim is to give convincing arguments as to why we must remodel our economic system to fit the reality of today's world, or be prepared to suffer the consequences as the whole thing collapses around us. The financial crash of 2008 should be seen as a warning; a tremor in the foundations of the free-market system. The real earthquake is still to come.

Part One

Why Things Are Bad

1 Three charts

Summary of the problems

The fundamental problems affecting the global economy – and in particular the most developed regions of the world – can be summarized in three charts. Figure 1 shows how the world has grown beyond its means, or to put it another way, why we're not as wealthy as we thought we were. It shows how somewhere in the region of a third of the world's supposed wealth doesn't actually exist, because a substantial part of the recent growth in the global economy was founded on nothing more solid than the credit bubble – a bubble that, despite a partial deflation in 2008, has resumed its growth, fuelled now by public debt rather than private debt.

The following chapters go into more detail, but for now I'll explain this chart in simple terms: real wealth must come initially from the earth, before having value added by human ideas and labor, so there should be a close correlation between the amount of wealth in the world and the quantity of raw materials extracted from the earth. The lines on the graph show this link clearly until the 1970s, after which time the line representing the economy (wealth measured in terms of Gross Domestic Product, or GDP) begins to rise more quickly than the line representing mineral extraction.

This is because the economy is being inflated by credit, and most of this credit has been created artificially by banks. The additional wealth that is supposedly boosting the economy doesn't really exist, which means that currencies have become overvalued in relation to minerals. This in turn means there will have to be a correction at some point, because ultimately the only thing giving money its value is its relationship to the real wealth that it supposedly represents. We have effectively borrowed this growth from the future and, one way or another, we will have to pay it back.[1]

Figure 2 shows how technology, combined with the element of competition inherent in the free-market system, has improved productivity to the point where manufacturing no longer creates

Figure 1

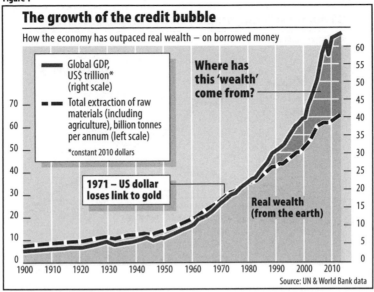

enough jobs – and never will, unless we make radical changes to the system.

Although this chart draws on US data, the trend is the same throughout the developed world – and even in the developing world, though the process might be less advanced in other nations.

Figure 3 shows how the wealth that *does* exist is no longer being spread around enough; how wealth is becoming more concentrated in the hands of those who are already wealthy.

We see how earnings in the US and Europe became more evenly distributed from the 1950s to the late 1970s, after which point the richest 1% increased their share of total earnings from less than 10% to over 20%, in the US at least. In Europe the trend is the same, though the inequality is less pronounced (this is my own estimated average for what is now the European Union, using available data). This inequality is linked to the first two charts because much of this wealth has been 'made' in the booming financial sector, and before that – before it ended up in bank accounts and investment funds – it came from the profits of

15

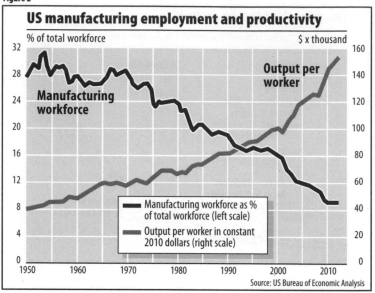

Figure 2

US manufacturing employment and productivity

large corporations that benefited from the increasing productivity of industry. Higher output with fewer workers means more profit for executives and shareholders. And we should bear in mind that this wealth came originally from natural resources, more than half of it in the form of crude oil, as I will demonstrate in Chapter 8.

The economy – which is really just the name we give to the wealth-creation process – might seem like a very complex system these days, but it still follows a simple pattern: natural wealth is taken from the earth, has value added by industrial activity, and is then distributed, via those industrial workers, throughout society. Traditionally, this wealth was spread around in the form of payment for goods and services, which created other jobs, which in turn led to more demand for industry, feeding a virtuous cycle of economic growth.

But lately something has gone wrong with the system: real jobs are in decline, not as much wealth is being spread around, and the value of that wealth, or at least of money, has been eroded by the boom in credit.

Figure 3

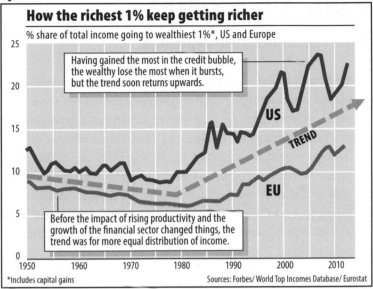

How the richest 1% keep getting richer

% share of total income going to wealthiest 1%*, US and Europe

Having gained the most in the credit bubble, the wealthy lose the most when it bursts, but the trend soon returns upwards.

US

TREND

EU

Before the impact of rising productivity and the growth of the financial sector changed things, the trend was for more equal distribution of income.

*Includes capital gains

Sources: Forbes/ World Top Incomes Database/ Eurostat

This failure of the system is linked to the ever-diminishing proportion of real industry relative to the financial sector. Banks accumulate more wealth than is needed for investment by productive industry and therefore use it to profit from unproductive investment, resulting in more debt creation and less job creation.

So the causes of the economic sickness we are now suffering from are actually quite easy to diagnose, once we cut through all the fat and jargon to reach the heart of the problem. In the following chapters I expand on these three points to show how they relate to every aspect of the economy and how they affect us all, from the humblest laborer to the billionaire chief of a global conglomerate.

1 A consideration is made here for fuel-efficiency gains and the recycling of resources, particularly metals, which can result in more wealth being created from a given unit of raw material. However, although metal recycling now accounts for approximately half of all metals used in industry, the world total of around 280 million tons per annum represents less than half a per cent of total natural resource use by volume, taking into account all fossil-fuel extraction and agricultural produce. The bulk of mineral use consists of low-value construction materials, and until very recently these were rarely recycled. I show the effect of these factors later on in Figure 15.

2 What is wealth?

Basic economics; GDP explained

To understand what has really gone wrong with the economies of the developed world, it might help if we give some thought to the concept of wealth. Riches, abundance, prosperity, even just a general feeling of well-being or happiness: all these can be thought of as wealth.

By some measures (for example, the World Bank's 2006 report, *Where is the Wealth of Nations?*) wealth includes 'intangible capital', as well as the stuff we might normally think of as wealth, such as property and money. By 'intangible capital' the World Bank means human potential, as defined by the quality of education and the political and social institutions of the nation in question.

These are difficult things to measure of course, so economists and governments calculate the wealth of nations in terms of Gross Domestic Product, or GDP, which is an approximation of the final output, in money terms, of all economic activity. GDP has become a global standard as an indication of a nation's wealth, primarily because it's the only measure widely available and, when adjusted for the purchasing power of different currencies, allows for a useful comparison between countries.

So the GDP figure has become important as an indicator of the health of a nation, as well as its wealth – if the figure rises, we have a growing economy, which governments and economists think is good; and if it falls, we have a recession, which is bad.

Things are not quite so clear-cut as this might suggest, however. For a start, GDP figures are not a very good indicator of a nation's real wealth, as I will explain in Chapter 4. In addition, growth cannot go on forever, because before very long, almost certainly during this century, we will start to run out of resources.

Rich Mother Earth

Real wealth comes from the earth. It always has done and, as long as there are human beings living on this planet, it always will. The problem is that, at some point in recent history, we lost sight of this fact. We came to believe, for example, that the financial sector of the economy created wealth, when all it has ever done is to shift wealth around. It creates money, but that is an entirely different thing. In fact, creating money is part of the problem.

From a time before the human race had developed enough to have anything resembling an economy, and indeed right up to the middle of the last century, most people would have understood that real wealth had to come from the earth. What would we have, if we had not grown the crops, reared the animals, caught the fish, chopped down trees, dug minerals and fuel from the earth? Nothing.

Well, that's not quite true, of course. We'd have a pristine natural environment, so in that respect we'd have everything, but we'd still be living in caves and eating grubs. Looking at this in purely economic terms, we'd have no economy, no 'assets', no wealth in the accepted sense.

We are products of the earth. We dug raw materials from the earth and, using human ingenuity and labor, we added value to those materials – we turned the earth's natural wealth into something useful. Through industry, we turned crops into food, reared livestock on the soil's bounty, turned animal skins, flax plants and cotton into clothing. We built houses and factories from timber and stone and clay, learned how to make cement from limestone, how to make steel from iron ore. We invented machines that made it possible to make more things more easily, using coal, and later oil, as fuel. And all of this came from the earth, to be enriched by human ideas and hard work.

A simple equation:

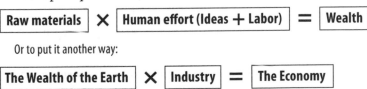

Raw materials × Human effort (Ideas + Labor) = Wealth

Or to put it another way:

The Wealth of the Earth × Industry = The Economy

I don't mean to imply that this is a mathematical or scientific equation; the values are not absolute, rather they are concepts with variable optimum inputs. The main point is that neither the raw materials nor the labor have what we would call 'value' by themselves. The gold or iron-ore buried in the earth, the undisturbed soil or the virgin forest: this natural wealth only acquires its value, to us humans at least, when we apply human labor and turn it into something useful. And the labor itself is useless without the natural resources to work with.

So we see that no wealth can be created without both materials and human effort, and this has important implications for the future, as technology makes industry ever more productive.

Whichever way we look at it, there is no economy until we extract the raw materials from the earth, and this would have been perfectly clear to anyone who cared to give it some thought, until economics started to get more complicated, say around 50 years ago. At this point some of the more obvious truths began to get submerged beneath a rising tide of prosperity, and beneath the corresponding rise of the service sector, which now employs over three-quarters of the workforce in many Western countries, yet creates no real wealth.

This brings us back to one of the fundamental problems affecting the major economies of the developed world. In order to understand this problem fully we must first endure a brief lesson in simple economics.

Back to basics

In traditional economic teaching, the economy is divided into three sectors: Primary, Secondary and Tertiary.

The Primary Sector is concerned with the extraction or harvesting of natural resources and includes agriculture, forestry, fishing, mining and oil-drilling.

The Secondary Sector is concerned with turning these raw materials into something useful. This means industry – processing, manufacturing, construction.

The Tertiary Sector is everything else, and is usually referred to as the service sector. It includes retail, transport, finance, marketing, healthcare, leisure and entertainment.

Sometimes these days a fourth sector is added to cover knowledge-based intellectual services and government activities, but this is an unnecessary complication. To create a new category for them is to miss the main point of the original three-sector classification:

1) Take the natural wealth from the earth.
2) Use human ideas and labor to turn that wealth into something more useful, thus adding value and producing 'tangible' wealth.
3) Distribute that wealth amongst the population through payments for services, thus creating a wider economy.

Certainly there is a lot of crossover between sectors: industries such as publishing and information technology, for example, have large elements of manufacturing as well as services, and some big oil companies straddle all three sectors. But the main point still stands: are the majority of workers productive or non-productive? Or, to put it another way, do they work mostly out on the land or in factories, or do they work in shops and offices? It used to be classified by clothing – blue-collar or white-collar – but that distinction has faded with time, and with the T-shirts and jeans of Silicon Valley.

This is all very simplified of course – a significant proportion of service workers drive trucks and buses and trains, for example. Another distinction can be made between private and public ownership. In the US and Europe these days, most direct government employment is limited to the service sector, in areas such as social welfare, health, education, defense and law enforcement. In many other countries the state owns major oil companies, aircraft manufacturers and so on, in which case it is involved in productive wealth creation. But the type of ownership doesn't affect the points I'm trying to make.

As an economy develops, more raw materials are taken from the earth, more crops are grown and more goods are produced, resulting in overall growth in the economy and continued

Figure 4

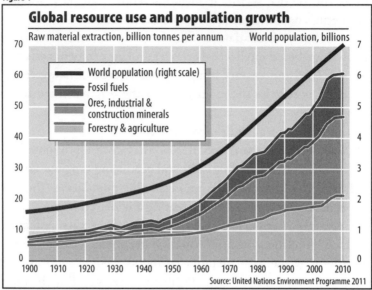

Global resource use and population growth

Raw material extraction, billion tonnes per annum · · · World population, billions

- World population (right scale)
- Fossil fuels
- Ores, industrial & construction minerals
- Forestry & agriculture

Source: United Nations Environment Programme 2011

expansion of the workforce. Figure 4 shows how the world's population grew in the 20th century, and how that growth was supported by the extraction and harvesting of the earth's natural wealth.

As the population grows, demand for goods increases, more jobs are created and the cycle feeds itself. As Henry Ford understood when he raised wages so that his employees could buy Ford cars, the workers are also the consumers.

A developing economy moves from reliance on the Primary Sector, through an expanded Secondary Sector until eventually the majority of its workforce is engaged in the Tertiary Sector.

This transition occurs because human ingenuity, when applied to the needs of these developing industries, leads to increased mechanization, which brings productivity gains in the first two sectors. The wealth of an industrial society accumulates over time, and this wealth supports the growth in services.

Figure 5 illustrates the development of the US economy from 1850 to the present day. We can see the trend away from working on the land, the rise and fall of factory work (with a boost during

Figure 5

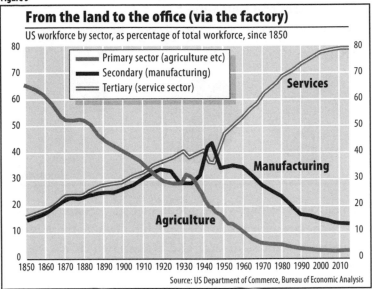

From the land to the office (via the factory)

US workforce by sector, as percentage of total workforce, since 1850

- Primary sector (agriculture etc)
- Secondary (manufacturing)
- Tertiary (service sector)

Services

Manufacturing

Agriculture

Source: US Department of Commerce, Bureau of Economic Analysis

the Second World War) and the eventual domination of the service sector. This can also be read as a move away from the wealth-creating sectors to the wealth-distributing sector. We see also how the trend begins to flatten out as the development cycle reaches its limits, or even overshoots its limits, as I will explain later.

I use the US as an example of a developed economy because of its size and the variety of its industry, and also because it provides reliable historic data, but the pattern for countries such as Britain and France is similar. We can see the same pattern in a different way by looking at three countries at different stages of development in 2010, as shown in Figure 6.

So most developed countries these days rely overwhelmingly on the service sector for the bulk of their economic activity, and especially for employment. There are a few exceptions to this rule, however. Canada and Australia, for example, have large mineral-extracting industries, and the German economy still has a substantial manufacturing base. And it just so happens that these three countries were less affected by the crash of 2008, because they earn more real wealth.

Figure 6

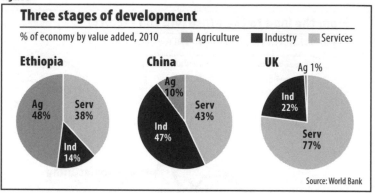

Germany exports high-value goods such as cars and machine tools to the booming economies of China (where there is new wealth from manufacturing) and Russia (which has wealth from oil and gas).

I would suggest, therefore, that the economic problems affecting most developed nations today are primarily a result of the decline in the primary and secondary sectors relative to their overall economies. Too much reliance has been placed on the service sector for employment, and, although during the boom years the service sector created millions of well-paid jobs, the wealth still had to be created originally by the primary and secondary sectors. We lost sight of this fact.

We came to believe that the financial services 'industry', for example, created wealth, when all banks really do is take wealth that has already been created in the real economy, much of which is now held in large investment funds (in other words, other people's savings and pensions), and try to profit by lending that money, or by borrowing more money against it (leveraging) and speculating in things like derivatives, in the hope of making still more money. But this whole business, which according to GDP figures adds around five trillion dollars a year to the global economy, does not actually create a penny in real wealth. The nature of derivatives, which form the bulk of financial trading these days, is such that when one trader gains, someone else must lose. This is comparable to the more obvious forms of gambling, only worse, because the loser might not be another gambler, but rather an innocent investor, or pretty much anyone (more on this in later chapters). Does the betting shop or the casino create wealth? Of course not.

So that five trillion dollars wasn't really new wealth at all – it was a combination of wealth that already existed and credit that had been artificially created by leverage. A lot of that existing wealth will have crossed international boundaries, so in that respect nations such as Britain and Switzerland gain, but, from a global perspective, financial services don't create wealth. What they create is debt.

As the proportion of actual wealth creation in the economy declines relative to wealth that has accumulated from past industry, as it inevitably must do, the dynamics of the global economy change with it. The influence of the financial sector grows at the expense of the productive sector, with unfortunate consequences for the majority of the world's population.

Yes, banks provide a useful service to industry, and have done for thousands of years, but since the 1970s, after money lost its link to gold, the bulk of banking activity has been increasingly detrimental to the economy. If it weren't for the rapid growth of the financial sector, the last recession would not have happened – or at least it would have been a lot less severe, and the Eurozone wouldn't be in the mess it's in now. The credit bubble gave us artificial growth, and now we must return to reality. The value of the dollar, and currencies generally, has been falling, and will have to keep falling until the amount of supposed wealth in the world corresponds to the amount of real wealth that's been created. This has serious implications for the global economy over the next decade or two, as the long-term trend for falling prices, as shown in Figure 7, goes into reverse.

I'll return to the issue of rising prices later, but first I want to think a bit more about the balance between the productive and non-productive sectors.

Figure 7

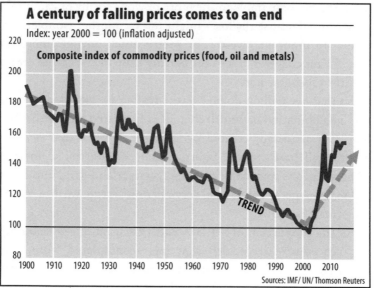

A century of falling prices comes to an end

Index: year 2000 = 100 (inflation adjusted)

Composite index of commodity prices (food, oil and metals)

TREND

Sources: IMF/ UN/ Thomson Reuters

Different kinds of wealth

Perhaps I should clarify this point about wealth creation, because although in some respects it might seem obvious, I have a feeling that some politicians and economists might disagree with me when I suggest that what amounts to almost 80% of the British economy, according to GDP figures, doesn't create any wealth. Is it really possible that 20% of the workforce – around 10% of the population – is supporting the rest of us?

Well, no, it isn't. For one thing, Britain imports wealth from other nations via the City of London, and for another thing, as I've already mentioned, GDP figures give the wrong picture.

Let's think for a minute what service jobs involve. Whether you're a shop assistant, a hairdresser, a bus driver, a waiter, a banker, a marketing manager, you aren't really *creating* wealth. All you are doing is taking money from your customers in exchange for a particular service. Even if you're a doctor or a lawyer, a police officer or a judge, the same principle applies –

you are paid for providing a service. That service enriches the economy, certainly.

A teacher, for example, provides an invaluable service. Perhaps more than any other worker, a teacher adds a great deal of what I referred to earlier as 'intangible capital' to the economy, and therefore to the nation. But the reason we call it *intangible* capital is that teachers add a kind of value that we can't see or touch, and therefore can't really measure. The whole nation – business especially – benefits from a good education system, which is one reason why we shouldn't begrudge paying for it in taxes.

But it should be clear enough that, to pay those taxes, there must be some real wealth entering the economy. If everyone worked in education or the health service, or any other service, where would the wealth come from?

A more obvious example still is the army. For as long as there have been city states and other organized societies, there have been armies to protect them from attacks by 'barbarians' or rival armies. But armies had to be equipped and soldiers had to be fed, which meant either a raid on a neighboring state's gold supplies or a tax on landowners, or possibly both. One of the first forms of taxation was the demand by Persian emperors and other ancient rulers for a portion of the harvest to feed the army. And effectively, this still goes on today: the produce of the earth, and of industry, is still the source of all government revenue.

That isn't what the figures will tell you, of course. A breakdown of UK economic output as measured by GDP suggests that less than 1% of the nation's wealth comes from agriculture, 16% from manufacturing and over 30% from financial and associated services. Most of the rest comes from other services. So if Britain is a nation of shopkeepers and bankers, where does the real wealth come from?

Investment banking is totally dependent on large funds of accumulated wealth, all of which must have come from industrial activity of some kind. It's not easy to trace the source of private wealth, but there are enough clues around to give us a general picture. A lot of the money that finds its way into the City of London, for example, originates in Middle Eastern oil or Siberian gas fields.

In fact, as I will explain in more detail later in this book, more than half of all wealth in the world today has come from oil.

3 What happens to wealth?

The vanishing trillions

For most of the world's population, the accumulation of wealth is something that happens only to other people: rich people. Even the prospect of buying a modest home is way beyond reach for the vast majority of the global population. Day-to-day existence is the best that can be hoped for: another meal for the family, another week's rent paid to the landlord, another shirt for a child.

According to a United Nations report from 2006, half the world's adults had assets of less than $2,200, which meant the poorest 50% owned barely 1% of all wealth between them, while the richest 2% of adults owned over half the world's assets. The UN researchers estimated that total household wealth at the beginning of this century was in the region of $125 trillion. A more recent report by Credit Suisse gives a figure of $240 trillion for 2013, which would work out at over $50,000 per adult, if it were evenly distributed. The bank estimates that the richest 1% now own 46% of the world's wealth, and the latest data from the World Economic Forum (as of November 2013) puts this closer to 50%.

Figure 8 shows how wealth has accumulated over the last decade or so. [Credit Suisse actually gives a lower figure than the UN for 2000. These are only educated guesses, as actual figures aren't available; wealthy people, and Swiss banks, being understandably secretive about their accounts.] This chart, using Credit Suisse data, shows how the world's privately held wealth has almost doubled this century. If one thinks about it, this is an astonishing fact, assuming these figures are correct. How is it possible that the same amount of wealth has been created in one decade as was accumulated in all of past history?

The short answer: it isn't possible. Although the boom in China explains some of the rise, this increase in wealth is partly an illusion, linked to the related trends of rising credit (which

Figure 8

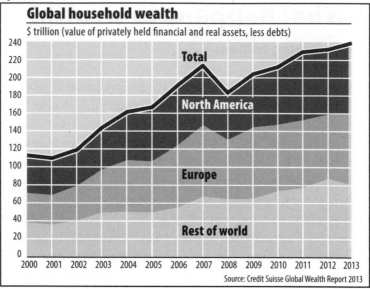

Global household wealth

$ trillion (value of privately held financial and real assets, less debts)

Total

North America

Europe

Rest of world

Source: Credit Suisse Global Wealth Report 2013

leads to higher asset prices) and devalued money (especially the US dollar). I will return to these themes in detail later in the book, but first we can still learn something useful from this chart, because although it might be misleading in some respects, in other ways it is accurate enough. For example, the chart shows how wealth is split roughly into thirds between North America, Europe and the rest of the world, which means of course that it's very unevenly distributed, as we might expect. The US, with 4% of global population, has 30% of all wealth and over 40% of all individuals with $50 million or more.

What we find, in other words, is that wealth is highly concentrated among relatively few very rich people, and, as I noted in the opening chapter, this inequality is increasing.

Figure 3 showed how the richest 1% were grabbing ever more of the world's wealth, leaving less for everyone else. Figure 9 shows the huge gains seen by the wealthiest 10% in Britain and the US, especially since 1980, compared to the rest of the population, whose incomes have actually fallen in recent years, to the point where most people are earning less, in real (inflation-

Figure 9

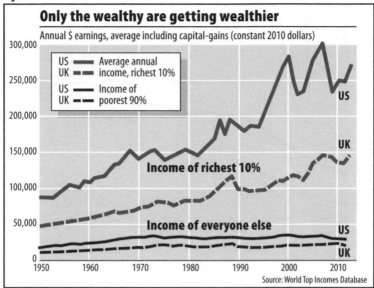

Only the wealthy are getting wealthier

Annual $ earnings, average including capital-gains (constant 2010 dollars)

US ━━ Average annual
UK ■ ■ ■ income, richest 10%

US ━━ Income of
UK ─ ─ poorest 90%

Income of richest 10%

Income of everyone else

US

UK

Source: World Top Incomes Database

adjusted) terms, than they did in the 1970s.

It isn't possible to get such accurate data for most countries but, although the equivalent figures for Europe might show less of a gap between the rich and everyone else (because Europe generally has a more even spread of wealth), the trend in most of the developed world is for declining wages in real terms, as Figure 10 shows.

This trend for declining earnings for the majority, while the rich get richer, coincides with the decline in manufacturing jobs that we saw in Figure 2. As the number of jobs in industry falls relative to output, the share of corporate profit that goes to owners and executives increases and the share that goes to the general population falls. Combine this with the rise of the financial sector, where a relatively small workforce – traders and fund managers and so on – earn large incomes, as can be seen in Figure 11, and we begin to see why income inequality, and especially wealth inequality, is increasing.

There are various ways of looking at the gap between the very wealthy and the rest of us, but they all show the same trend: the

Figure 10

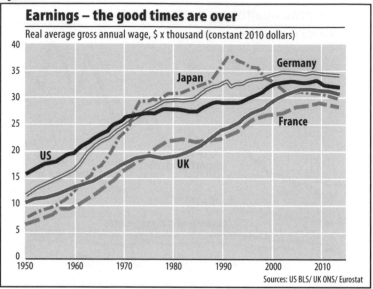

Earnings – the good times are over

Real average gross annual wage, $ x thousand (constant 2010 dollars)

Germany

Japan

France

US

UK

Sources: US BLS/ UK ONS/ Eurostat

rich are getting richer while the middle classes of the developed world get poorer and everyone else – the really poor – struggle along on next to nothing, as they always have done. Something has gone seriously wrong with the idea that free-market capitalism is the best way to spread wealth.

Yet in the relatively recent past, over the last half-century or so, a vast amount of wealth has been made in this world, all of it originating in the earth before being turned into something useful by industrial workers. So what's gone wrong with the system? How can so much of the earth's wealth, most of which comes from natural resources that can't really 'belong' to any one person – should surely belong equally to everyone – end up in the hands of so few?

To answer this question, we first need to distinguish between different types of wealth. For most of history the real wealth was in the land. In ancient civilizations, and much of Europe until quite recently, most land was claimed by the ruler of the state, or the Crown. Under the feudal system, the monarch could grant the rights to parcels of land to his barons, or lords, in return for their

Figure 11

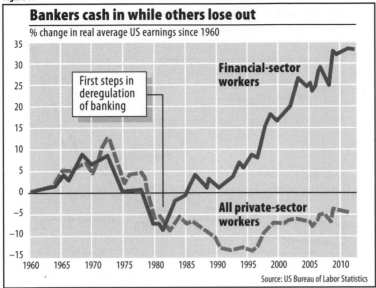

Bankers cash in while others lose out

% change in real average US earnings since 1960

First steps in deregulation of banking

Financial-sector workers

All private-sector workers

Source: US Bureau of Labor Statistics

military service. The lords, who became tenants-in-chief, could then sub-divide this land among their own favored knights, who could in turn sub-let to other lesser mortals, and so on. In this way, over centuries, the land ended up as estates in the hands of the aristocracy, who either farmed the land themselves or rented it to other farmers, either for money or a share of the crop – as in sharecropping, a form of land tenure common throughout much of the world.

So the old money – the wealth of the old aristocracy of Europe – came from ownership of agricultural land, and also, in the last two centuries, from land that became more valuable as it was gradually absorbed into the growing towns and cities. This wealth passed down the generations, though some of it went to the government as taxes. But although it caused much anger among the 'proletariat', or at least among those intellectuals and revolutionaries who took up the cause of the proletariat, the inherited wealth of the aristocracy wasn't that great compared to the new wealth that came after industrialization; the wealth of the capitalist owners of industry. Even the wealth of the

33

Figure 12

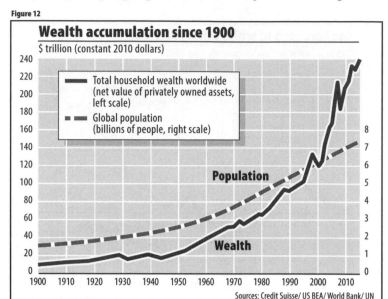

19th-century industrialists doesn't look all that significant when compared to recent levels of wealth accumulation, mainly because of inflation; a millionaire of 1850 had the status of a billionaire by today's standards. And, more to the point, there are far more very wealthy people around now.

Figure 12 shows an estimation of private wealth accumulation over the last century, based on the reports I've already mentioned, plus a few other sources as indicated. I've also plotted the world population. We can see how wealth has grown much more quickly than population, especially in the last two decades.

We can also see how the value of this accumulating wealth occasionally falls with the fortunes of stock markets and house prices; hence the blips around the times of the 1929 Wall Street crash and the crises of 1997 and 2008. But we also know that no real wealth was actually lost in these crashes; no buildings or gold bars were destroyed, nor bank-vaults full of cash burnt to ashes. The falls were numerical only, in the perceived values of companies and houses, which had been pushed beyond their true value by unrealistic expectations and the eagerness of banks to lend. Even when a bank fails, no real wealth is lost. As with the stock market, some people might lose money, but other people must have gained that money. In the case of company stock, the person who sells a share certificate when the price is high gains, while the buyer, if the price falls, loses.

If you have savings in a bank that fails and you're told that your money has somehow disappeared, the chances are that it went on a bad loan. But where did that money actually *go*? What happened to all the money lost in the crash of 2008?

Figures in the ether

Various estimates have been made of the 'cost' of the recent financial crisis. The International Monetary Fund (IMF) reckoned in 2009 that $12 trillion had been lost, while in 2012 the US Treasury Department gave a figure of $19 trillion. Either way, it's a huge amount of money. But what does it really mean? Where did that $19 trillion disappear to? Outer space?

All it really means is that the wealth of the world after the crash was valued at $19 trillion less than it was before the crash. But not one single penny coin was actually lost. All the real wealth – all the actual solid stuff like houses and factories and gold bars and even banknotes – still exists, exactly as it did before the crash. The losses are all a matter of figures in the ether, so, yes, in a way the money did end up in outer space. But, more to the point, it never really existed in the first place.

That $19 trillion was the credit bubble, or at least a part of it. In other words, the global financial system was responsible for creating $19 trillion out of nothing over the previous decade or so. In fact, according to my calculations regarding the difference between GDP figures and the real wealth of the global economy, as shown in my first chart, the credit bubble amounted to considerably more than $19 trillion. At its peak, the GDP figure for the world as a whole was overstating real economic output by over $20 trillion annually, and this situation had been going on for well over a decade, and is still going on now. The credit bubble hasn't really burst, it just deflated slightly.

I return to this problem in more detail later in the book, because I think this overestimation of real economic activity has serious consequences for us all and is the main reason that parts of the world, especially Europe, will have to adjust to a new economic reality. In these difficult times – times in which the majority of the population in the developed world will continue to experience declining income in real terms (adjusted for inflation) – we need to look again at certain values.

The boom times are over and they won't be coming back, and the main reason for this is the lack of real jobs, a shortage caused by the increasing productivity of industry, which in turn is linked to the growth of the financial sector, a sector of the economy that has no apparent interest in job creation but a very great interest in debt creation.

There has been a massive fraud committed by the banking sector generally, one in which the wealth that should belong to everyone has been taken by the rich. It wasn't a planned theft, and no particular person or organization is to blame; it's just the way things have worked out, a direct result of the free-market capitalist system, an inevitable consequence of the accumulation of ever more wealth in the hands of the few. It can't go on for much longer.

I don't mean that in a moral-outrage sense, though obviously I think it's a bad thing. I believe that there are practical reasons why this situation cannot continue for much longer. The dynamics of the economy have changed greatly over the past few decades, in a way never seen before. The proportion of genuine wealth creation relative to total wealth has been falling. The rise of the banking sector has resulted in the credit bubble, and although this might have deflated slightly during the crash of 2008, as long as central banks keep paying off one type of debt by creating another type of debt, the problem can only get worse.

This transition from an industrial society to a financial society – from one that produces real wealth to one that produces credit – is obviously unsustainable. The free-market capitalist system is rapidly approaching its inherent limits. For the last two centuries, the developed world has thrived on industrial growth but, for the last three decades, that real growth has been increasingly overshadowed by a financial system that depends on the creation of credit for profit, while at the same time relying on real industrial growth to generate enough wealth to pay those debts. We have become dependent on economic growth, but continuous economic growth is impossible.

4 Something out of nothing

An investigation into values

The creation of artificial wealth is bound to have a significant impact on the economy. By 'artificial wealth' I mean the creation of money by banks in the form of credit, as happened in a big way leading up to the 2008 financial crisis, or by governments in the form of 'quantitative easing', the process by which central banks buy government debt (bonds etc) from banks and other institutions with newly created money, as undertaken after the crisis.

One effect, as I've already tried to show, was to boost economic activity by as much as $20 trillion annually in the years leading up to the 2008 crash. In Figure 13 I've taken the information on real wealth creation – based on raw-material extraction, as shown in Figure 1[1] – and used it to plot a line representing my estimation of GDP without the credit bubble. This is simply the line that GDP would have followed if it had continued to grow at its long-term trend rate, which, allowing for efficiency improvements and a gradual reduction in the waste of resources, happens to correlate very closely with raw-material extraction. This is, of course, what one might expect, and follows the trend that my first chart showed for most of the previous century, until money lost its link to gold in 1971, after which time the financial sector of the economy began to expand quite rapidly.

The chart shows the build-up of this artificially created wealth: the loans that led to the inflation of asset prices, especially housing, which in turn contributed to the inflation of the credit bubble. By adding up the difference between the two lines for each year, I arrive at a figure that represents the bubble. This figure is in the region of $200 trillion, and at the time of writing (early 2014) the bubble still appears to be expanding.

$200 trillion seems a lot of money to have been created out of nothing, and I am inclined myself not to believe it. Although the method I used to reach this figure seems sound enough, the whole thing obviously requires careful investigation.

Figure 13

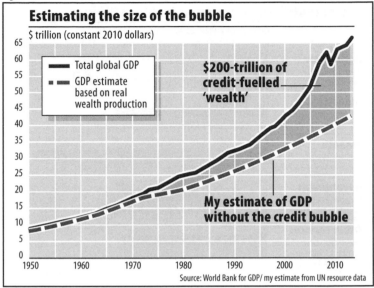

Estimating the size of the bubble

$ trillion (constant 2010 dollars)

Legend:
— Total global GDP
■ ■ GDP estimate based on real wealth production

$200-trillion of credit-fuelled 'wealth'

My estimate of GDP without the credit bubble

Source: World Bank for GDP/ my estimate from UN resource data

First, I think we should look more closely at GDP, which, as I mentioned earlier, is not an accurate reflection of real wealth creation. [When I talk about total world Gross Domestic Product, as I do here, I really mean the gross output of the global economy. The word 'domestic' no longer applies in the global sense, but I shall continue to refer to it as total world GDP, because it is arrived at by combining national GDP figures.]

GDP is theoretically a measure of annual industrial output, but it includes all economic activity, whether productive or not. As well as including spending based on debt, which has been my main point so far, it also includes a great deal of unproductive output based on general activity within the service sector, including government spending on health, education and defense, only a small percentage of which involves real wealth creation (mostly the spending that goes into construction of public buildings, plus some manufacturing related to equipment and the defense industry). Because of this, the figure for real wealth creation – what we might call productive GDP – has always been much lower than the official GDP data would suggest. We can see this

Figure 14

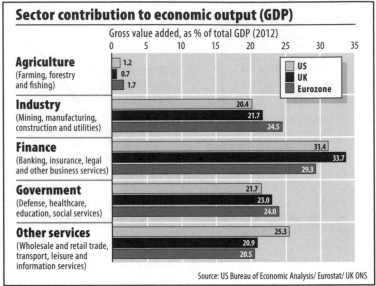

Sector contribution to economic output (GDP)

Gross value added, as % of total GDP (2012)

Source: US Bureau of Economic Analysis/ Eurostat/ UK ONS

in Figure 14, which gives a breakdown of economic activity in the US, UK and Eurozone, according to official GDP figures.

The data suggest that agriculture represents just 1.2% of the US economy, by value added. For Britain the figure is a mere 0.7%, while the financial sector apparently adds over 30%, when grouped with related activities such as insurance, accounting and legal services (banking by itself is around 10%).

Even taking the lower value, one might conclude from this information that banking is more than 10 times as important to the UK economy than is agriculture, and business services generally more than 30 times as important. In GDP terms, this is obviously the case. But out there in the real world, on the ground as it were, away from the City of London's square mile, it seems an absurd statistic. Who would you prefer to be without, bankers and lawyers, or farmers?

Even in Britain there is still a lot of farming going on, with 69% of the land either cultivated or grazed, though this isn't enough to feed everyone (40% of the food eaten in Britain is imported). But the US is the biggest agricultural producer in the world, or third biggest after China and India, depending on how you measure it. US agriculture feeds over 300 million people and still has enough left over to export a quarter of its produce to the rest of the world. You only have to pass through the vast American heartlands to see the obvious importance of this huge industry. Yet according to the figures, it represents only 1.2% of the economy. So what's wrong with these statistics?

The problem lies in the way GDP is calculated. Gross Domestic Product is a measure of the final output of a nation's economy, and represents the market value of all goods and services produced in one year. In 2010, for example, the net contribution of US agriculture to the economy was around $170 billion. But this figure then feeds into the food-processing industry, where value is added by turning the raw produce into food that people can eat. The value added to agricultural produce is now reflected in the manufacturing figures, the food-processing sector of which shows an output figure of $800 billion. This food is then distributed by the retail sector, where it adds another $500 billion to GDP figures. So a more accurate reflection of the importance of agriculture, when measured by value to the US economy, would be $1,470 billion. This would represent around 10% of the economy rather than 1.2%, with 15% of US jobs dependent on agriculture.

But this is to be expected; we already know that the primary sector is vital to industry, and industry to services. That's how the economy works, as I explained in Chapter 2. The distortion of GDP figures really occurs because of the inclusion of economic activity brought about by the spending of accumulated wealth and newly created money (credit, or debt), whether by the private sector or by governments. According to the same set of figures that gave us agriculture as 1.2% of the US economy, we have a total government contribution of 22%, and financial and other business services, including insurance, law and real estate, giving a total of 32%. How is it possible that the government has created more wealth than farming and industry? It isn't, of course. No real wealth can be created by finance, insurance or government – nor by any other service. All they can do is reallocate wealth that's already been created by the primary and secondary sectors of the economy at an earlier period than the GDP figures imply.

In other words, although GDP figures are calculated so as not to count the same new wealth twice in one year (in the way I showed above, with the wealth of agriculture feeding into processing and then retail) they *do* count the industrial wealth of the past, over and over again. The apparent wealth-creating activities of the service sector, which make up such a large percentage of developed economies these days, are really just a recycling of the wealth of past industry.

In addition to this, although most investment income is excluded from GDP figures (in recognition of the fact that such 'rent' is not genuine output), there is a different measure of the so-called wealth added to the economy by the financial sector. A strange concept devised by the United Nations in 1993 attempts to account for the 'intangible' wealth created by banks using a system that translates the financial risk from loans into output.[2] So the more debt a bank takes on, the more it apparently contributes to GDP.

Services add value by assisting the real wealth creators to produce their goods, certainly, but that value is already reflected in the figures for real industrial output. We see therefore that GDP figures are seriously flawed as a measure of real wealth creation, and this distortion must surely be reflected in policy decisions based on these figures.

Another example of how GDP figures seriously understate the importance of primary industry is in mineral extraction. A 2009 study by PricewaterhouseCoopers (PwC) of the US oil and natural-gas industry arrived at the results shown in the following table.

Contribution of Oil and Natural Gas Industry to US economy (2007)		
Source: PwC report for American Petroleum Institute, Sept 2009		
Employment:	9.2 million workers	5.2% of total
Value added to GDP:	$1,037bn	7.5% of total

PwC concluded that the sector accounted for 7.5% of total US GDP, compared to the 1.5% shown in official GDP statistics. But even the PwC estimate still uses the same flawed data for overall GDP measurement. In other words, the total GDP figure from which they calculate the sector's 7.5% contribution still includes the supposed 54% for the financial and government sectors, plus another 25% or so for all other services that, as I've already pointed out, are merely recycling past industrial wealth. If we remove these from the picture, we find that the US oil and gas industry makes up 37% of the real economy.

This failure by economists and politicians to appreciate the inadequacy of GDP figures seems quite pervasive. For example, the data for mineral extraction that form the basis of my first chart, and which set me off on this investigation, come from a 2011 United Nations report called *Decoupling Natural Resource Use from Economic Growth*. In this report, the authors state:

'These data indicate that globally, natural resource use during the 20th century rose at about twice the rate of population, but at a lower pace than the world economy. Thus resource decoupling has taken place "spontaneously" rather than as a result of policy intention. This occurred while resource prices were declining, or at least stagnating. Further research is needed on this relationship between "spontaneous" relative decoupling and declining resource prices.'

In other words, the authors fail to understand why the economy apparently grew faster than the rate of natural resource use would suggest it should have done. They obviously didn't make the connection to the growth in debt, yet I would suggest that the connection is quite clear. Because spending on credit requires no industrial activity, it uses no natural resources; the debt is created by leveraging the accumulated wealth of past industry. Or, to put it another way, new money is created from past activity. This is not to say that it doesn't *result* in any use of natural resources – some of this new money is bound to be spent on industrial goods, and therefore will boost industrial production, and consequently the use of raw materials. But my point is simply that the credit is created from nothing, as distinct from money that has been *earned* by real work.

Although some of this artificial wealth will be spent on real goods, a lot more of it goes into services and inflated asset prices, particularly housing. Although construction uses resources, the inflation of house prices does not; a house of a certain size requires the same resources, however much it sells for. Yet inflated selling prices result in a general feeling of rising wealth and raise GDP figures by boosting economic activity, especially in the financial and real-estate sectors.

If we look again at that chart of GDP and mineral extraction, this time adjusting the baseline slightly so that both graphs start at the same point (Figure 15), we see even more clearly the link between natural resources and economic growth. The link begins to break some time around 1971, when the dollar, and subsequently all money, broke away from the gold standard.[3] Adjusting the baseline might seem like cheating, but all we are doing here is comparing growth rates. The scales are not the same, but that doesn't matter: there is a strong correlation between the growth of resource use and the growth of the economy, as one might expect. The only surprising thing, as the UN researchers found, is that GDP apparently starts to grow without resources, and I have explained this as being the debt bubble. [I also show here the relatively small gains from increased material recycling, reduction in waste and fuel-efficiency improvements.]

At the start of this chapter I calculated the size of the bubble at $200 trillion, a figure I considered too high to be believable. However, if we add up the GDP figures for each year going back to 1900 (in constant 2010 dollars), we get a total of around $1,760 trillion. This means that the total wealth ever produced, up to the year 2013, according to GDP figures (in today's money), is around $1,800 trillion (the figures become relatively insignificant before 1900). Now I've already shown that GDP

Figure 15

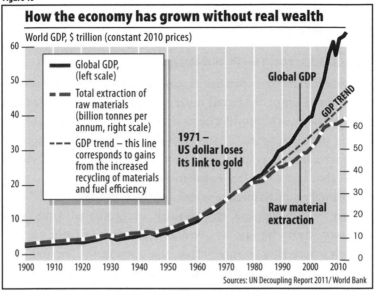

figures are a gross over-exaggeration of true wealth production, because they keep recycling wealth that was created in previous years, and therefore this figure of $1,800 trillion will also be grossly exaggerated. But it does at least explain how we might get that $200-trillion figure as the measure of the debt bubble. In GDP terms, $200 trillion of credit-fuelled growth starts to look quite plausible, as long as we remember the key point that it doesn't represent *real* wealth.

If we compare my figure of $1,800 trillion for total accumulated GDP with the earlier figure we had for total private wealth in the world – around $240 trillion in 2013, according to Credit Suisse data – we might begin to understand the relationship between output in terms of GDP, and the amount of actual wealth in dollar terms that ends up accumulating in banks. But in reality, the situation must be more complicated than this. Some wealth must get lost along the way – assets such as property crumble with time – and also private household wealth doesn't represent all the wealth in the world. What about state-owned wealth? Obviously, I must investigate this matter further. I return to this theme in Chapter 8, but first I must answer another question I think this chapter raises.

So what's wrong with old wealth?

Because the service sector has expanded to become the dominant force in the economy, based on the recycling of past industrial wealth, the ratio of productive to non-productive GDP has been falling in recent years. I can show this in Figure 16 simply by plotting a line corresponding to the proportion of total global GDP that has come from real industry (in other words, from the primary and secondary sectors of the economy).

One might suppose that wealth accumulated from past industry would be just as good as that created from current industry, but this is rarely the case, primarily because this accumulated wealth tends to end up in banks and other financial institutions as private investment. Unless investment goes towards the development of the real economy (ie, non-financial business) – and most of it doesn't these days, because there's far

Figure 16

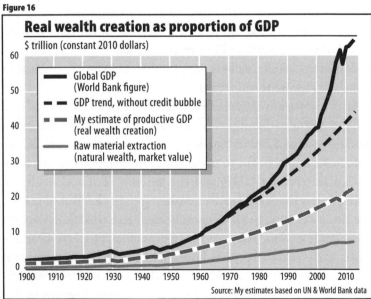

Real wealth creation as proportion of GDP

$ trillion (constant 2010 dollars)

Global GDP (World Bank figure)

GDP trend, without credit bubble

My estimate of productive GDP (real wealth creation)

Raw material extraction (natural wealth, market value)

Source: My estimates based on UN & World Bank data

more old wealth held in funds than is required for productive investment – then it doesn't create jobs. All it creates is debt.

This process of debt creation is at the heart of the world's economic problems. Not only is it linked to the reduction in real jobs and the resulting impoverishment and inequality in society, debt creation is also harmful in less obvious ways. Because so much economic activity is now based on the spending of credit rather than on genuine wealth that's already been 'earned', it is effectively borrowed from future earnings. There are two negative aspects to this borrowing from the future.

First, even if a debt-fuelled economy sees an increase in genuine production due to the spending of this borrowed money, this production itself is also borrowed from the future, because production is bound to decline as debts are repaid; consumers will have less money to spend in the future.

Second, the debt-fuelled boosting of asset prices gives a false sense of increasing wealth. This new 'wealth' has no basis in reality because it is based purely on the increase in credit, and this in turn must have consequences for the value of money, because the value of anything follows a simple formula:

$$\boxed{\text{Value}} = \boxed{\text{Utility}} \times \boxed{\text{Rarity}}$$

(Utility being a combination of usefulness and desirability)

So if money has become less rare while its utility has barely increased (because its utility – its *real* usefulness – must be a function of its purchasing power, which in turn is related to genuine economic growth, and this hasn't risen anything like as much as the money supply) then its value must have fallen. To look at it another way, while the amount of real wealth was rising moderately with genuine industrial output, the amount of money being pumped into the economy was expanding much more rapidly.

There is only so much real wealth in the world at any one time and, however much credit banks might create through leveraged lending, or governments might pump into the banks through quantitative easing (more on this in Chapter 12), it doesn't add one penny to that stock of real wealth. So all it can do is dilute the value of money, like adding water to wine. Just as the wine will be lower in strength, so will the money, and this must inevitably lead to higher prices.

A quick word about inflation

Inflation is commonly understood these days to mean the rise in prices caused by the devaluation of each monetary unit. It would be more correct to say that rising prices are the result of inflation and that the actual inflation is the growth in the amount of money in the economy relative to real economic activity.

An easy way to understand the relationship between the amount of money in circulation and its value is to go back to the commodity analogy.

Say a bushel of wheat has traded for an ounce of silver for several years – this being the accepted market rate, according to the principle of supply and demand – but then farmers start to grow more wheat so they can exchange it for more silver. The effect will be to cause a shortage of silver, raising its price relative to wheat. Each bushel of wheat will then be worth less, when measured in silver terms.

Now try it the other way – an ounce of silver will buy a bushel of wheat. What happens if more silver is mined and gradually finds its way into people's pockets, via the local market? The demand for wheat increases because people can buy more. Wheat becomes scarcer so prices rise. Farmers might plant more wheat next season to meet the increased demand, but that's only possible if they have the land. If they don't, then the cost of wheat stays higher and you have price inflation.

The same thing applies to money supply: if governments print more money than the economy merits, the price of commodities must rise to compensate for the new demand. The money is devalued. Inflation of the money supply beyond genuine

Figure 17

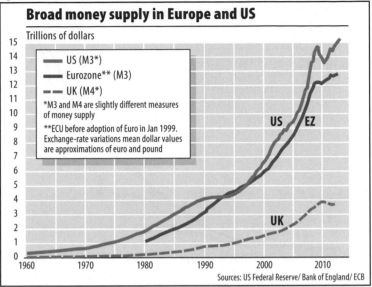

Broad money supply in Europe and US

Trillions of dollars

— US (M3*)
— Eurozone** (M3)
– – UK (M4*)

*M3 and M4 are slightly different measures of money supply

**ECU before adoption of Euro in Jan 1999. Exchange-rate variations mean dollar values are approximations of euro and pound

US   EZ

UK

Sources: US Federal Reserve/ Bank of England/ ECB

economic growth results in rising prices.

The rise in money supply seen in Figure 17 is mostly due to rising wealth and economic activity, and only partly to inflation (this chart is not inflation adjusted). There should be a close correlation between money supply and GDP – otherwise it must mean a change in demand for money relative to output – but the two don't actually move together. If, for example, we plot US GDP, unadjusted for inflation, against the broadest measure of money supply, which just happens to be very close to GDP in actual dollar terms, we see a close fit (as in Figure 18).

But we see also that the money supply has been rising more quickly in recent years. At the time of writing, we haven't seen the full effect of this inflation of the money supply, because most of this newly created money is being held by banks and other financial institutions and hasn't entered the real economy. The high demand that caused the last boom – demand fuelled by credit – has collapsed since the crash, but the supply side of the economy takes longer to adjust. Weak demand relative to supply keeps prices down.

Figure 18

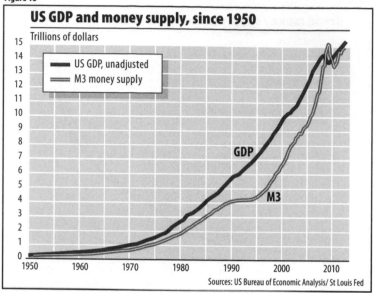

We have had a trend of falling commodity prices over the last half-century (as shown in Figure 7), due to rising efficiencies on the supply side related to globalization and the increase in market size. Prices recently have been up and down like a rollercoaster, partly due to speculation, but this hasn't resulted in a big rise in most consumer prices in the long term. However, the trend is turning upwards and is likely to rise more steeply as oil and mining companies, and farmers, demand a fair price – a price that takes account of the falling value of the dollar and of money generally.

This has not affected these primary producers significantly yet, because their costs haven't risen all that much (the cost of equipment and labor and so on). But at some point there has to be a readjustment. It is inevitable that prices will rise, because although the value of money has fallen, the value of the earth's natural wealth hasn't changed – except in so far as resources have become scarcer, which will itself also cause prices to rise.

There might not appear to be any particular law that governs the relationship between the value of natural resources and

Figure 19

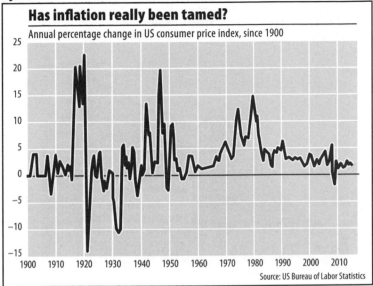

money – supply and demand is hardly a scientific equation – but there ought to be a general consensus that links the scarcity of resources to the price, which must eventually feed through to the markets.

It's true that markets aren't actually all that good at valuing commodities, partly because of the influence of speculation – betting on future prices influences those prices, just as betting on a racehorse changes the odds. There's a tendency towards a herd instinct that pushes the trend too far upwards, followed by an overreaction when it becomes obvious that prices have risen too much, sending the price too low, much the same as happens with stock markets.

One might suppose that the true value of something like oil, for example, shouldn't vary greatly, both demand and supply being fairly constant. The former rises and falls with changes in the real economy, but not by all that much relative to the total quantity produced, as shown in Figure 20. Supply is depleted gradually by extraction, and can be temporarily reduced by production problems in a certain region – a war in the Middle

Figure 20

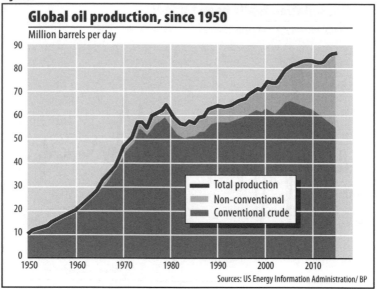

Global oil production, since 1950

Million barrels per day

Legend:
— Total production
■ Non-conventional
■ Conventional crude

Sources: US Energy Information Administration/ BP

East, for example. It can also be boosted by new fields coming into production. But these are not wild variations compared to the overall quantity of oil available from operational fields.

If we look at the oil price over the last half-century, as shown in Figure 21, we see that the price hardly varied until the dollar, and therefore oil, lost its link to gold in 1971, at which point producers began raising prices to compensate for the fall in the dollar's value. Unrest in the Middle East added to the uncertainty and caused price spikes in 1973 and 1979. Prices fell as production increased in the 1980s and 1990s, then rose sharply in the boom up to 2008, driven by speculation as well as rising demand. So the price is obviously not governed purely by the true value of the product, and in fact might bear little relationship to it.

But ignoring these wild fluctuations, the trend for commodity prices is bound to turn upwards. Global demand will keep increasing as long as the population keeps rising and emerging economies continue to grow, while many commodities are gradually being used up. At the same time, money is more abundant than ever.

Figure 21

Oil price since 1950, adjusted for inflation

$ per barrel (in 2012 dollars) Arabian Light till 1984, then Brent Crude

1971 – dollar loses its link to gold

Source: US Energy Information Administration/ BP

Easy money is cheap money

I look more closely at the subject of prices in Part Two, but for now I want to return to the debt problem. The credit bubble hasn't really gone away: it only deflated slightly, and has since blown up again in a different form. With the government bailout of the banks, some private-sector debt has been converted into public-sector debt, which has hit a record level, greater even than was experienced at the end of the Second World War, even though there was nothing this time that remotely resembled the global crisis that made such debt unavoidable in the 1940s.

This has serious implications for the wealth of future generations, because surely public-sector debt is merely private-sector obligations carried into the future, in the form of future tax revenues. We talk about public and private sectors as if they are quite different things, but in the end the state is just the people; a collection of individuals. And unless it has somehow become possible to get something out of nothing, debts always have to be paid, one way or another.

Whether all this means we are in for another major financial

Figure 22

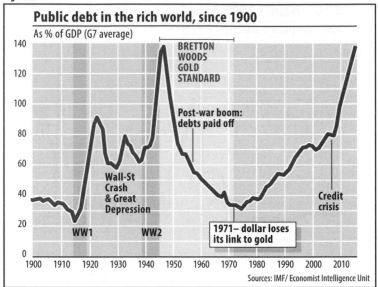

Public debt in the rich world, since 1900

As % of GDP (G7 average)

BRETTON WOODS GOLD STANDARD

Post-war boom: debts paid off

Wall-St Crash & Great Depression

WW1

WW2

1971– dollar loses its link to gold

Credit crisis

Sources: IMF/ Economist Intelligence Unit

shock, or whether the difference between perceived wealth and actual wealth can somehow be reconciled more gently over time, I wouldn't like to guess, though if I were a gambler I'd put my money on another crash.

One thing, however, seems fairly certain: the amount of real wealth in the world today is considerably less than the figure suggested by Credit Suisse or any other financial institution, because the banks are measuring assets in terms of money that has been devalued by the credit bubble and subsequent inflation of the money supply, even though that devaluation hasn't yet fed through into the economy.

Why hasn't all this new money fed through into the economy? Because the banks aren't doing anything with it. With interest rates effectively zero, the banks aren't lending because there's no profit in doing so. They have been building up their reserves instead, which is a good thing, but doesn't alter the fact that money has been devalued.

The idea that governments should stimulate demand by keeping interest rates close to zero is self-defeating. The lack of demand isn't caused by the cost of borrowing. How could it be, when interest rates are already so low? The lack of demand is caused by the reduction in the real wealth of the majority of the population, which is linked to the shortage of real jobs and the related decline in real wages.

The credit boom boosted demand with debt-based consumer spending – the growth in GDP was artificial, as I've shown. So the answer can't be to increase demand through more borrowing. The answer is to accept lower demand, because this is the *real* level of demand, and concentrate government policy on creating jobs instead of creating more debt.

There is a fundamental relationship between money and work: when we exchange money, we are ultimately exchanging our labor, and although this doesn't necessarily apply in practice in the modern world, the principle is still relevant, for reasons I shall explain in Part Three.

But there's an even bigger issue behind all this, connected to the increasing dominance of accumulated wealth over produced wealth, as seen in the rise of the financial sector relative to real industry. It is this rise that led to the increase in lending, encouraged by ever-lower interest rates – a glut of cheap money that in turn led to the credit and house-price bubbles, and I think this has major implications for the future of the global economy, and for the future of civilization in general.

Representations of wealth, such as money, *must* be linked to the real wealth created by industry. Money has no other claim as a measure of wealth. Government promises mean nothing if the government cannot back the promise with real wealth. The rise of the financial sector to a position of economic dominance over real wealth-creating industry poses a serious threat to the value of money everywhere, and to the economy in general.

The whole concept of making money from assets such as property and other financial investments, rather than from real industry, is deeply flawed. No real wealth can be created this way; all that happens is wealth is transferred from the borrower to the lender, which usually means from the middle classes to the rich, and this of course reduces the spending power of the majority while increasing the wealth of the financial sector, creating a vicious circle of unsustainable credit creation.

When we take into account the ever-rising productivity of manufacturing and the associated reduction in the industrial workforce, we begin to understand the fundamental problems facing the developed economies of the world. I'll come back to this after the next chapter. But before we go any further, we need to think a bit more about money and, in particular, what gives money its value.

1 The data for global mineral extraction, which forms the basis of Figure 1, comes from a 2011 United Nations report entitled 'Decoupling Natural Resource Use and Environmental Impacts from Economic Growth'. The authors of this report in turn based their work on research undertaken by Fridolin Krausmann and colleagues at the Austrian Institute of Social Ecology, who made the following points regarding data reliability: 'According to broadly accepted principles of material flow accounting, we accounted for the extraction of all types of biomass, fossil energy carriers, ores and industrial minerals as well as for bulk minerals used for construction. Extraction by definition also includes the biomass grazed by domesticated livestock, used crop residues and the tailings that accrue during the processing of extracted ores. Resources extracted but not used (eg overburden in mining, excavated soil, burnt crop residues etc) have not been accounted for. We think our data provides a consistent picture of the overall size and composition of global materials use, and their change over time. Our results match well with other estimates of global material flows covering the period 1980 to 2005.'
2 The United Nations System of National Accounts (SNA) is a global set of accounting rules for nations compiling statistics, and was updated in 1993 to include Financial Intermediation Services Indirectly Measured (FISIM).
3 For more about the link between gold and money, see Chapter 5.

5 The value of money

A brief history of money and debt

It might seem as if money is just printed by the government and circulates around the economy indefinitely, via the banks, but for several reasons this is not the case. A balance must be maintained, because the quantity of money in circulation affects its value. As the economy expands, more money will be required to keep up with demand. A shortage of money will constrain overall economic activity relative to primary output, subduing demand and forcing down the price of goods; this is what we call deflation. On the other hand, if the government, or indeed the banking system, creates more money than the real wealth of the economy merits, the lower its value must become, as I explained in the previous chapter. So the value of money can vary almost day to day.

In fact money itself, being just an IOU from the government – a promise written on a piece of paper – has no intrinsic value at all these days. Its value is related to its usefulness as a medium of exchange, and therefore depends on how much of something else it will buy, and this in turn depends on a complicated series of relationships between commodities and currencies, which in turn depends on the relative strengths of national economies, which in turn depend on commodity prices, which in turn...

Perhaps we should look at it another way. A dollar is worth a dollar because the US government says it is. Okay?

Better still, let's go back to the beginning.

A goat and two shekels

The first forms of money were commodities that were in common use and had a generally agreed value relative to other goods, and which therefore became accepted as payment. The most obvious examples are coins made of gold, silver or copper, but before coins came into general use people used all kinds of things: seeds, tobacco, rice, salt, tea, grain, linen, even goats.

The value usually depended on the weight, which is why so many currency units are still called lira (from the Latin *libra*) or pound. The original pound sterling, introduced to Britain in the 12th century, was equal to one troy pound of sterling silver. (Silver currently costs around £200 per pound, by the way). The troy weight system is still used for precious metals, as in the troy ounce of gold. The name comes from the French town of Troyes, an important trading center since early Roman times.

Historical evidence suggests that the first unit of currency was the shekel of Mesopotamia, which came into use around 3000 BCE. Shekel probably referred to a weight of barley initially, but by 550 BCE a coin had been introduced by the king of Lydia (in what is now Turkey) to make life easier for traders. These gold discs were stamped with an official seal to certify their purity and weight, giving them a readily accepted value. They also had the advantage of being easy to carry around, and they didn't rot away, unlike most commodities. The use of coins quickly spread throughout ancient Greece. By around 350 BCE, Aristotle was writing about the concept of non-commodity money, such as we use today: 'Money exists not by nature, but by law,' he explained.

Aristotle was one of the first philosophers to write about economics, and in particular the value of money. In trying to explain how we arrive at an agreed value when exchanging goods, and how money makes this process easier, he concluded that money provided a measure of value determined by need, or demand, rather than the value being intrinsic to the goods themselves. Value is subjective – we each put different values on goods because our perception of a thing's usefulness or desirability varies – but demand, for the purposes of trade through the market, requires a standard unit of measure, and money provides this. The price represents a threshold determined by wants; if you want something enough, you'll pay the price.

Coins were also used in China and India by Aristotle's time, possibly earlier, but these were more like bronze tokens than true coins, as they weren't marked by an official stamp. By 280

BCE, the Roman Republic had begun minting coins in gold, silver, brass and copper. Initially these coins were stamped with the image of the goddess Roma, but by Julius Caesar's time they featured the emperor himself. These early Roman coins had an intrinsic value in their content of precious metal, though as coins they tended to be worth around twice that value.

Later coinage issued in Europe and elsewhere had a lower content of precious metal relative to its face value, allowing the issuing government to mint more coins from its limited supply of gold, silver or copper. This process of 'debasement' of coins reduces the value of the coinage. This in turn causes inflation, which is bad for the citizens, because their money will buy less, but can be good for the government because its debts will be devalued along with the currency.

The first banknotes

Around 2500 BCE, when the shekel was being used as currency in Mesopotamia, there was also a form of credit money authorized by the Babylonian kings, who used clay tablets to record transactions of some kind. It is thought that these clay tablets, hundreds of which have been found in temple ruins, were receipts for barley paid to the temple as a tax, and there is evidence to suggest that they were also traded as a form of 'IOU', in which case they would have been the first form of banknote, and as such the first form of actual money, predating coins by two millennia or more. This would mean that the first forms of money were also the first forms of recorded debt; so the link between money creation and debt creation might be as old as money itself.

Paper money was first introduced in China around the eighth century, as a form of receipt used by merchants who didn't want to carry large quantities of coins around. The merchant would deposit coins with a trusted person – the banker – who would write a note confirming that a certain number of coins had been deposited, or a certain weight of gold. This note could then be exchanged for goods. The person who sold those goods, on presentation of the note to the banker, or any other banker in the region, could then redeem the coins.

In the case of clay tablets, paper currency and coins that lacked intrinsic value (in other words, were not worth their weight in gold), money was representative of a value rather than actually holding that value itself. This 'representative money' acted like a certificate to show that a certain amount of gold or silver (or grain in the earliest cases) was stored at the central bank, or treasury, in the way that a note for one pound sterling could be exchanged for one troy pound of sterling silver. In effect, it was a promise by the government, or the bank on the government's behalf, to hand over that amount of bullion.

By the 19th century, most of the world's currencies had become 'representative' by being linked to the gold standard, and remained so until the 1970s, after which time money became nothing more than a government promise, known as 'fiat' money, from the Latin for 'it shall be'.

The gold standard

Gold has been valued as a commodity, both for jewelry and as coinage, for thousands of years, and has for a long time been accepted everywhere as a trusted currency, thanks to a proven record of holding its value. Along with silver, gold was the standard medium of payment for international trade well into the 20th century. Its value is guaranteed by its rarity.

Like all elemental metals, gold was formed in space by nucleosynthesis, the process by which a nuclear explosion, a collapsing star for example, creates new atomic nuclei.

Relatively small quantities of these metals combined with more abundant elements in the formation of planets, as happened with Earth. Because of its weight, gold sank deep within the molten mantel of the newly formed planet. The traces we find today have mostly been thrown up from the mantel by deep volcanic activity. It is also likely that some of the heavy metals found near the surface of the earth, including gold, come from asteroid impacts, most of which occurred around four billion years ago.

Figure 23

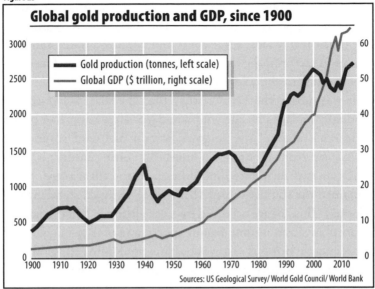

Global gold production and GDP, since 1900

- ▬▬▬ Gold production (tonnes, left scale)
- ▬▬▬ Global GDP ($ trillion, right scale)

Sources: US Geological Survey/ World Gold Council/ World Bank

Unlike the mineral wealth that we use as fuel, or metals lost through industrial process or corrosion, nearly all the gold that has ever been mined, around 175,000 tonnes by 2014, is still around today, mostly in the form of bullion or jewelry. Around 2,500 tonnes are mined every year, and this quantity is limited by the physical constraints of the mining process, so although it has generally risen with economic growth, the rate of gold production doesn't greatly change.

At one time silver was more popular for coinage in Europe, being more available than gold but still scarce enough to hold its value. Silver ingots had been used as a medium of exchange in China since around 200 CE. As world trade began to increase in the 16th century, in particular between China and the Spanish and Portuguese, silver became the standard method of payment.

Silver dollar coins became popular. The term 'dollar' was originally the English term for the German 'thaler' – an abbreviation of the name of a place where silver was mined in what is now the Czech Republic. This region of Bohemia was part of the Holy Roman Empire in the 16th century, a time

61

when most European currencies had become debased and were therefore unpopular with traders. The thaler was recognized as one of the few reliable silver coins and became a trade standard, remaining so until the end of the 19th century, when Germany replaced it with the gold mark.

It was during the 19th century that the silver standard was gradually replaced by the gold standard, after silver had begun to lose its value relative to gold. Britain had used silver coins exclusively from around 770 until the 14th century, when a gold coin was introduced in addition to the silver coins. Silver remained the standard until 1816, when the gold standard was adopted. This change occurred because although Britain paid for imports in silver, income from exports was mostly in gold, and consequently Britain's reserves became predominantly gold.

The US used both gold and silver until 1873, when it adopted the gold standard. Germany switched to gold around the same time, and as gold became the dominant currency for world trade other countries followed suit.

Under a gold standard, all money has a value linked to gold, whether it be paper money or coins made of silver or any other metal. This effectively creates a fixed exchange rate between different currencies using the gold standard.

It also means that a country must retain a substantial amount of gold to back up its currency. The US Federal Reserve, for example, before the US abandoned the gold standard in 1971, was required by law to hold enough gold to back at least 40% of the total value of notes in circulation. This limited the ability of the government to manipulate the money supply, which can be seen as both good and bad; it keeps inflation down, but also constrains a government's options when using monetary policy to boost the economy, by lowering interest rates, for example (because interest rates affect the value of the currency).

Since gold stopped being the *de facto* global currency, exchange rates between national currencies have varied according to the relative strengths and weaknesses of different economies, encouraging currency speculation and causing uncertainties in the pricing of goods, making international trade more complicated.

It was to eliminate such complications that the European Union introduced a single currency. Unfortunately this only succeeded in causing other complications, because it doesn't really work to have a single currency while at the same time having lots of different governments. I will return to this theme later, but first we must take a quick walk through the woods.

The last link is broken

It was because of this unpredictable volatility between the currencies of different nations that the Bretton Woods system of monetary control was set up in the summer of 1944. Just three weeks after the D-Day landings, delegates from the 44 allied nations took a break from the horrors of the Second World War and met in a grand hotel in the peaceful mountains of Bretton Woods, New Hampshire. With the end of the war finally in sight, US President Franklin D Roosevelt and British prime minister Winston Churchill were determined to avoid the economic problems that followed the First World War, and which to some extent had caused the war still raging in Europe and the Pacific as they gathered.

Their goal was to create a new world order that would speed up post-War reconstruction and ensure lasting peace, and ultimately prosperity. John Maynard Keynes, the British economist, was one of the principal negotiators, along with senior officials from the US Treasury. They focused on two key issues: how to pay for the rebuilding of Europe, and how to form a stable exchange-rate system. For these purposes they set up the International Bank for Reconstruction and Development (later renamed the World Bank) and the International Monetary Fund.

Keynes was in favor of a single world currency, but the US insisted that fixed exchange rates should be linked to the dollar, which was itself linked to the price of gold. The US was by this time the only strong economy remaining in the world and, as most of the money that went into the new bank would come from the US, it became by far the most dominant player in this new world order.

The Bretton Woods agreement established a rules-based system of international finance that helped to restore confidence in world trade, resulting in a US-led economic revival and the boom years that endured, on and off, throughout the second half of the 20th century.

It worked initially because dollars flowed to Europe in the form of loans and grants (the Marshall Plan) and, as Europe recovered, it imported goods from the US, thus helping the American economy to keep expanding. As worldwide demand for US goods increased, this in turn led to rising US demand for raw materials, which benefited the economies of some mineral-rich nations.

But the Bretton Woods system had a few drawbacks, the biggest of which, for the US at least, was that gold was tied to the dollar at $35 per ounce, while the free-market price could vary. US policy was to try to keep the gold price close to $35 by maintaining the dollar's value, but this proved impossible. If the free-market price of gold rose higher than $35, as it did whenever the dollar looked threatened by some event (the Cuban Missile Crisis of 1962, for example, sent gold up to $40 per ounce) there was nothing to stop other nations from converting their dollar holdings into gold at $35, then selling the gold for the higher price, a practice known as arbitrage.

By the mid-1960s, a resurgent Europe was becoming less tolerant of America's unprecedented power and influence. France, in particular, under President Charles de Gaulle, didn't trust the US government's ability to maintain its currency's value, and used dollars earned from exports to build French gold reserves, further depleting US supplies.

Burdened by the increasing cost of fighting the Vietnam War, the US could no longer guarantee to exchange all dollar holdings for gold. Its reserves had fallen to around 20% of total dollars in circulation, down from 55% in 1946, when the US held $26 billion in gold (over 60% of global reserves).

In May 1971, West Germany, wary of inflation and unwilling to devalue the mark to prop up the dollar, pulled out of the Bretton Woods agreement. Other countries, notably France and Switzerland, exchanged more dollars for gold.

On 15 August 1971, with US gold stocks down to $10 billion or so, President Nixon ended the convertibility of dollars into gold, a move that became known as the 'Nixon shock'. This brought an end to any semblance of a gold standard and meant the dollar became fiat money, soon to be followed by all the currencies that had been tied to it. From this period onwards, the value of most major currencies would be free to float, dependent only on the fortunes of their parent countries in relation to other nations. The price of gold quickly went up, from $35 an ounce in 1971 to $190 by the end of 1974.

As good as gold

There is no particular reason why the value of money should be linked to gold, but there is a very good reason why the quantity of money in circulation needs to be determined by something real, something related to economic activity by the real wealth of industry. Because of its rarity and long history of desirability, which guaranteed its value, gold provided a useful benchmark from which money could be valued.

Whether or not we should return to some form of gold standard is a subject that provokes even more disagreement amongst economists than most other aspects of the economy, but there's no doubt that today's financial problems could not have occurred if the gold standard was still in force, because there's no way that banks could have created so much credit. The gold standard linked the value of money to genuine wealth creation, because governments had to acquire the gold (either by mining it

Figure 24

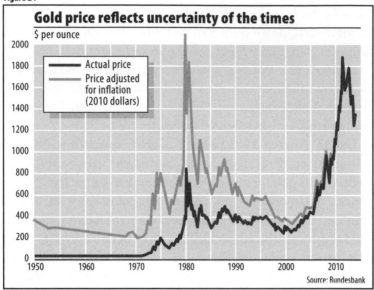

Gold price reflects uncertainty of the times

$ per ounce

Legend:
— Actual price
— Price adjusted for inflation (2010 dollars)

Source: Bundesbank

or exporting goods that could be exchanged for gold) before they could print more of the paper stuff.

There is obviously a need for some form of standard that ties money creation more closely to genuine wealth creation, but it might be the case that gold is just too valuable to be used now, with money being so abundant and gold so rare. Since the end of the gold standard, the price of gold has fluctuated wildly because of speculation, but overall has shot up, as Figure 24 shows.

Gold can be traded in the same way a currency is traded, and is often bought in times of uncertainty, when currencies, especially the dominant US dollar, risk losing value through inflation. But the fact is that the value of everything, including gold, can vary relative to everything else, according to the simple free-market principle of supply and demand. The market does the valuing, which is supposedly a good thing because in theory it is the market, meaning the market traders collectively, that has the most information, and can therefore make the most accurate judgments.

But this fluidity of prices means there is no fixed value to anything, including money. And we know that markets get things wrong sometimes, that they are prone to herd instincts and can be influenced by heavy trading and deliberate attempts at price manipulation. This reliance on the market means that governments are constrained in their actions by concerns that certain economic policies will affect the value of their national currency, which in turn affects the economy.

Out of control?

Again we return to this point: that with no fixed values, the economy is governed by complicated interactions between millions of players in the global marketplace. The whole economic system has grown so large and complex that no single authority has any control or even much influence. None of it is planned; things just happen on the general basis of supply and demand, which in turn is governed by self-interest, getting the best price – by the profit motive.

The free-market system has worked quite well for much of history; better than the 'planned' economies of communist nations anyway, for the most part. But something has changed in the last decade or two. The market for goods and money has become truly global in a way that it never was before, and in the process it has become less accountable and less regulated.

As the proportion of accumulated wealth has risen relative to produced wealth, so the ability of governments to influence national economies has declined, because accumulated wealth, when in the form of money or financial investments at least, can be moved around easily. It often ends up in countries, or even small island dependencies such as the Cayman Islands or Channel Islands, that deliberately attract wealth by promising not to tax it, and which encourage transnational corporations to register with them by offering favorable secrecy laws and minimal regulation.

The wealth of industry, on the other hand, has traditionally been more fixed; located in a real place in a real country, where there is still some governmental control over what goes on. Industrial

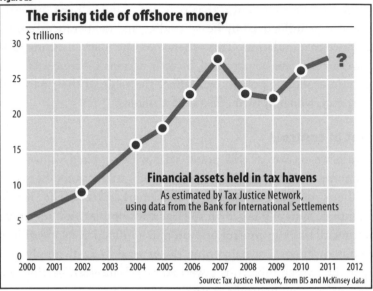

Figure 25

The rising tide of offshore money

$ trillions

Financial assets held in tax havens

As estimated by Tax Justice Network,
using data from the Bank for International Settlements

Source: Tax Justice Network, from BIS and McKinsey data

wealth fed into the economy because it created jobs and made the majority a little wealthier, and, until recently, most of the profits of industry were reinvested in the economy, creating more jobs.

This has begun to change however, as large transnational corporations become wealthier and more dominant. Jobs can be created where labor is cheapest, companies registered where taxes are lowest. And rising productivity, as I mentioned earlier, means fewer jobs. More of the profits can be kept by company owners and executives. I examine this trend in more detail later in the book, but with regard to the value of money, the point is that governments have very little control over national currencies in the truly global free-market economy, even though it is governments that supposedly guarantee the value of money. Most monetary policy these days is limited to the setting of interest-rate targets and the issuance of money, and even these critical functions are to some extent beyond government control.

I will return to the matter of accumulated wealth later in the chapter, but first there is another important topic that needs to be addressed, and this is the system of money creation itself.

There has never been a perfect monetary system. Perhaps because of the subjective and relative nature of value, such a thing is impossible. But the system we have now is very far from perfect.

Fractional-reserve banking

It might not be a term that sets the pulse racing, but fractional-reserve banking lies at the heart of the monetary system of most countries these days. It refers to the fact that banks only need to hold cash reserves that represent a fraction of their customer deposits. It works on the basis that not all customers are going to withdraw all their cash at any one time, so there is no need to hold that amount in the bank. Banks can therefore lend out more money than they actually possess, which adds ready cash, or 'liquidity', into the economy.

The amount that must be held in the bank, known as the reserve ratio, is set by the central bank and is usually somewhere between 20% and zero. The reason it can be zero, which is theoretically the case in Britain for example, is that the central bank will always provide funds to commercial banks when they are short of cash. In practice, British banks hold around 3% of deposits and the rest is either lent out or invested in other ways. The US has a reserve requirement of 10% on some instant-demand accounts, but none on other longer-term deposits.

With a 10% reserve ratio, for every $100 a bank holds in deposits, it can lend out $90 and keep $10 in reserve. But that $90 loan might be invested somewhere else, enabling another bank to hold $9 and lend out $81. This process can theoretically go on until the initial $100 deposit has resulted in $900 of new money in the form of loans, although this is unlikely to happen to the full extent, as at some point the money will most likely be spent rather than reinvested.

This uncertainty as to how much money will be reinvested and how much kept as cash, or spent, means that when a central bank creates money by crediting (lending to) commercial banks, it has no way of knowing what multiple of that money will eventually find its way into actual circulation. The reserve ratio acts as a limit to money creation, but the complexity of the system makes it a very crude and unreliable tool.

The effect of all this 'leveraging' (the process of multiplying money by creating credit out of thin air) is not very different from the ancient practice of debasing gold coins with copper to make the sovereign's gold supplies last longer. Both processes, unless backed up by a corresponding increase in real economic output, have the effect of devaluing the currency.

Not so efficient

I made the point earlier that the gold standard provided a fixed link between money and real economic wealth, and that such a link would have prevented the formation of the credit bubble, which in turn would have prevented today's economic problems from developing. But, even without a gold standard, if the banks had been forced to hold higher reserves it would not have been possible for them to lend so much money, so this also would have reduced the likelihood of such a financial crisis.

This lax regulation has its origins in the City of London in the late 1950s. The foreign-exchange department of the Bank of England, which was self-governing but had to agree to increasing controls on trades in pounds sterling, began trading in dollars internationally, to avoid such regulation. The British government, which had close ties to the City, chose to let the Bank do so, and counted this market for international deposits and loans (which became known as the Eurodollar market) as 'offshore'.

Thus developed an unregulated but quite legal trade, theoretically based offshore but actually using banks located in the City of London. It wasn't long before these banks started opening branches in real offshore territories, in particular the Bahamas and the Cayman Islands. In 1963, the US government tried to limit the flow of dollars overseas by introducing a tax on the interest from foreign securities, but the unintended result was to send US banks flocking to London's offshore accounts, where they could avoid tax altogether. The US asked Britain to tighten regulation on these offshore banks, but the Bank of England resisted such measures and, when US banking interests also exerted influence on politicians, the matter was quietly dropped.

A bigger change came with London's 'Big Bang' of 1986, which wasn't really deregulation so much as the discarding of a system based on honor and trust (as well as restrictive practices), in which investment bankers were partners who shared the risks as well as the rewards. The new 'anything-goes' culture that followed this change was actually more regulated (because the honor-based system didn't need much regulation) but in such a way as to leave huge loopholes, which were quickly exploited by the new wizards of finance.

The Big Bang was an essential step in Britain's transformation from fading industrial power to global financial center; from producer of wealth to magnet for wealth produced elsewhere. The City's square mile, and its outgrowth in Canary Wharf, part of London's redundant docklands, became the focus of international currency dealing, bond and derivatives trading, insurance and other financial services. Once the busiest port in the world, handling 50,000 ships per year at its 19th-century peak, trade now goes through 500 banks instead. Unfortunately, for the majority at least, this is the wrong kind of trade.

Banking is supposed to be a service to industry, a means of providing funds for investment in the real economy. Real investment involves the expansion and modernization of industry; the construction of new factories, farms, infrastructure, housebuilding: the process of economic development and the creation of jobs. Real investment has nothing to do with speculating on exchange rates or profiting from other people's wealth to make personal fortunes that don't contribute to the real economy.

Bankers try to justify these activities by claiming they provide more funds for industry at lower rates, using the 'efficiency of the

Figure 26

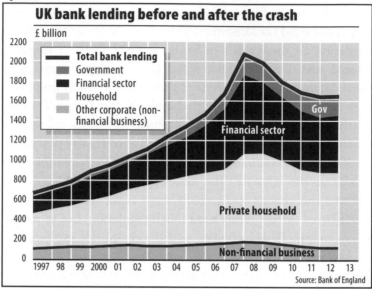

UK bank lending before and after the crash

£ billion

Legend:
- **Total bank lending**
- Government
- Financial sector
- Household
- Other corporate (non-financial business)

Labels on chart: Gov, Financial sector, Private household, Non-financial business

Source: Bank of England

markets' argument, but there hasn't been a shortage of funds for sound industrial investment for decades, as my next two charts show, and as wealth keeps accumulating faster than the economy can grow (as I explain in Chapter 8), there isn't likely to be.

The only thing in short supply is real work, yet the financial sector is responsible for killing jobs by encouraging corporations to become more productive and more 'efficient', so they can make more profit for the owners and banks at the expense of everyone else (investment banks being major shareholders), and also by ensuring that as little tax as possible is paid on these profits and inflated earnings.

Two types of debt

As I said earlier, money can be lent for productive or non-productive purposes. When a commercial bank lends money for genuine business expansion, the debt is eventually paid off with the resulting boost in real earnings. This is productive debt; it boosts the economy. But lending for purposes other than business expansion results in non-productive debt, and this is

Figure 27

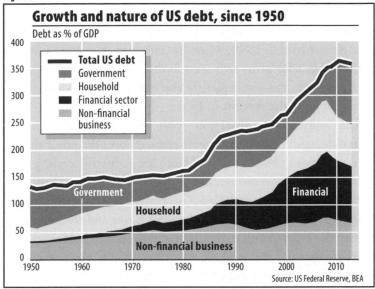

Growth and nature of US debt, since 1950

Debt as % of GDP

Legend:
- **Total US debt**
- Government
- Household
- Financial sector
- Non-financial business

Source: US Federal Reserve, BEA

predominantly the type of lending undertaken by investment banks and other financial traders and investors. Non-productive debt creation is by definition a zero-sum game; because no wealth is created this way, any gains must involve losses elsewhere. This means that any asset growth boosted purely by unproductive credit is inherently unsustainable, as we have seen with stock-market and house-price bubbles.

As the ratio of real industrial investment to financial investment declines – as the latter grows much larger in relation to the former, as shown in Figure 26 (for the UK) and Figure 27 (for the US) – then the ability of the economy to service the debts declines with it. This has been happening since the 1980s; the financial sector generally has been attempting to profit from rising asset prices rather than from real investment in industry. But in the long run, this is impossible, because the rising asset prices represent rising debts, which in the end will have to be paid, in the process bringing down the asset prices, as happened in Japan in the 1980s (more of this in Chapter 13).

The profits made from such unproductive investments are 'unearned', as was recognized by the economist-philosopher John Stuart Mill in 1848, when he criticized the *rentier* income of landlords, who 'grow rich even in their sleep'. There is no real work involved, and consequently there is no value added to the economy; quite the reverse, in fact.

The central-bank obsession with controlling inflation, or indeed deflation, through interest rates, ignores the point that it is this attempt by banks to profit from unproductive lending that causes the growth in unsustainable debt, which in turn threatens to bring about serious inflation. Governments and central banks should have been limiting unproductive lending and debt creation, as they did before bank deregulation, rather than holding down interest rates and encouraging more borrowing, most of which results in the wrong kind of debt. As the two charts show, the growth of unproductive debt is a recent phenomenon.

So how did banks get into this business of wrecking the economy through unsustainable debt creation?

Financial times

With all the negative publicity concerning the financial sector since the crash of 2008 – the infamous bankers' bonuses, excessive rates of pay generally, the fixing of lending rates and so on (criticism that was entirely justified, to the point that several top bankers have been forced to resign and few have tried to defend their practices) – it would be easy to forget the vital role that banks play in the economy. Businesses need loans to invest in capital – in factories and machinery and anything else that requires large sums of cash – just as people need mortgages to buy houses and loans to buy cars. So banking is an essential business, and also one of the oldest.

As already noted, a form of banking – in which priests or monks lent grain or other commodities to merchants – predated the use of actual money. The earliest evidence of this kind of banking activity dates to Mesopotamia around 2500 BCE. In

Sumeria, for example, the state agreed loans in grain, olives or dates, on condition that the loan was repaid within a year, plus a bit extra – at an interest rate of around 20%. This food bank helped people to survive between harvests. And during this period, wealthy individuals sometimes stored their gold in the temple for safe keeping.

The idea of holding other people's money and lending it out to farmers or traders goes back to around 500 BCE, and occurred in different civilizations as a result of the growth in trade. Records show that some form of banking existed in ancient Greece and also in the Roman Empire, China and India.

Roman emperors recognized the importance of banking as a way of regulating money. Merchants had to change foreign currency into Roman coins. The moneylender set up a stall near the marketplace, on a bench known as a *bancu* – the origin of the word 'bank'. The practice of charging interest on loans, and also of paying interest on deposits, developed in a regulated environment, with bankers competing to offer the best rates.

As the Roman Empire declined and Christianity spread, banking became more restricted, because the charging of interest (known as usury) was considered by early Christians to be immoral. The Jewish faith also forbade usury amongst its own people, but permitted Jews to charge interest to non-Jews. This point, combined with the difficulty that Jews often had in finding other work in a non-Jewish society, encouraged them to concentrate on the business of lending money.

By the 14th century, in Renaissance Italy, Jewish traders had moved into the grain-trading business of Lombardy, setting themselves up, in the tradition of the Roman moneylenders, on benches around the trading halls and squares of the main towns, offering loans to farmers while accepting the future grain harvest as collateral.

As this business grew, the Jewish merchants began offering insurance against crop failure, and they also took deposits in the form of bills of settlement. The funds from these deposits, which were held for merchants until they needed them to settle grain trades, could be lent out to other farmers, as long as the bankers kept enough to settle other deals. If they didn't, they risked a broken bench (Latin *bancus ruptus*, from which we get the term bankrupt).

When wars disrupted business in Italy, some of these Jewish bankers migrated northwards, taking their merchant-banking practices into Germany and eventually the Netherlands and Britain, often becoming goldsmiths as well as bankers, charging fees for storing other people's gold in their vaults. The goldsmith would write a deposit receipt, which the owner would then show when wanting to take out some gold. As with those eighth-century Chinese banknotes mentioned earlier, it became the custom to use these deposit receipts as currency in themselves, instead of carrying the actual gold around. A goldsmith would hand over the specified quantity of gold in exchange for the note, whether it was presented by the original depositor or by someone else.

By lending out more money, or bank notes, than they held on deposit, bankers had begun to create money out of nothing. For example, if a merchant deposited a pound of gold with the bank, they received a note for that pound. The note represented the gold, and could itself be used as money. At the same time, the banker could lend out some of the gold to a farmer who needed to buy seed, and who would repay it with interest after the harvest had been sold. If the merchant returned for the gold, or spent the bank note and another trader wanted to redeem that note, the banker would repay the pound of gold from other deposits.

Thus begins a process by which the banker makes money – the interest on loans – from lending out gold that belongs to someone else. The business depends on taking in more gold to cover the repayment of previous deposits. The banker is effectively creating money, but also getting stuck into a cycle of debt creation that is dependent on new gold coming into the bank. The system works as long as new wealth is being created in the economy. If people stop bringing in gold, the banker can no longer repay all the depositors and goes bankrupt.

The banking system today is little changed in principle, apart from the addition of central banks, which supposedly guarantee the deposits of the nation's citizens. The main difference is one of scale. The financial sector has grown into a dominant force that affects everyone's lives, and the effects are mostly bad. Figure 28 shows the growth of debt in various countries.

The grand illusion

Wealthy people don't *need* to borrow money. When the wealthy borrow, it's usually because they can use the money to make more money. This is what banks do.

The really poor of the world don't borrow either, because nobody will lend money to a person who has no assets, and no prospects of earning more than pennies. It is mostly the middle classes that borrow, though one of the features of the credit boom was that banks had started lending to people on the margins of

Figure 28

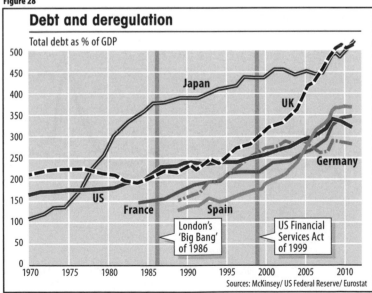

Debt and deregulation

Total debt as % of GDP

Japan

UK

Germany

US

France

Spain

London's 'Big Bang' of 1986

US Financial Services Act of 1999

Sources: McKinsey/ US Federal Reserve/ Eurostat

poverty, people who wouldn't have been granted mortgages in the days before bank deregulation.

But effectively, the financial system represents a massive transfer of wealth from the middle classes to the very rich. In the boom years, the middle classes were happy to accept this, or at least they mostly didn't question it, because they were buying houses that were going up in value. They were becoming quite wealthy themselves, and even if this wealth was tied up in the value of the houses they lived in, and therefore wasn't actually available for spending, the banks were happy to offer new loans based on that increasing equity. The good times kept rolling along on this rising tide of debt.

There was only one problem: the whole thing was an illusion and the credit bubble had no basis in reality. As I've already pointed out, the real wealth of the economy was growing at a much lower rate than GDP figures implied.

As the banks invented increasingly elaborate ways of profiting from the build-up of wealth, both real and artificial, they lost

Figure 29

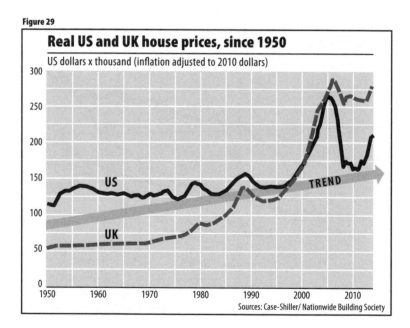

Sources: Case-Shiller/ Nationwide Building Society

sight of the true value of the assets they were using as collateral. In particular, they lost sight of the true value of housing, as shown in Figure 29, but to some extent they also became detached from the true value of everything else, including money.

Perhaps the problem goes so deep that it's impossible to see from a skyscraper window but, whatever the reason, these high-flying traders and gamblers appear to have lost sight of a simple truth: there is no real value to be gained from unproductive credit creation and speculation. Such activity is not real work, which perhaps explains why so many traders can't wait to take their final bonuses and move on to something more genuinely rewarding.

6 Betting naked

The growth of finance; derivatives explained

As we have seen, a change occurred during the second half of the 20th century, as the golden age of real industrial expansion gradually turned into a more tarnished age of financial expansion. The economies of the developed world came to rely less on making things and more on shifting accumulated wealth around. Even large industrial corporations moved into the finance game, as it became easier to make a profit from lending money than from making real stuff. General Motors, for example, was making two-thirds of its profit from its finance division by 2004 and, in the same year, Ford made a loss on car manufacture but a billion-dollar profit from its credit business.

Global competition hit the manufacturing industry much harder than it did the financial sector, where the costs of labor and materials are less significant. The whole concept of productivity and efficiency that has been such a driving force in the real economy – the survival-of-the-fittest mentality that requires job-cutting to stay competitive – hardly applies to investment banking, where one trader can make millions simply by pressing a few keys on his keyboard, just as long as his luck doesn't run out.

But it is exactly this lack of real jobs and industry that makes the growth of the financial sector so damaging to the real economy. When banks made most of their money by lending to industry for investment in new wealth-creating business, or by lending to the middle classes so they could buy homes and cars, they had a direct link to the real world. It was in bank managers' interest to make sure their customers prospered.

All that changed during the 1980s and 1990s. Thanks to new legislation forced through by the influential executives of Wall Street and the City, many of whom had close links to government in both the US and UK, liabilities became limited. Commercial banks began to indulge in practices that had previously been

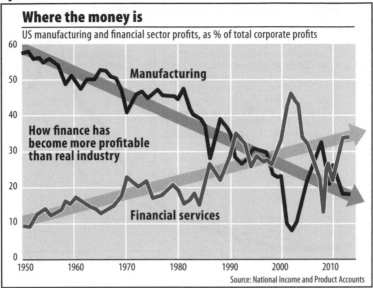

Figure 30

Where the money is

US manufacturing and financial sector profits, as % of total corporate profits

Manufacturing

How finance has become more profitable than real industry

Financial services

Source: National Income and Product Accounts

limited to investment banks, resulting in a new bonus culture in which managers and traders got rich using other people's money. Combined with new technology that made international trading and speculation much easier, this led to a rapid rise in what has come to be known as 'shadow banking'.

As wealth accumulated and more of the banks' profits came from speculation, bankers began to lose their traditional link with the real economy. They were amassing more money than was needed for real investment, and they began to devise increasingly unorthodox methods of using that money to create more money. The big banks also began to acquire stakes in other companies on a scale never seen before, to the point where, according to a 2011 report by the Swiss Federal Institute of Technology, a small network of the biggest transnational banks and other mostly financial institutions – what the researchers called a 'super-entity' of 147 closely linked companies – controlled 40% of the global economy in terms of revenue.

This trend towards massive wealth accumulation in a select group of transnational banks (which really means a relatively

Figure 31

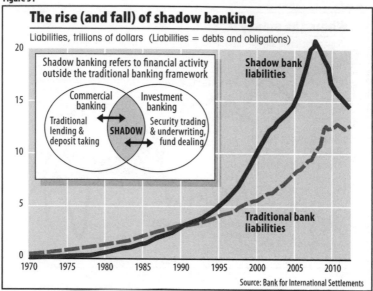

small group of influential owners, executives and investors) has distanced the banks from their traditional high-street banking activity – real investment on the ground, as it were – and focused their attention on making much bigger profits through share dealing and speculation, a trend that can be seen in the growth of the derivatives market.

A derivative is a type of contract between two parties, the value of which is 'derived' from an underlying asset; it has no value in itself. The contract specifies a future date at which an agreed transaction will take place, but the nature of that transaction varies, depending on the type of contract.

The most common are 'Forwards' or 'Futures', where one party agrees to buy an asset, and the other to sell it, at a future date, but at a price specified at the time the contact is made. Another type is an 'Option', which means the buyer has the right, but is not obliged, to buy the asset at the agreed price.

The asset in question can be anything that is traded, but the most popular these days are currencies, equities and commodities. Interest-rate and exchange-rate contracts make up the bulk of derivative trading, which means that a huge chunk of financial activity consists of betting on the future strengths of currencies relative to each other. As Figure 32 shows, the derivatives business grew rapidly, to the point where the notional values being traded far exceeded the underlying asset values (and also far exceeded the US regulated limit, which American banks got round by operating from their London offices).

This recent explosive growth in the trading of various complex forms of securities stemmed from the technological revolution that brought us the internet, without which such huge volumes of information 'sifting' would be impossible. The general idea is to profit from the change in price of whatever it is one is dealing in, either over time, as with futures, or almost instantly, as with the process of arbitrage – taking advantage of the temporary price difference between different markets. To the traders sitting at their computer terminals, it can seem like an exciting game, not so different from online gambling.

One such derivative 'instrument', to use the trade jargon, is

Figure 32

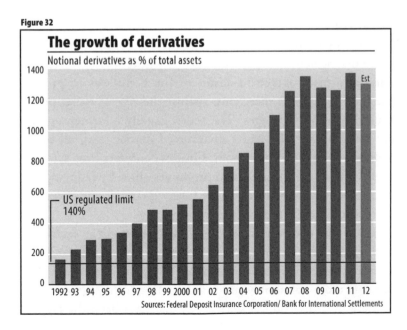

The growth of derivatives

Notional derivatives as % of total assets

US regulated limit 140%

Est

1992 93 94 95 96 97 98 99 2000 01 02 03 04 05 06 07 08 09 10 11 12

Sources: Federal Deposit Insurance Corporation/ Bank for International Settlements

the Credit Default Swap (CDS), a form of default insurance on bonds issued by corporations or governments. Most of the $30-trillion annual trade in these CDS contracts is undertaken by speculators who have no interest in the underlying protection, but merely want to profit from buying and selling contracts as the prices shift according to the perceived risk. Such purely speculative CDS dealing is termed 'naked' trading.

The traders typically make large bets against a government or corporation meeting its payment obligations. Naked CDS trading can increase the risk of default by raising borrowing costs, as happened to Greece, for example. The trade lacks regulation and has been much criticized, being implicated in the failure of many large financial institutions, some of which had to be bailed out with taxpayers' money.

I will leave the moral judgment on such naked speculation to others, but one thing I feel reasonably sure about: there is no real economic value to any of this activity, and certainly no real wealth creation involved.

Futures past

Derivatives evolved in the 18th century as contracts to buy a particular agricultural product, such as wheat or rice, at a future date, at a price agreed in advance. The point was to protect the buyer, usually a merchant, against the risk of rising prices caused by crop shortages. The seller, usually a farmer, agreed the price because he had a guaranteed market and, all being well, would make a good profit. Futures contracts thus served a useful purpose for traders and producers alike, by reducing the uncertainty over products whose future quantity, and therefore price, could not be reliably predicted.

These days the transaction can either be through an exchange, such as the Chicago Mercantile Exchange, or 'over the counter', meaning the two parties negotiate directly with each other. The latter is more commonly used, as it is free from regulation. It is these over-the-counter derivatives that have been the biggest

Figure 33

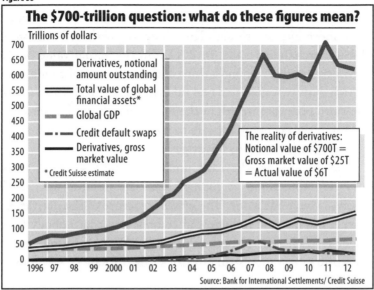

The $700-trillion question: what do these figures mean?

Trillions of dollars

Legend:
- Derivatives, notional amount outstanding
- Total value of global financial assets*
- Global GDP
- Credit default swaps
- Derivatives, gross market value

* Credit Suisse estimate

The reality of derivatives:
Notional value of $700T =
Gross market value of $25T
= Actual value of $6T

Source: Bank for International Settlements/ Credit Suisse

source of bank failures in recent decades, the failure often being blamed on a 'rogue trader' (effectively an online gambler who got a bit carried away, and whose luck ran out).

In 2011 the Bank for International Settlements announced that the total amount of over-the-counter derivatives outstanding had reached a new record of $707 trillion (which looks like this, by the way: $707,000,000,000,000), which was more than 10 times total world GDP (around $63 trillion in 2011 – see Figure 33).

One reason these sums are so huge is that they represent commodities or currencies that will never actually change hands, and can be traded any number of times by different traders at the same time – hence the absurdly high 'notional' value. Also they include two-way bets. The trader isn't actually at risk of being asked to pay the full amount gambled because if one bet loses the other must win; the bets are 'hedged'.

So a notional value of $700 trillion represents a gross market value of around $25 trillion, which is what the contracts would be worth if they had to be settled on the day. Taking out the bets that offset each other, this gross value is reduced to an actual value more like $6 trillion. This compares with $18 trillion of global merchandise trade (in 2011). So the actual value of the derivatives trade is around a third of the trade in real goods, even though derivatives have no real value in themselves. This ratio of one-third phantom wealth in the financial sector relative to real wealth in the economy appears to have some significance, as we will discover later in this investigation.

And for anyone who can't understand how so much trade goes into something as intangible as an interest rate, don't worry – you aren't alone. The whole structure of the derivatives market has become so huge and complicated that nobody fully understands it. These are the things that Warren Buffet, one of the world's most successful investors, called 'financial weapons of mass destruction'.

Obscure as this business might seem, there is one thing we can be fairly certain about: all this apparent economic activity in things that have no real value has distorted the overall picture, as far as the true value of the world's wealth goes. It just isn't possible to create wealth out of nothing; an obvious point, I know, but I feel it is worth repeating nonetheless. When these traders make themselves or their banks some money from such speculation, they are taking that money from someone else. If one trader gains, someone else must lose. Sometimes, as with Greece, a whole nation loses.

7 From warehouse to whorehouse

Early industry and the dawn of trade

Without real wealth to back it up, money has no value. Or, to go back one stage further: without real wealth, there is no economy and no civilization. It is perhaps worth reminding ourselves how we ended up where we are now, trading worthless contracts and gambling with money that doesn't exist. The modern world seems so complex; so random and confusing. Looking back to simpler times, gaining a historical perspective as it were, might help us to understand things better.

In the beginning

Since the story of economics must start somewhere, we might as well start at the beginning. Once upon a time the world was a green and pleasant land, full of lush forests, pure rivers and an abundant variety of life. Making their way slowly towards the top of the food chain were our ancestors, the early humans. They lived off wild fruits, nuts, birds' eggs, dead animals they found lying around, seafood if they were near the coast.

As their brains developed, they figured out ways of killing animals using sharp pieces of stone and sticks. About a million years ago, humans became hunter-gatherers rather than just scavengers. They began to make tools such as axes and spearheads out of flint, a hard sedimentary rock that splits into sharp pieces, to help them kill larger animals. They lived nomadic lifestyles, following herds around.

People were smaller in those days and still resembled the apes from which we've all evolved, even though the earliest human ancestors had split from chimpanzees about five million years earlier. So humans have been around a long time in one form or another, but as far as the economy goes, they took a while to get started.

Figure 34

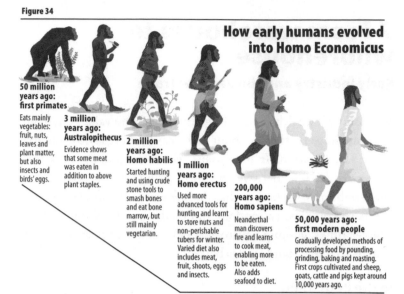

How early humans evolved into Homo Economicus

50 million years ago: first primates
Eats mainly vegetables: fruit, nuts, leaves and plant matter, but also insects and birds' eggs.

3 million years ago: Australopithecus
Evidence shows that some meat was eaten in addition to above plant staples.

2 million years ago: Homo habilis
Started hunting and using crude stone tools to smash bones and eat bone marrow, but still mainly vegetarian.

1 million years ago: Homo erectus
Used more advanced tools for hunting and learnt to store nuts and non-perishable tubers for winter. Varied diet also includes meat, fruit, shoots, eggs and insects.

200,000 years ago: Homo sapiens
Neanderthal man discovers fire and learns to cook meat, enabling more to be eaten. Also adds seafood to diet.

50,000 years ago: first modern people
Gradually developed methods of processing food by pounding, grinding, baking and roasting. First crops cultivated and sheep, goats, cattle and pigs kept around 10,000 years ago.

Homo sapiens began to evolve as a distinct species around 200,000 years ago. A combination of factors around 50,000 years ago – the requirements of tool-making, living in large social groups, sexual selection – resulted in an increase in brain size and greater intelligence among humans. Tools became more sophisticated and people began to fish as well as hunt. Simple boats, resembling canoes, had been invented by this time.

People had also begun to use pigment for self-decoration and for painting cave walls. They made jewelry and wore clothing made from animal skins; this coincides with the migration of modern humans out of Africa and into the cooler climates of Europe and northern Asia, as shown in Figure 35.

It was also around this time that different groups of humans began to barter goods, perhaps swapping tools for animal skins, fancy shells for precious stones or pieces of shiny metal. The concept of trade was born.

Humans start to settle down

Around 12,000 years ago, towards the end of the last ice age, many regions of the world began to experience longer

Figure 35

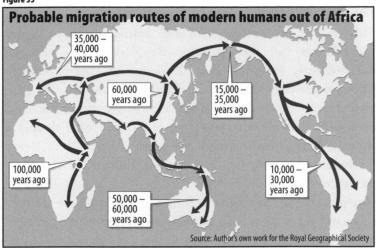

Probable migration routes of modern humans out of Africa

35,000 –
40,000
years ago

60,000
years ago

15,000 –
35,000
years ago

100,000
years ago

10,000 –
30,000
years ago

50,000 –
60,000
years ago

Source: Author's own work for the Royal Geographical Society

dry spells. This change in climate favored plants that died off in the dry season, leaving a dormant seed or tuber that would grow again when the rains came. This resulted in a large supply of wild grains and pulses of which the human population, still nomadic hunter-gatherers at this time, could make good use.

Following this change, some societies began to stay in one place, most likely around a spring or other water source where animals also gathered, and where the fertile land supported a variety of plants that could feed both animal and human populations. These plants and animals – the wild ancestors of cattle for example – were subject to a process of domestication. In other words, humans started to control them.

At some point, probably around 10,000 years ago in southeastern Turkey and what is known as the Fertile Crescent of the Middle East, humans began experimenting with the cultivation of wild wheat. By 9,000 years ago (7000 BCE), wheat cultivation had spread to Mesopotamia (an area roughly equivalent to modern-day Iraq) and in the next few thousand years it reached India, Greece and the Nile Delta, then Spain via North Africa and Germany via eastern Europe.

The first industry

This process of settling down and cultivating crops, which archeologists call the Neolithic Revolution, also occurred independently in other areas. Evidence has been found in China of rice cultivation around 7000 BCE, and by 5000 BCE agriculture – mostly the planting of rice, sorghum and flax – had become established in various parts of Africa, from Ethiopia in the east to the Atlantic coast in the west.

There is also evidence, from around 4000 BCE, of orange-tree cultivation in the Indus Valley of what is now Pakistan, plus peas, barley, figs, dates and mangos, followed by cotton a thousand years later. Also during this period, there are signs of yam cultivation in Papua New Guinea and maize in Central America, followed by potatoes, tomatoes, beans, peppers and squashes, all in the Americas.

Greece probably had a food-producing economy by 7000 BCE, with wheat and barley cultivation and also domestication of sheep, goats and pigs. In the next few thousand years, these practices would spread throughout Europe. The first evidence of enclosures for animals comes from Ireland circa 5000 BCE, where farmers built stone walls to stop their sheep from wandering off into the bog. Cattle evolved, in several different regions, from a large bovine animal known as the auroch, which originated in India but roamed wild over much of Asia and North Africa by early Neolithic times, when they first became domesticated. And some time around 4000 BCE, on the grassy steppes of the Ukraine, humans tamed the horse.

With this domestication of crops and animals came settlements, and with the harvesting of grain came the need for storage. Stone granaries are thought to have been constructed around 10,000 years ago in the Jordan Valley, where evidence of stocks of barley and fig seeds has been discovered. These would have been the first warehouses.

Other signs of production and storage come from the Zagros Mountains of northwestern Persia, where the earliest evidence of wine production has been discovered, in the form of an organic residue in a clay jar, circa 5000 BCE.

So it would appear that food production began around 10,000 years ago in several areas of the world, soon to be followed by wine production from wild grapes and the spinning of cotton into yarn. Industry had begun.

The first states

As these settlements grew and began to compete with each other for resources, alliances developed. Groups of people banded together and formed military forces for protection against other groups. By around 4000 BCE in Mesopotamia, the Indus Valley and the Nile Valley, some of these alliances began to take on the form of early states, with governments and administrators as well as armies. These early civilizations started to expand, waging wars and capturing neighboring settlements.

The first signs of trade also come from this period in Mesopotamia. This region around the Tigris and Euphrates rivers is sometimes referred to as the 'cradle of civilization' and,

Figure 36

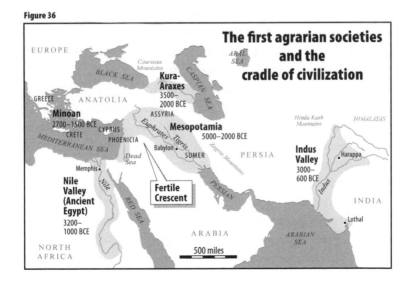

91

until the fall of Babylon in 539 BCE, was home to the Sumerians, Babylonians and Assyrians.

Early cultural developments in the region include one of the first written languages, Sumerian, and consequently some of the first books: inscribed clay tablets from around 3200 BCE. The Sumerians also played music on one of the first stringed instruments, an early version of the lyre (a kind of prototype harp). Records from Sumeria show that priests in the city of Urak were operating a bordello by 4000 BCE. So, yes, prostitution really is one of the oldest trades: the whorehouse is almost as old as the warehouse.

Technological innovation was in evidence here too, with the invention of the potter's wheel, and possibly the first wheeled vehicles, which are known to have existed in Sumeria since 3500 BCE, and possibly earlier.

The Babylonians gave the world its first philosophers, mathematicians and astronomers. They also gave us the first business tycoons, for it was in this cradle of civilization that the first significant economy developed.

The first economies

Before these developments in Bronze-Age Mesopotamia, which saw the beginnings of urban society, each small settlement had to produce everything it needed: families grew their own crops, tended their own herds of sheep and goats, made their own tools, weapons, clothes and jewelry. But it was around this time that people began to exchange goods; to trade grain for lambs or pots or clothing. Markets were set up in convenient locations: at the crossing of paths between different groups of farmers or alongside a settlement, by a source of water; anywhere that people gathered.

The settlements grew and the markets became established. Some farmers began to specialize in certain crops or animals rather than trying to produce everything they needed themselves.

This period also marks the transition from the Neolithic

to the Bronze Age. Although copper had been discovered in northern Mesopotamia around 9000 BCE, and independently in other areas perhaps a bit later than this, it didn't have much use other than for jewelry, being too soft for weapons and tools. It was only after some early genius figured out that when melted down and mixed with tin, copper forms a strong alloy (which in Europe, at a later date, became known as bronze) that the value of copper began to be appreciated.

The Anatolian region proved to be rich in copper, but it was a civilization to the east of Anatolia and north of Mesopotamia, in the Caucasus, that first made use of bronze, influencing the whole region. This civilization, known as the Early Trans-Caucasians, or Kura-Araxes (after the two main rivers), had by around 3400 BCE begun to develop an economy based on farming and livestock grazing. They built mud-brick houses, harvested grain, cultivated fruit trees and domesticated cattle, sheep, goats and dogs, and, by 3000 BCE, horses too. These horses would have been captured from the herds of wild horses that roamed the steppes of southern Russia, to the north of the region.

There is evidence of trade with Anatolia and Mesopotamia. The distinctive pottery of the region has been found as far away as Syria and Israel, and metal goods from the Kura-Araxes, including bronze tools and weapons, are known to have been traded with surrounding cultures.

The first trade routes

As settlements grew in importance and the idea of markets became established, trade began to develop between cities in different regions. There is evidence of trade between the civilizations of Mesopotamia and the Indus Valley, a distance of 3,000 kilometers or so, from around 3000 BCE.

It's not clear exactly when humans began to ride horses. There are 3,000-year-old rock carvings in Tibet that show men on horseback, so it's possible that a few of these early traders rode horses or donkeys, but most would have had to make these long and

Figure 37

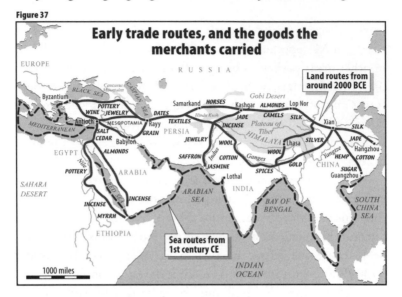

dangerous journeys on foot. The incentive was the profit to be made from luxury goods: spices, fancy textiles, jewelry, precious metals.

Towns grew up on these trade routes, catering to the merchants and their intermediaries. Some of them grew rich on this trade. By 2000 BCE there were networks of trade routes linking Mesopotamia with Anatolia and Egypt as well as the Indus Valley and northern India, and over the next thousand years these would link up with civilizations in other parts of India and into China, as shown in Figure 37.

Early transport

By this time the ancient Egyptians had domesticated the African wild ass, the ancestor of the modern donkey, and this animal soon became a popular beast of burden on the trade routes, being hardier than the horse. Donkey breeding developed into an important business in Mesopotamia after 2000 BCE. Camels were also used for carrying goods, but the donkey became the pack animal of choice.

Also around this time, or possibly a little earlier, the wooden-spoked wheel was invented. Carpenters built simple two-wheeled carts that could be pulled by horses or donkeys, and also bigger four-wheeled carts. Oxen were used for heavy duties, including the pulling of a primitive plough. The carts were of limited use, however, as the only roads at the time were a few stone-paved city streets. Tracks evolved gradually, connecting the main towns of Mesopotamia.

By 3000 BCE, boats were being used for carrying goods across and along the rivers of these early civilizations. The first maritime trade began around 1500 BCE, when the early Phoenicians built vessels to sail around the Mediterranean, from what is now the Lebanon, to Cyprus, Greece, Egypt and further west along the coast of North Africa. The shipbuilding industry was born.

Empires arise

The Phoenicians grew wealthy by trading cedar wood and also dyes, in particular a purple dye made from the shell of a type of sea-snail. Cyprus became an important source of copper and was colonized in the south by Phoenicians and in the north by Greeks. Egypt was also becoming an important sea-trading nation, its merchants crossing the Red Sea to the Arabian Peninsula. The ancient Egyptians traded papyrus and wool for gold, ivory and ebony from the lands around the southern end of the Red Sea. They also imported frankincense and myrrh, the aromatic gum resins used to make incense and perfumes, from southern Arabia.

Trade also developed in various stretches of coastal waters around the horn of Africa, the Persian Gulf, the Arabian Sea and along the coasts of India and China. By 1000 BCE in India and China, the first empires were being built, soon to be followed by the great empires of Persia, Greece and Rome.

So we can see that by the beginning of the Common Era, a time when the Roman Empire had come to rule much of Europe, most of the requirements of a modern economy were already in place. Agriculture was well established in many regions of the world, and this would have kept a majority of the population employed in one way or another, earning at least enough food to live on. Mining had become an important industry, and around this time Roman engineers pioneered hydraulic mining methods, enabling large-scale extraction of iron, lead, copper, silver and gold.

By 100, Romans, Egyptians and Greeks were trading goods directly with India and China, both by sea and across Arabia. Although the people would have been unaware of it at the time, the process that we now call globalization had begun. Without any planning and without any barriers, the market economy, based on production and trade, had become established as a natural progression in human development. People had begun to accumulate wealth. Real wealth.

8 Measuring wealth

Why oil rules the world

Wealth is a difficult thing to measure. We can give monetary values to assets such as property, and to crops and minerals, based on market value, but in the end all values are subjective and therefore arbitrary; we all value things according to our own needs and desires, which differ from those of other people and also change over time and even with mood. As we established in Chapter 5 (concerning money), it is the value of one thing relative to another thing that matters, and this relationship is governed by the utility (the combination of usefulness and desirability) and the scarcity of those things.

As I mentioned earlier, the process of wealth accumulation begins with the extraction of raw materials from the earth, and this natural wealth has value added by the industrial process, by the application of human ideas and labor. In Figure 38 I attempt to compare various related aspects of wealth, in the hope of understanding better the relationships between them.

Reading the chart from the lowest values upwards, we start with an approximation of the current dollar value of all wealth taken from the earth each year in the form of minerals, crops and so on, which in 2012 came to around $8 trillion (roughly as follows: oil & gas $5 trillion, coal and other energy $1 trillion, agricultural and forestry production around $1.5 trillion, and the remaining half trillion from other minerals).

Next up, we have total world GDP, which in 2012 was around $70 trillion. Then we have the Credit Suisse figure for total household wealth, which, unlike the two lower lines, is an accumulation rather than an annual production figure. Roughly alongside this we have the thick solid line that represents my own estimation of real wealth accumulation, as explained in the next paragraph. And I've also plotted world population because, although the scale is of a different value, the relationship of population growth to wealth creation is

Figure 38

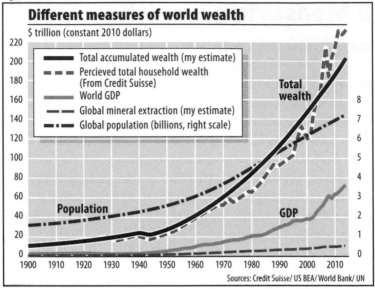

significant, as I explain below when I link it to per-capita GDP.

My estimation for total 'produced' wealth differs from the Credit Suisse figure because I include public wealth as well as private (or 'household' wealth, as it's usually called). Private wealth includes most corporate wealth, because the value of shareholdings and equity is included in these household wealth figures – in other words, everything that isn't owned by the state must be owned by private individuals (we'll ignore the issue of natural wealth for this purpose) – but it doesn't include state-owned businesses and state property. State property, which would include most of the world's infrastructure, is not an easy thing to put a value on, but it's a relatively small figure when compared to the $200 trillion or so of private wealth – I'm guessing it would be somewhere in the region of 10 per cent, or $20 trillion. I have ignored the concept of human or 'intangible' wealth, which I mentioned in Chapter 2, as it doesn't constitute anything solid that we can measure, despite attempts by the UN and the World Bank to do so.

The net result is that my graph of total accumulated wealth gives a slightly lower figure for 2012 – around $200 trillion – than Credit Suisse gives for household wealth. This is because I've knocked off $60 trillion of private wealth, for the reasons I explain elsewhere (in Chapter 12) concerning the overvaluation of money relative to real wealth, but I've also added sovereign wealth funds (including foreign reserves) of $20 trillion, plus my estimate of state-owned property, also $20 trillion.

My main point in compiling this chart is to show that real wealth accumulates steadily as the population grows and more stuff is produced, and this wealth doesn't really fluctuate with the fortunes of property and stock markets. And because of this accumulation we see total wealth rising at an ever-increasing rate relative to economic activity – a rate that is linked to population growth and the fact that, on average, people have been getting wealthier, as shown by the measure of GDP per capita, which represents economic output per head of population (Figure 39).

This average figure tells us very little about the wealth of individuals – as I've already pointed out, wealth is very unevenly

Figure 39

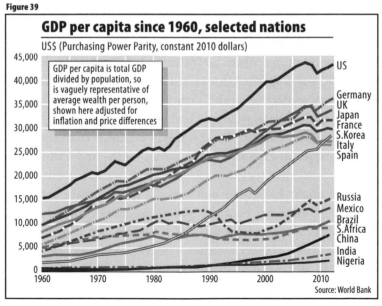

99

distributed – but it gives us an indication that, because wealth accumulates, and because we consume more as we become wealthier (therefore leading to a higher rate of production in the economy) wealth increases at a higher rate than population, by a ratio of more than three to one in recent times.

Over the period 1950 to 2010, world population rose from around 2.6 billion to 7 billion, a multiplication factor of 2.7, while global GDP, adjusted for inflation, rose from $6 trillion to $63 trillion, roughly a factor of 10. So wealth, in GDP terms at least, grew at a ratio of 3.7:1 compared to population growth. Put simply, this means that wealth per person, on average, has risen by around $100 per year in real terms over the last 60 years. But this average hides a much more complicated picture.

The accumulation of wealth

After the Second World War, the US economy was the first to expand, so Americans were the first to experience this boom in wealth. And this was real wealth creation, based on the solid foundation of industrial activity on a level never seen before, boosted by rising oil production. During the 1950s and 1960s this golden age of prosperity spread to Europe and Japan, and to a lesser extent the world in general. By the 1970s, the US boom was running out of steam as the growth in consumer demand eased off. Although the US was still the world's biggest economy by far, new centers of wealth creation had appeared in Europe and the Middle East, where oil had begun to flow.

At this time, half the world was still excluded from this free-market capitalist expansion. The Soviet Union and China were closed communist societies and, although wealth within these societies might have been more evenly spread, there wasn't so much of it. And much of the rest of the world, from India to Africa and Latin America, was still very poor.

By the 1980s, as the economies of the West became increasingly developed, all that industrial wealth, along with new Middle Eastern oil money, fed into the banking system and boosted the service sector, which continued to expand at a much higher rate than productive industry. The ratio of produced wealth to accumulated wealth, in terms of GDP, began to decline, as I showed in Figure 16.

We see this trend even more clearly in Figure 40, which shows how manufacturing, a sector that covers the majority of real industrial activity, accounts for a diminishing percentage of total annual GDP figures in the US and UK, as accumulated wealth finds its way into the financial sector following the demise of the gold standard and the subsequent deregulation of the banks.

If we compare this to my chart showing total global GDP divided into productive and unproductive output, which I reproduce here in a slightly different form (Figure 41), we can see how a change takes place during the 1970s, when the proportion of unproductive economic activity becomes greater than that of wealth-producing industry. In other words, the service sector overtakes real industry as the dominant force in the economy.

This effect led to the belief amongst economists and politicians that finance had become more important than real industry to

Figure 40

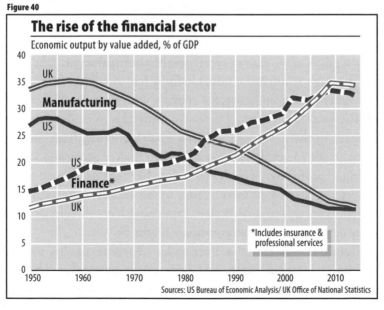

101

Figure 41

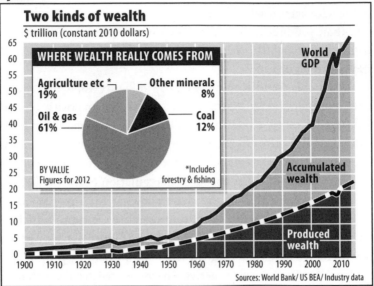

Two kinds of wealth

$ trillion (constant 2010 dollars)

WHERE WEALTH REALLY COMES FROM

Agriculture etc *
19%

Other minerals
8%

Oil & gas
61%

Coal
12%

BY VALUE
Figures for 2012

*Includes
forestry & fishing

World GDP

Accumulated wealth

Produced wealth

Sources: World Bank/ US BEA/ Industry data

the developed economy; that we had entered a post-industrial era, in which almost everyone could work in services, while the dirty business of making stuff was left to developing nations. This attitude, which gained prominence during the 1980s (the era dominated by UK prime minister Margaret Thatcher and US president Ronald Reagan) failed to take into account the fact that services alone cannot create wealth, nor ultimately jobs.

Although it might be possible for a few small nations – the Bahamas and Luxembourg, for example – to live very comfortably off the wealth of others, it is surely a mistake to expect a larger country to thrive without a strong wealth-creating base. While global trade in goods and some services makes economic sense, trying to profit from wealth made elsewhere seems rather a risky concept. Unless a country wants to be totally dependent on activities outside its jurisdiction, some wealth creation must take place close to home, wherever home might be.

Figure 41 also includes a reminder of where all this wealth originates – in the earth, and from oil in particular. The pie chart shows industrial resources as a percentage of total resource extraction, by value, for 2012. In other words all wealth produced that year – wealth from industry worldwide – began with these resources, which had value added by the industrial process, turning $8 trillion worth of raw materials into an output of $20 trillion. We might therefore conclude that the application of human ideas and labor increases the value of raw materials, on average, by a factor of 2.5, at least in market terms.

The importance of energy

We can also see that the majority of natural resources by value are used to provide energy, bearing in mind that most agricultural production ends up as food, which is of course energy for humans and cattle. Cotton and other fibers for clothing amount to less than 5% of agricultural output, while the proportion of oil that goes into plastics and other materials is also in the region of 5%. So although Figure 4 showed industrial and construction minerals making up around 40% of natural-resource extraction by volume, by value these only represent around 10% of the total, as most of these minerals tend to be high in bulk and low in value, especially compared to oil (one gets an idea by comparing the cost of a gallon can of petrol and a concrete block of the same size).

So what we find is that, measured by value, and including food, almost 90% of mineral extraction – the source of all real wealth creation – goes to supplying energy. Leaving out food, we get a figure of 73% for the contribution of fossil fuels alone.

A note with regard to my earlier equation:

| Raw materials | $\times$ | Human effort (Ideas $+$ Labor) | $=$ | Wealth |

It is important to stress that, in the context of industrial activity, the raw-material element should be measured by volume rather than value. We are not concerned here with the market price, but with the provision of the resources that enable industry, and therefore work, to take place. My point is that no wealth can be created without industry, and no industry can take place without raw materials.

A question of value

In fact, the value of raw materials can't really be measured in monetary terms. Although there is a connection between the value of money and the wealth derived from raw materials, the earth's natural wealth can't really be reduced to mere numbers, in the same way that we can't put a value on life. The market price of commodities is just that; the price decided by the market.

One might justifiably claim however, that if $8 trillion worth of raw materials are transformed into an industrial output of $20 trillion, then the value of the raw materials to the economy is $20 trillion. At the same time, one can go and dig up some clay or limestone for free. Value in this context is a tricky concept; I make the point elsewhere in this book that the real value is derived from the work – the industrial process – that turns these resources into something useful, hence the importance of energy. But the fact remains that the entire global economy is totally dependent on these natural resources.

I touched on the subject of value in Chapter 4, defining it as a function of utility combined with rarity (utility being a combination of usefulness and desirability). Is value the same thing as worth?

One might argue that something – anything – is worth what someone will pay for it, but this doesn't necessarily correspond to true value. The selling price, or market value, is dependent on supply and demand, which in turn is influenced by *perceived* value, which fluctuates according to factors ranging from the state of the economy to fashion. If a house, for example, was worth $500,000 in 2006, but only $400,000 in 2009, did it really lose value? It lost market value, certainly. But did it become less useful? This seems unlikely, as the house hadn't actually changed in any way. Did it become less rare? Not really. One might argue that it became less desirable – certainly that is what the market was saying. But I would suggest that the true value didn't change. The house was never really worth $500,000. The market overvalued the house before the crash because demand was boosted by credit. The market failed to see that the rise in selling price had no basis in reality.

The true value of a house is related to the wealth-creation process involved in its construction (the quantity of raw materials and labor that went into it) plus the value of the land. The value of the land will be a function of our utility-and-rarity formula, but again we must distinguish between true value, which can be gauged by long-term trends, and market value, which fluctuates more wildly. It is understandable that more people want to live in London than in the Outer Hebrides, for example, so it is to be expected that a house otherwise identical should be worth more in London, even though the construction process might be the same.

Another example of the market's failure to value things is provided by levels of pay. I have already tried to show how value is connected to 'usefulness', and in a free market this ought to be reflected in earnings: the more useful a job, the higher the reward should be. But the market fails to recognize this value, and awards pay levels based purely on the only thing it understands: supply and demand, as determined by the profit motive.

There might be a relationship between the supply-and-demand element and usefulness, in the sense that usefulness, or 'utility', includes desirability, but the market's interpretation of desirability is far too shallow, because the market, being just a random collection of buyers and sellers, has no way of accounting for true value, only for immediate gain. The profit motive – which tends to be a short-term consideration (though it doesn't have to be) – distorts true values.

At a very simple level, we can see in a real marketplace how perceived value fluctuates wildly according to individual needs. Towards the end of the day the traders at my local market – a traditional street market – will sell off fruit and vegetables very cheaply, because they don't expect to find any more buyers and they don't want to have to take the stuff away and dump it. Supply has exceeded demand. We buyers can get great bargains because, although the fruit and vegetables have lost value as far as the market trader is concerned, in reality they are just as tasty and nutritious as the stuff people were buying for twice as much an hour earlier. It's a sensible arrangement – I'm not suggesting otherwise. I'm merely pointing out that there's a mismatch between the market price and true value, brought about by changes to the supply-and-demand situation and the trader's perception of profit. In a case like this it doesn't matter, but there are instances where it can have serious consequences.

When it comes to rates of pay, for example, this distortion becomes more significant. Banks and investment funds will pay very highly for market traders of a different kind: the sort who are able to bring in huge profits by speculating in derivatives markets. Despite the fact that these traders are effectively gambling and their results are based more on luck than skill (all they really need is a good knowledge of the markets, and some idea of what's going on in the world generally), those who have had a good run of luck can make vast sums of money. In this case, the demand for 'lucky' traders exceeds supply; the banks compete with each other for their services – or at least they did in the boom times – and because the banks can make a lot of money from such traders, they value them highly.

Yet the true value of these speculators to society is zero, or even less than zero, because they have a negative effect on exchange rates and commodity prices – another case of distorting true values. The business they are in, being unproductive and dependent on debt creation, is partly responsible for the problems we face today. In reality, a garbage collector, for example, is far more useful to society than a derivatives trader or hedge-fund manager who gets paid a hundred times his or her wage.

The same kind of thing can be seen throughout the business world: a distortion of pay scales so that reward bears no relation to real usefulness. The free-market capitalist system fails to recognize true value, and I shall return to the implications of this later.

A word about sovereign wealth funds

In my previous calculations of total world wealth (as shown in Figure 38), I mentioned an estimate of $20 trillion for sovereign wealth funds, which are state-owned investment funds, and, as such, don't feature in household wealth assessments.

An interesting point about sovereign wealth funds is that 60% of this wealth comes from oil and gas. Perhaps that isn't surprising, considering many of them are based in the Middle East, or in places like Russia, Norway and Alaska. The funds constitute the investment of a nation's natural wealth: profit from the sale of minerals that have been in the earth's crust since its formation, or formed over millions of years, in the case of petroleum deposits; investment by the state for future contingencies; a recognition that the natural wealth isn't going to last forever and can't be replaced.

Figure 42

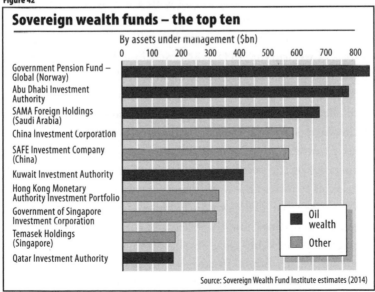

Source: Sovereign Wealth Fund Institute estimates (2014)

But sovereign wealth funds represent only around 10% of the natural wealth that's been extracted from the earth, most of the rest having been spent or invested elsewhere, most of it ending up in private hands, via the oil companies, mining conglomerates, banks and industry generally.

Much of this wealth was exploited by the corporate sectors of the developed nations of the West. Also, it was acquired relatively recently, so the wealth of large communist states of the past, such as China and the Soviet Union, doesn't figure very highly here. The industrial wealth of the last four decades, which accounts for two-thirds of total wealth in the world today, was mostly made by private companies. The major exceptions are the large state-owned oil companies of oil-rich nations, the largest of which, Saudi Arabia's Aramco, is by far the wealthiest corporation in the world, in terms of assets (though not in terms of revenue – see Figure 43).

But even the wealth of state-owned oil enterprises often finds its way into the financial sectors of the West – into the merchant banks of London, New York and Switzerland, where it makes more money for its owners, and for investment bankers. Although there is no data available to show where the world's wealth originated, it is clear, when you look into it, that those sovereign wealth funds are actually quite representative of the sources of wealth; that in fact, as I mentioned earlier, over half of all the wealth ever created has come from oil and gas.

It's not so much that sovereign wealth funds are set up mainly by oil-rich states, more that oil-rich states have the biggest share of the earth's natural wealth, and therefore the most cash to invest in funds. Another way of confirming the overwhelming importance of the petroleum industry, when it comes to wealth creation, is to look at the world's biggest corporations by revenue.

We can see that, of the world's 20 highest-earning corporations, 11 are oil companies, and these account for 61% of total revenue – a figure remarkably close to the 60% contribution of oil to sovereign wealth funds. In addition to these 11 oil companies, there are also two commodity trading companies and two energy suppliers. And there is nothing new about this situation, as the Fortune list from 1960 shows (Figure 44; though at that time only data for the US was available).

Taking this fact into account, plus the figures in my previous chart showing how fossil-fuel extraction now accounts for over 70% of real wealth creation by value (Figure 41), I think it is reasonable to estimate that around 60% of all the wealth ever created in the world originated in the earth's oil and gas fields.

Figure 43

Where the real money is made

Top-20 corporations worldwide 2012, by revenue

	Company	2012 revenue ($ billion)	Business sector
1	Royal Dutch Shell	485	**Oil & gas**
2	Exxon Mobil	453	**Oil & gas**
3	Wal-Mart Stores	447	Retail
4	BP	386	**Oil & gas**
5	Sinopec Group	375	**Oil & gas**
6	China National Petroleum	352	**Oil & gas**
7	Saudi Aramco	311	**Oil & gas**
8	Vitol	303	Commodities
9	State Grid (China)	259	Energy supply
10	Chevron	246	**Oil & gas**
11	ConocoPhillips	237	**Oil & gas**
12	Toyota Motor	235	Auto manufacture
13	Total	232	**Oil & gas**
14	Volkswagen Group	222	Auto manufacture
15	Japan Post Holdings	211	Conglomerate
16	Glencore International	186	Commodities
17	Gazprom	158	**Oil & gas**
18	E.ON	157	Energy supply
19	ENI	154	**Oil & gas**
20	General Motors	150	Auto manufacture

Sources: Fortune Magazine, Forbes, company reports

The black-gold bounty

Nothing happens without energy and, although most forms of energy can be traced back ultimately to the sun, much of the fuel we use now is taken from the earth, whether it be coal, oil, gas, wood or the food we grow to fuel ourselves. Just as the Industrial Revolution of the 19th century was powered by coal, the economic revolution of the 20th century was fuelled primarily by oil.

Although oil wells were drilled in southern Russia in 1848 and in Poland in 1854, the development of the oil industry really began in 1859, when the first commercial oil well was drilled in the US state of Pennsylvania. The oil was distilled into kerosene (or paraffin) and used mainly for lighting, replacing whale oil. The residue from the distillation process was used as asphalt. The industry remained relatively small-scale until the rise of the motor car in the early 20th century, by which time large reserves of oil had been discovered in Texas and California.

Oilfields were by then also being developed in Russia and the Dutch colony of Indonesia (where Royal Dutch Shell was formed). BP began life in Iran in 1908, as the Anglo-Persian Oil Company.

The rapid growth of the US economy throughout the middle decades of the 20th century coincided with the development of its domestic oil industry. The US was the world's dominant oil economy for much of the last century; the biggest producer by far until the 1970s. It was oil that made possible the quick development of its massive industrial base during and after the Second World War. The boom of the 1950s and 1960s (the 'golden era') was fuelled by oil. The growth of the US automobile industry and the rapid construction of its highway network, the huge defense and aeronautical industries; the general feeling of optimism and prosperity that spread throughout the economy: all this wealth had its origins in

Figure 44

Fortune top-20 US companies 1960

By revenue

	Company	1960 revenue ($ million)	Business sector
1	General Motors	11.2	Auto manufacture
2	Exxon	7.9	**Oil & gas**
3	Ford Motor	5.4	Auto manufacture
4	General Electric	4.3	Conglomerate
5	US Steel	3.6	Steel
6	Mobil	3.1	**Oil & gas**
7	Gulf Oil	2.7	**Oil & gas**
8	Texaco	2.7	**Oil & gas**
9	Chrysler	2.6	Auto manufacture
10	Esmark	2.5	Food
11	AT&T Technologies	2.3	Telecommunications
12	DuPont	2.1	Chemicals
13	Bethlehem Steel	2.1	Steel
14	Amoco	2.0	**Oil & gas**
15	CBS	1.9	Broadcasting
16	Armour	1.9	Food
17	General Dynamics	1.8	Aircraft
18	Shell Oil	1.8	**Oil & gas**
19	Boeing	1.6	Aircraft
20	Kraft	1.6	Food

Source: Fortune Magazine

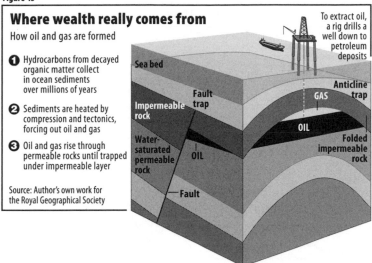

Figure 45

Where wealth really comes from
How oil and gas are formed

① Hydrocarbons from decayed organic matter collect in ocean sediments over millions of years

② Sediments are heated by compression and tectonics, forcing out oil and gas

③ Oil and gas rise through permeable rocks until trapped under impermeable layer

Source: Author's own work for the Royal Geographical Society

the earth in the form of 'black gold'. Without oil, it wouldn't have happened.

Having become so reliant on oil, the US government, as some of its own wells began to dry up, encouraged its oil industry to look to the Arabian oilfields for an alternative supply. US oil companies were the first to develop the drilling technology and were essential partners when it came to oil exploration around the Persian Gulf. The giant Saudi state oil company, Saudi Aramco, started life in 1933 as a subsidiary of Standard Oil of California. This subsidiary evolved into the Arabian American Oil Company – hence the name 'Aramco'.

While US companies were profiting from their technological lead in the Persian Gulf, the Soviet Union was developing its own massive oilfields. As Figure 46 shows, the USSR soon overtook the US as the biggest oil producer, and Russia and Saudi Arabia now swap places at the top of the chart.

The dip in Soviet production during the late 1980s occurred as some of its oil became more difficult to extract. The US government had banned the export of America's superior drilling technology to the USSR during the Cold War, knowing that the Soviets were

111

Figure 46

Top 5 oil producers, since 1900

Crude oil production, million barrels per day

Sources: US Energy Information Administration/ Institute for Energy Research

reliant on revenue from oil exports – a 1985 CIA report estimated that 25% of Soviet oil was exported, accounting for over half of all the country's hard-currency earnings – and consequently the US put pressure on Saudi Arabia to reduce oil prices. The policy was successful – the loss of oil money contributed to other failures within the Soviet system and led to further pressures for reform, and ultimately to the break-up of the Soviet Union.

I mention this only because it gives another example of the importance of oil. Although the Soviet system was considered to be inefficient, it was only when oil production began to decline that the system failed. Up to that point, it was by no means clear that the communist system wouldn't prevail. Nearly all modern economies, whatever the political regime, are reliant on oil to power industry. Russia is still extremely dependent on oil and natural gas exports, as are many other nations, from Arabia to Venezuela, by way of Nigeria and Norway (Figure 47).

I made the point earlier that GDP statistics tend seriously to underestimate the importance of oil to the economy. I have a feeling that some governments and even economists tend to

Figure 47

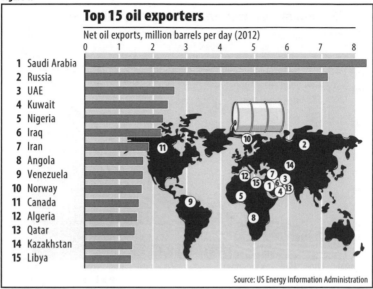

Top 15 oil exporters

Net oil exports, million barrels per day (2012)

1 Saudi Arabia
2 Russia
3 UAE
4 Kuwait
5 Nigeria
6 Iraq
7 Iran
8 Angola
9 Venezuela
10 Norway
11 Canada
12 Algeria
13 Qatar
14 Kazakhstan
15 Libya

Source: US Energy Information Administration

underestimate it too, otherwise they wouldn't put such faith in the ability of a finance-dominated service economy to grow without a wealth-producing base.

Figure 48 shows 110 years of energy use and GDP growth in the US. We can see the importance of oil and natural gas to the expansion that took place from the 1920s onwards. But we can also see that something changes around the end of the 1970s, after which point the economy appears to grow more quickly than ever, but without using as much energy.

In the next chart I zoom in on these later years and rebase the scales, so we can see more clearly this surprising development (Figure 49). Although there is a drive at this time for an increase in fuel efficiency – people started buying smaller cars, for example, spurred on by rising oil prices – this factor alone can't account for such a sudden reduction in energy needs. The data comes from a 2012 report by the US Energy Information Administration, and the researchers hint at the expansion of the service sector and the relative decline of manufacturing, but acknowledge that something else is at work, without being able to say what it is:

Figure 48

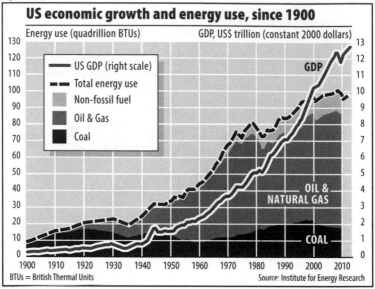

'Other factors unrelated to efficiency improvements contributed to a relative decline in energy use of 17% between 1985 and 2004.'

I suggest that the answer is related to my first chart (as shown in the inset of Figure 49); the economy booms because of the credit bubble. Spending on credit doesn't require energy because the creation of debt through the leveraging of accumulated wealth doesn't require real work. And most of the real industry that resulted from the debt-fuelled consumer boom didn't use US energy because it took place in China. The patterns of the two charts are similar because they are both telling the same story.

Of course the close correlation between energy use and economic growth is exactly what one might expect – as already noted, industry is totally dependent on energy. This point is also of great significance when evaluating the potential for further growth in the global economy, considering that, with the ever-rising demand for a limited resource, a gradual decline in oil supplies seems inevitable in the not-too-distant future. And from an environmental perspective, reduced oil consumption is an essential goal.

Although economists talk about the 'resource curse', in which countries that are rich in natural resources, especially oil, fail to develop other industries because they earn so much from commodity exports, the reality is that oil extraction has brought more wealth into the world than any other resource.

As far as the environment goes, this is not a desirable situation. Our dependence on fossil fuels is probably the greatest dilemma facing civilization right now. As we switch to renewable energy supplies, as we must do eventually, less real wealth will be created. Solar and wind power, for example, are effectively free once the infrastructure is set up, so the only wealth creation involved is in the manufacture and maintenance of the equipment required to harness this 'free' energy, and to distribute it. This point might seem debatable, to say the least: one might expect cheap and clean energy to be a huge benefit to industry, and so it will be, for the industries that make use of this energy. But my point is that the oil industry itself will gradually decline in importance, and our wealth-creating capacity will decline with it.

Figure 49

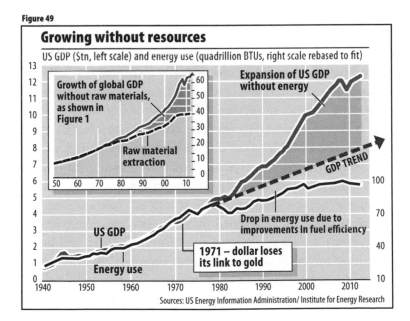

Sources: US Energy Information Administration/ Institute for Energy Research

One way of understanding this is to think of the wealth that a country such as Saudi Arabia has made from oil. Without oil, the Saudis would be poor; there is little else the country can produce, being mostly desert. But what if the Saudis covered that desert with solar panels and exported the electricity? Certainly they might earn some income in this way, but nothing like the amount they make from oil, because the resource of sunshine is so abundant, while at the same time being difficult to 'transport' very far. The electricity would have a value only to those neighboring nations, if any, that couldn't produce it as cheaply themselves. And the Saudis would have to manufacture the solar panels to create the wealth that comes from all the work involved, otherwise all that added value would go to whichever nations developed the solar-panel industry.

This brings us back yet again to the fundamental relationship between natural resources, work, wealth and money. Material wealth, as expressed in monetary terms, is a function of the amount of work involved in the industrial process; essentially, money represents an exchange of labor. The reason so much wealth comes from oil is that there is so much industrial activity involved in the whole process of exploration, extraction, refining, distribution and so on, and because oil is so vital to our current way of life, while at the same time being increasingly scarce and difficult to extract. None of these criteria apply to renewable sources, at least not to anything like the same degree.

It is an unfortunate fact that any activity that is less harmful to the environment tends to involve less wealth creation, simply because it requires fewer resources and less real industry. As oil consumption declines, whether because it is running out or because it becomes too expensive to extract, less and less real wealth is going to be pumped into the economy. We will find a substitute for oil as a source of energy, but there will be no substitute for oil as a source of great industrial wealth, unless that substitute comes from the earth, which seems unlikely.

Ignoring for now thermal energy, which, like solar energy,

is potentially abundant and cheap, the only really usable form of energy remaining in the earth in greater quantities than oil and gas is coal, and the burning of coal is even worse for the environment than the burning of oil. That doesn't mean it won't get used of course – it probably will, under the current system – but, taking a sensible and realistic approach to this problem, there is little hope for continued economic growth in the future.

We need to start thinking seriously about a whole new economic system, one that doesn't depend on growth for prosperity. And we need to redefine our concept of wealth, towards a less materialistic form of prosperity.

Part Two

Why Things Are Going To Get Worse

9 Wealth and work

Marx and the productivity problem

We have become accustomed to the idea that, overall, things tend to change for the better in this world. Economies grow as they develop, industry becomes more productive, people become wealthier, even as populations expand. Each generation ends up better off than the previous generation. At least, that's what happened in the second half of the 20th century.

But it didn't happen that way for most of human history, and it isn't happening any more. For a lot of families now, the younger generation has no hope of earning their parents' level of income. In fact, the second half of the 20th century was almost certainly an anomaly, a happy coincidence of abundant natural wealth, heavy industrialization powered by cheap oil and, starting from a low base after years of war and hardship, a self-sustaining increase in demand for goods and services. It couldn't go on forever, and now it has ended.

In the previous chapter I made the point that accumulated wealth – wealth from industry past that is now invested in the financial sector – doesn't lead to significant job creation. Real job creation, even in services, requires the produced wealth of real industry. Banking has never been a labor-intensive business and, despite the fact that the financial sector has thrived on accumulated wealth, new technology means it is becoming even less dependent on actual workers. And although some of this past wealth will be reinvested in real industry, the percentage that goes to job creation is declining as industry becomes ever more productive.

Productivity is a measure of output relative to input, and tells us how efficiently a business is run, in the same way that fuel consumption reflects energy efficiency. As wages are one of the main costs of industry, higher labor productivity means lower costs and helps a company to compete in the global marketplace: the higher the output per worker, the greater the profit for a given sale price of the goods produced. The other main costs – raw materials and capital (factory construction and machinery) – are relatively fixed, so provide less scope for cost-cutting. So we can see why economists and business leaders always stress the importance of raising labor productivity.

One might suppose that if manufacturing were to become so productive that it employed only two per cent of the working-age population to make everything the world needs, it would still be creating just as much wealth as when it required 10 times as many workers. After all, that's what happened when agriculture became more productive. Food output continued to rise while workers who lost their jobs on the farms found higher-paid work in the new industries.

This was how many economists and politicians viewed the situation during the boom years of the 20th century. There was a general feeling that increasing productivity was entirely for the good, that more wealth would be created and workers could find better jobs in the service sector – nice clean office jobs, instead of all that dirty industry. We could all work fewer hours for more pay, with longer vacations and earlier retirement, as all this wealth accumulated and spread around the economy.

But the reality turns out to be different. As I explained in previous chapters, the economy requires a substantial foundation of genuine wealth-creating industry to support the non-productive sector, and this industry cannot thrive without a certain level of employment, because it is only through the employment of workers that the wealth is spread around and demand for products is sustained. When workers moved from the fields to the factories, they went from the old wealth-creating sector to a new wealth-creating sector, and in the process created a lot more wealth. But, as I explained in Chapter 2, when it comes to services, it doesn't work like that.

The rise of the machine

The idea of replacing workers with machines is almost as old as civilization itself. The first ox-drawn ploughs were invented in Mesopotamia around 5000 BCE, though things didn't progress much in agriculture (the largest source of employment by far until recent times) until the 18th century. A much bigger change came with the Industrial Revolution of the late 18th and early 19th centuries, when the mechanization of the British textile industry, combined with the development of the steam engine, brought in massive improvements in productivity.

The cottage industry that had existed until the mid-1700s, in which home-based artisans produced cloth from wool or flax, was transformed into the mill-based cotton industry of the 1800s. This new industry soon became a source of great wealth, relative to the old agricultural existence. British ships imported bales of raw cotton, first from India and then from America, and the mills of the north of England, powered initially by streams and then by local coal, produced cloth that was exported to mainland Europe and around the empire.

In the process, the living standards of the masses began to rise and the population, previously constrained by disease and lack of food, began to increase in number. Throughout this age of industrial expansion, the development of steel and other innovations led to the invention of machine tools that helped to make the new industries more productive. The gradual adoption of the mechanized farm tractor, beginning in the late 18th century, boosted food production, but also accelerated the transition from a rural, agricultural existence, in which most people worked on the land, to a more urban, industrial way of life.

The number of people earning more than a subsistence wage (just enough to survive on) began to grow; a new middle class emerged, and with it a demand for services. The service sector expanded to take advantage of this new wealth.

In Figure 5 I showed how the US evolved from a

Figure 50

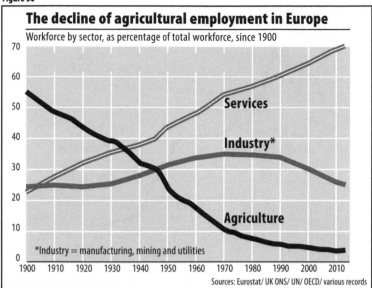

The decline of agricultural employment in Europe

Workforce by sector, as percentage of total workforce, since 1900

Services

Industry*

Agriculture

*Industry = manufacturing, mining and utilities

Sources: Eurostat/ UK ONS/ UN/ OECD/ various records

predominantly agricultural economy to an industrial and then a service economy. Figure 50 shows how the same historical pattern occurred in Europe, a decade or so later than in the US.

The beat of heavy metal

When it comes to real wealth creation, the heavier the industry the better. The more raw materials used, the more labor needed, the more wealth is created. 'Where there's muck, there's brass,' the first industrialists of the north of England liked to say (brass being slang for money) and this is still a popular saying in the region, though most of the muck has gone now, and most of the brass has gone with it. Call centers are clean environments; the wealth is created elsewhere.

At the peak of the Industrial Revolution, the tall chimneys of those northern mills (the 'dark satanic mills' of William Blake's famous poem, 'Jerusalem') belched smoke from their coal-fired engines into the valleys of the Pennines around Manchester, while the workers toiled away inside the factories and in the nearby coal mines, and also in the distant cotton fields of the

Figure 51

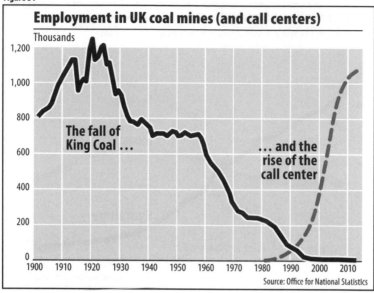

Employment in UK coal mines (and call centers)

Thousands

The fall of King Coal …

… and the rise of the call center

Source: Office for National Statistics

southern US, where the raw material for this new wealth grew.

In the early 20th century, as productivity increased and jobs were lost on the land and in the old industries that had grown with the Industrial Revolution, especially textile manufacture, workers found employment in new manufacturing: in shipbuilding, railways, coal mining and steel making, or in the nascent car industry. By the end of the Second World War, the global economy, like much of Europe, lay in ruins. When the War ended, there followed a huge demand for almost everything: food, clothing, construction materials, anything that would help people rebuild their shattered lives.

The one country that could satisfy this demand was the United States, which had taken over from Britain as the world's industrial superpower, partly because of the War. The US manufacturing industry, having struggled through the Great Depression of the 1930s, a depression that was partly a result of lost agricultural jobs, was revived during the War by government spending on armaments. When the War ended, the factories made a quick transition to producing cars and washing machines and television

Figure 52

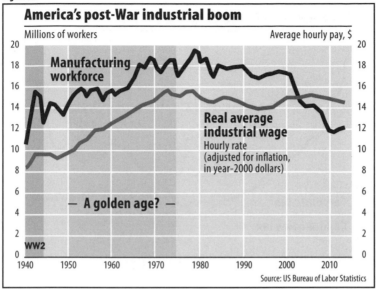

America's post-War industrial boom

Millions of workers   Average hourly pay, $

Manufacturing workforce

Real average industrial wage
Hourly rate (adjusted for inflation, in year-2000 dollars)

— A golden age? —

WW2

1940   1950   1960   1970   1980   1990   2000   2010

Source: US Bureau of Labor Statistics

sets, and the American people bought them by the millions. For the first time in decades, everyone could find work, wages were rising, everything was looking good (Figure 52).

As noted in the previous chapter, the US had the advantage of abundant oil to fuel this post-War industrial and construction boom; a boom in which refineries, factories, interstate highways, shopping malls and suburban homes spread across the world's wealthiest nation. Americans might claim a certain inbred 'ingenuity' and an entrepreneurial predisposition to hard work, but the real source of their great wealth was the earth itself, of which the European settlers had just happened to claim a particularly rich slice. This earth contained not just oil, but a big chunk of the world's most productive farmland, forests, coal and lots of other minerals.

This post-War golden age coincided with the rapid rise of Hollywood, which, through its movies and newsreels, broadcast the American Dream across a world that waited eagerly (though often in vain) for its share of this new wealth.

With less fanfare but perhaps greater significance, the US

Figure 53

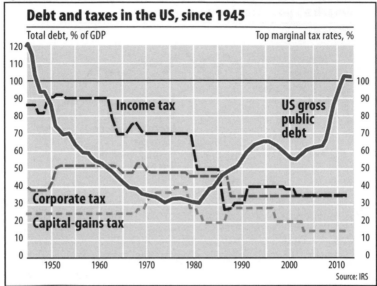

Debt and taxes in the US, since 1945

Total debt, % of GDP — Top marginal tax rates, %

Income tax

US gross public debt

Corporate tax

Capital-gains tax

Source: IRS

government raised tax rates on corporations and high-earning individuals during this period of rising prosperity, and paid off its war debts, as seen in Figure 53. In the immediate post-War years, when people remembered well enough the years of hardship and understood that the government had borrowed heavily to fund the war effort, paying taxes was the accepted price of freedom.

By the 1960s, this wave of prosperity had crossed the Atlantic and washed over most of western Europe, which had finally recovered from the ravages and rationing of war. The economies of Europe and North America averaged over 4% growth annually during the 1950s and 1960s, as production increased to meet demand (France would later christen the period from 1946 to 1975 *les trentes glorieuses*, marking 30 glorious years). Industrial wages rose faster than prices, and all this new wealth helped to create new jobs in the rapidly expanding service sectors.

Between 1950 and 1975, living standards in Europe and the US grew by an average of 3% per year. Unemployment fell to the lowest levels ever recorded.

Figure 54

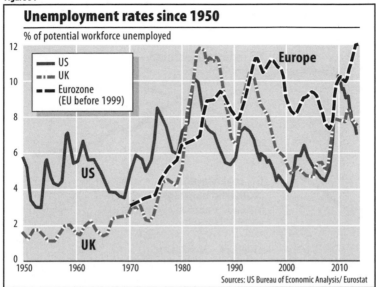

Unemployment rates since 1950

% of potential workforce unemployed

US
UK
Eurozone
(EU before 1999)

Europe

US

UK

Sources: US Bureau of Economic Analysis/ Eurostat

By the 1960s and 1970s, workers were getting used to the idea that they had power; they were an essential ingredient in this new prosperity, and they wanted their cut. Unions gained strength and wages rose to new peaks. For the first time in history, the working classes were becoming the middle classes. All this new wealth led to a boom in services: fancy new supermarkets and other retail outlets, leisure and entertainment centers; travel and holidays; luxury goods for the masses.

Civilization, in the developed world at least, had evolved from an existence in which the main concern was survival to a society in which survival was taken for granted, and the main concern had become advancement up the social ladder.

At this stage the wealth was still real. The rise in prosperity in this golden age was a direct result of industry employing more workers, adding more value to more natural resources, as seen by the correlation between resource use and GDP in Figure 15, and in Figure 55, which shows industrial output and wages in the G7 group of developed countries.

By the 1980s, however, the benefits of increased productivity

Figure 55

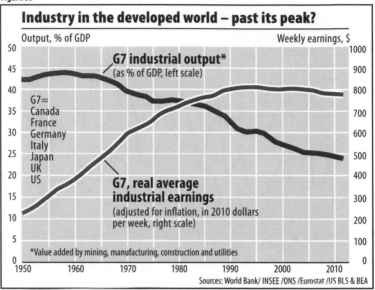

began to go more to the senior managers and to the shareholders, rather than to the workers. Wages on the shop floor stopped rising. At the same time, as more wealth found its way into banks and the financial sector gained influence, US and UK governments cut bank regulation at the behest of these new masters of growth. Priorities were changing; the economy was moving from dirty old industry to a new era of finance and business services. The bankers and the markets were taking charge.

Was Marx right?

With his 'surplus-value' theory, Karl Marx, building on the work of Adam Smith[1], suggested that labor was the sole source of economic value. He was making the point that industrial profit, being the difference between the input costs of industry (materials, labor and capital) and the sale price of the goods, is a function of worker input over and above the wage paid to the worker. The worker takes the raw materials and adds value by converting them into something useful, allowing the factory owner (the capitalist) to sell the product for a profit.

Marx also argued that the replacement of labor by capital (by which he meant the machinery used for production) resulted in a 'reserve army' of unemployed workers, holding down wages. This argument makes sense; for the unemployed, low pay is better than no pay. But then he develops his theory to suggest that, because labor is the only source of value, using machinery in place of labor must lead to a fall in profit. According to Marx, this encourages the capitalist to spend even more on machinery, or capital, and even less on labor, maintaining profit at the expense of the worker. He thought that this exploitation of labor, and the resulting class conflict, would eventually bring down the capitalist system.

At first glance, Marx's logic here seems a bit skewed, suggesting that if machines do the job instead of workers, the factory makes less profit. One might assume that the reverse is true, because in the long run the machines cost less than the workers; they don't demand pay rises and days off, or go on strike. In other words, they are more productive.

But Marx was right, for two related reasons. First, productivity gains result in lower costs, but competition between producers also drives down prices, so profits are kept down too. This is one apparent advantage of the free-market capitalist system: consumers benefit from the lowest possible prices.

Second, Marx was looking well beyond the factory walls, to society itself. In the long term, the increased productivity of industry, brought about by technological innovation, means that the reserve army of unemployed workers grows so large that it becomes a huge burden on the state, resulting in severe social disruption. As unemployment increases, society becomes poorer and the people have less money to spend on goods, so factory profits fall further.

It turns out that the apparent benefit of low consumer prices is a false saving; it is better to pay a higher price and maintain close to full employment.

But the expansion of the economy during the late 19th century, due to the productivity gains that Marx was criticizing, had the effect of obscuring the fundamental truth of his theory, as it would for most of the 20th century too.

Until recently, as I pointed out earlier, most workers who lost their jobs in the old industries found work in newer industries, often in the service sector. This is no longer happening, however, because, for the vast majority at least, there is no longer the excess wealth that in the boom times created a demand for services that people didn't really need. Also, services themselves are becoming more 'productive', as new technology finds its way into banks and supermarket check-outs and the internet reduces the need for various retail outlets (travel agents, bookshops, record stores and so on) – though 'productive' isn't perhaps the right word in connection with services, which don't really produce anything; 'efficient' might be a better word. But either way, the main benefit of the service sector to society – the provision of employment opportunities outside the realm of real industry, based on the wealth of that industry – is reduced by these efficiency gains.

Marx didn't foresee the huge rise in the service sector, which actually increased the wealth of the workers while the industrial economies were booming. The real wealth came from the raw materials, so when labor was replaced by machinery it didn't matter too much because value was still being added, just as long as people found work elsewhere. In a sense, the machinery represents an increase in the 'ideas' element of my wealth equation.

But even if the ideas element increases with new technology, the need for labor is decreasing at a faster rate. So could it be that Marx's predictions are finally coming true? Could it be that increases in productivity are finally leading to a permanent rise in the 'reserve army' of unemployed?

Figure 56 shows how the 2008/09 recession was different from previous recessions over the last half-century, in terms of

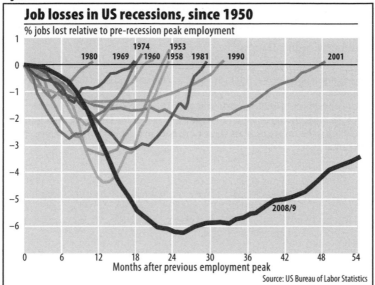

Figure 56

Job losses in US recessions, since 1950

% jobs lost relative to pre-recession peak employment

1974 1953
1980 1969 1960 1958 1981 1990 2001

2008/9

Months after previous employment peak

Source: US Bureau of Labor Statistics

US employment. In the past, the job market picked up as the economy recovered, but after the last recession, although the US economy began to grow again slowly, it did so without creating many new employment opportunities.

There's no doubt that the majority of people in advanced economies have been becoming poorer since the bursting of the credit bubble – incomes have been falling relative to prices. The main reason for this is the decline of industrial employment due to the rise in productivity, and the resulting decline in wealth distribution as more of the profits go to the very wealthy.

Usually after a recession there's a revival of demand as consumers start spending again, but this isn't happening any more. Throughout the world, especially the developed world, people have been feeling the effects of the credit crisis – the build-up of debt that fuelled the previous boom, and which we now have to pay for as the economy adjusts downwards to find its true level.

The developed world's golden era is well and truly over; capitalism is no longer capable of delivering the prosperity to

131

which we have become accustomed. It seems that, when it comes to his theory concerning the value of labor at least, Marx might have been right all along.

1 The Scottish philosopher Adam Smith is usually referred to as the first modern economist, and his work *An Inquiry Into the Nature and Causes of the Wealth of Nations*, published in 1776, the first modern book on economics. He wrote about the 'labor theory of value', though the idea that the labor that goes into something is the source of all its value goes back at least to Thomas Aquinas in the 13th century.

10 The technology dilemma

Why real jobs are in decline

Increases in productivity come mainly from technological innovation, and it was by leading the way in this field that the US gained its pre-eminent position in global manufacturing after the Second World War. But as unions gained power and competition increased from the newly revived industries of Japan and Germany, the US began to lose this advantage. Japanese car manufacturers, for example, took the US production methods and improved on them, and by the 1970s they were beating the US at its own game, making better cars with fewer workers. American industry fought back, and the battle to improve productivity goes on still.

The winners, at least initially, are global consumers, who get better cars, or whatever the product might be, at lower prices. The losers are the workers whose jobs are cut, and the old industrial strongholds like Detroit, where half the working-age population is unemployed and some residential suburbs now resemble wastelands.

So we can see that increasing productivity keeps prices low, which seems like a good thing, but only as long as new employment opportunities arise elsewhere. Certainly it can help a company, and even a nation, to be more competitive. It also means that the manufacturing labor force, though reduced in size, can at least survive in a higher-wage country, as wages decline in relation to output. But if there are no new jobs being created elsewhere in the economy, the result of increased productivity becomes higher unemployment, and the productivity of the economy as a whole declines. A wage earner, even at the lower end of the pay scale, makes a positive contribution to the economy. An unemployed worker, by contrast, is a drain on the economy, not only because of welfare payments, but also because of the cost in terms of increased crime and antisocial behavior, vandalism and so on, plus the less obvious costs associated with wasted education and blighted lives.

Figure 57

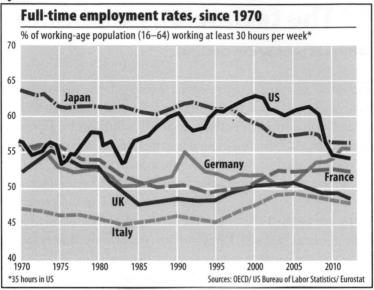

Full-time employment rates, since 1970

% of working-age population (16–64) working at least 30 hours per week*

*35 hours in US — Sources: OECD/ US Bureau of Labor Statistics/ Eurostat

When we reach the point where manufacturing requires very few workers, the only possible result, bearing in mind that the service sector can't flourish without a strong industrial base, is mass unemployment, followed by the decline of that super-lean manufacturing industry, which discovers now that there aren't enough consumers with enough money to buy its products. For the simple fact is that, if people don't have jobs, there is less wealth being distributed around the economy. Yet real jobs are in decline, to a greater extent than the unemployment figures might suggest.

Figure 57 shows how full-time employment is in decline relative to working-age populations as a whole. There is a trend towards part-time jobs, especially for women and older workers, which doesn't show up in the usual employment statistics, but is nevertheless highly significant, and is one of the reasons that average wages have been falling in real (inflation-adjusted) terms. Without these part-time jobs, the unemployment figures would look much worse. In the US, and in Europe as a whole, 20% of all jobs are now part-time, and in the UK the figure has recently risen to 28% (in 2013).

There is also a trend towards more self-employment (as shown in Figure 58), which again is partly a result of the shortage of full-time jobs. For many people with a skill, trying to make it on one's own is preferable to being unemployed, and governments often encourage such self-employment because it's better than adding to the dole lines. Self-employment is a good thing in many ways – the natural state for a worker, perhaps – but a lot of people who try this route end up with very low incomes, struggling along on what can easily end up being less than the minimum wage.

The result of these two trends is that the unemployment statistics hide a serious decline in well-paid jobs in the West, in the kind of employment that most people took for granted during the boom years.

To live is to work

Jobs mean more than just employment. This was what Marx meant when he said that labor was the source of all economic

Figure 58

Rise of the self-employed

Self-employment* as % of total employment (left scale)

US

UK

... but income is falling

Average annual earnings of self-employed
$ x thousand (right scale)

US

UK

*Includes self-employed incorporated (US)   Sources: UK ONS/ US Census/ Bureau of Labor Statistics

value: without work there would be nothing except the natural environment. Without work, we can't survive, and the natural wealth of the earth will remain forever in the ground. It seems likely that, in one sense at least, our hunter-gatherer ancestors must have spent most of their days working, just to provide themselves with enough food and shelter.

Human development has seen a process in which we spend a diminishing proportion of our time working just to survive, thanks to increasing productivity, but there's a limit to how far this process can go, partly because our expectations have risen along with our leisure time. We still need to work to create the real wealth that society depends on.

But even this doesn't explain the full importance of work. Not only is work the source of all economic value, in one sense it is the source of *all* value. We've become accustomed to defining ourselves by a trade or profession – he's a carpenter, she's a doctor, and so on – but this hides a more fundamental point about work. It doesn't have to involve such specialization, or even to bring in a wage. At one time work would have included a mixture of growing enough food to live on, building a shelter, making clothes from animal skins, while at the same time raising a family. All these things involve real work, but they are also the source of satisfaction and quality of life – the source of all value.

Work is not just a necessary function of the economy; it is also a vital part of our lives. It gives us a purpose, a reason to get out of bed in the morning, a sense of being needed, of being useful. It might well be that we aren't really needed and we aren't much use, but that's not the point. A society in which there is an ever-growing pool of idle people is a society heading for serious trouble. Younger people especially need to be gainfully employed, preferably learning a skill.

Ideally, everyone who wants a job should be able to find one, but under the current system that isn't going to happen. When we get to the stage where half the population aged 18-25 can't find employment, as is already the case in some European countries, then we're heading for a much bigger crisis than the one we experienced in 2008.

The decline in real jobs

So increasing productivity was seen as a good thing in the boom years of the last century, and still is by most economists and politicians. It helps industry to remain competitive, to be lean and mean. The logical conclusion of this reasoning is that a fully automated factory, one that could produce 50,000 cars per year, for example, with only a skeleton workforce of a hundred people, would be a fantastic achievement.

The absurdity of this policy is obvious from the employment perspective, but that's the way manufacturing has been heading anyway, as shown in Figure 59 (with regard to the US, but the trend is universal). The problem is the element of competition: in the global marketplace, survival of the fittest is the rule. The most productive manufacturer has the advantage, other factors being equal. And even if labor costs are not equal, a highly automated process is seen as the way to go. It guarantees build-quality and reliability, and it means you can build factories closer to markets without worrying too much about the local labor costs.

Manufacturers don't see their primary responsibility as providing employment, of course; they are there to make things, and in the process to make a profit. And as long as workers were finding jobs in the service sector, unemployment didn't seem to be a big problem. But things have changed since the 2008 crash and subsequent recession. Manufacturing has picked up slightly, but without creating new jobs. The service sector, however, is barely picking up at all, and there are obvious reasons for this.

For one thing, the growth in services over the previous two decades, or at least the two decades prior to 2008, had been in areas that depended on either the financial sector or on government investment, such as healthcare and education, as Figure 59 illustrates. But, as I pointed out earlier, such services

Figure 59

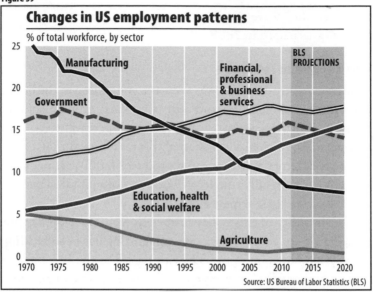

Changes in US employment patterns

% of total workforce, by sector

Manufacturing

Government

Financial, professional & business services

BLS PROJECTIONS

Education, health & social welfare

Agriculture

Source: US Bureau of Labor Statistics (BLS)

must be supported by the real wealth of industry. Economic growth has come up against a barrier erected by the very technology that led the last real growth spurt (the one before the credit boom). Not enough people are doing the right kind of work any more.

My own experience of work, which was mainly in journalism, is a case in point. A newspaper provides an interesting example of an industry straddling the manufacturing and service sectors; as a journalist I was providing a service, but at the same time I was adding content to a product that had to be manufactured. Huge rolls of newsprint were trucked into Fleet Street every night, and these had come originally from the forests of Scandinavia, by way of a factory that converted the trees into pulp and then into paper. The newspaper business made its money primarily from selling advertising space, and the nature of these ads showed where that money came from: car manufacturers, oil companies, brewers, big retail outlets, insurance, computer firms… in other words, a typical mix from what was at the time (this was the late 1970s into the 1980s) still a thriving industrial economy. For

Figure 60

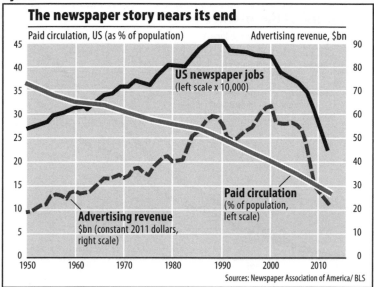

The newspaper story nears its end

Paid circulation, US (as % of population) — Advertising revenue, $bn

US newspaper jobs (left scale x 10,000)

Paid circulation (% of population, left scale)

Advertising revenue $bn (constant 2011 dollars, right scale)

Sources: Newspaper Association of America/ BLS

most of the 20th century, the world's newspaper barons gained wealth from advertising revenue and power from their editorial influence.

But, as Figure 60 shows, something began to change around the end of the century. By this time, technology had already led to job losses among many of the old newspaper trades: the compositors and Linotype operators and various other specialized printing skills that computerization had brought to an end. Such processes have been happening in other industries too, of course, ever since the Industrial Revolution, but in the newspaper industry it happened very quickly.

When I joined British national newspaper the *Daily Telegraph* in 1978, nothing much had changed since the 1930s, when most of the Fleet Street newspaper offices and printing works were built, and even then they were based on printing technology invented at the end of the 19th century. But, within a few years, new technology began making inroads into this cloistered little world and by the end of the 1980s the industry had deserted Fleet Street for new headquarters in London's Docklands,

Figure 61

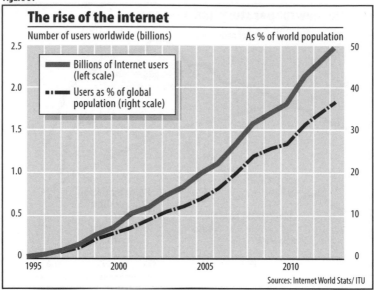

The rise of the internet

Number of users worldwide (billions)   As % of world population

- Billions of Internet users (left scale)
- Users as % of global population (right scale)

Sources: Internet World Stats/ ITU

where the inevitable transition to new technology took place.

By the beginning of the new millennium, with newspaper sales in decline and advertising revenue peaking, the internet began its inexorable rise, as shown in Figure 61. An important 20th-century industry found itself struggling to adapt to the new-technology revolution and, even if it does adapt to some extent (the struggle goes on as I write this), it will be a much leaner, poorer business.

The reality is that, as newspapers move from actually printing a physical product to offering content on a website, they cut out most of the manufacturing element and become almost entirely a service-sector business, employing far fewer workers and creating a lot less real wealth.

An unfortunate aspect of new technology, as ever-smaller machines and computers do more and more of the work, is that it leads to a reduction in both the use of raw materials and the jobs needed to make the products. And although the reduction in raw-material use is obviously very good for the planet, and therefore for our long-term survival prospects, the combination of these two factors inevitably results in less real wealth creation.

One final reminder of my equation:

| Raw materials | × | Human effort (Ideas + Labor) | = | Wealth |

So no real wealth can be created without raw materials. This means that as the devices get smaller, as of course they have done – think of the first computers that took up whole rooms, and which had less computing power than you get now in a laptop – they consume fewer natural resources. This is good of course, natural resources being finite, but in terms of the economy, it's not so good. Less real wealth will be created in the manufacture of a smaller device.

The same thing applies to cars (as I show in Figure 62), or anything else for that matter, from a box of matches to the building of a ship or a skyscraper – the heavier the industry the better, when it comes to real wealth creation.

This is not a question of sale price either. Just because the smaller computer might retail for a higher price than the bigger computer, it doesn't mean more wealth has been created. More

Figure 62

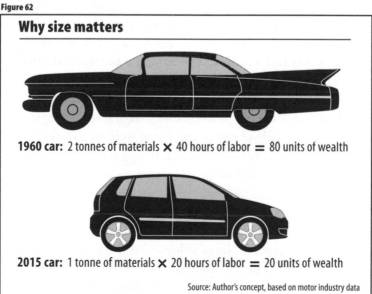

Why size matters

1960 car: 2 tonnes of materials × 40 hours of labor = 80 units of wealth

2015 car: 1 tonne of materials × 20 hours of labor = 20 units of wealth

Source: Author's concept, based on motor industry data

money is transferred from the consumer's bank account to the retailer and then to the manufacturer but, as I argued earlier, that isn't wealth creation, merely wealth redistribution.

Take the case of the bigger car. The usual higher selling price will reflect a product that requires more raw materials and more labor, and which therefore will have created more wealth in its making. Even if the economy car could be sold for more than the bigger car, perhaps because of its fuel efficiency, its manufacture would still have involved less wealth creation.

The huge gas-guzzling cars of 1950s and 1960s America were more than just flashy symbols of the new prosperity – they were an important element of that prosperity. Their manufacture had created a great deal of wealth, through high-value employment combined with large quantities of steel and chromium. This has obvious implications for the future, as we trade in our cars for bicycles.

Does high-tech mean low wealth?

The technology industry is big on ideas, but ideas in themselves don't create wealth without the manufacture of something. An idea, however brilliant, needs to result in something solid before it can create real wealth. So the music industry, for example, now adds less real wealth to the economy per unit sale than it did when it manufactured millions of vinyl discs – discs that required large hi-fi systems to get the best out of them.

This is one of the big problems with digital technology: now that we can download music and listen to it on a pocket-sized computer, there is far less manufacturing involved. The same thing applies to publishing: compared to traditional books, ebooks involve less real wealth creation. An even starker example of this is provided by the contrast between a full set of the *Encyclopedia Britannica*, which in its most recent book form required 32 large volumes, and the online version, which over 99% of buyers now choose – not surprisingly, given the difference in price and space required. The lower price reflects (though is certainly not equivalent to) the difference in the wealth-creation process. On the one hand, there's all the industry involved in forestry, the transformation of trees into pulp, the manufacture of 32 large books, transportation of the books to the shop, sometimes even a salesperson going door to door... On the other hand, all the knowledge contained in those 32 volumes goes onto a hard disk with a few strokes of a keyboard, and *voilà!*

A less complicated time

One way of explaining the essential relationship between raw materials and wealth creation is to go back to an earlier, less complicated time, when the economy was easier to understand: say, 300 years ago. A rich landowning farmer employs several servants to cook and clean his house, as well as the field workers who cultivate his crops and tend his animals. He pays them mostly in food and provides them with shelter, but he also gives them each a silver coin once a week.

The agricultural workers are employed in the primary sector and are an essential part of the farmer's wealth-creation process. The women who keep his house are in the service sector (they are servants, after all). He can create his wealth without these servants, but he prefers to pay them rather than clean his own house and make his own meals. He can better use his time managing the farm. The servants receive a little of the wealth that his other workers have helped him to create. They also contribute to the efficiency of the farm, enabling more wealth to be created, but if the farmer hadn't earned this wealth from the land in the first place, he would have nothing to give these servants. And when they spend their silver coins in the village store or in the pub, the workers spread a little of that agricultural wealth around the local community.

The crops that the farmer grows and the animals he rears are processed into food by other workers; the wheat is ground into flour, the milk made into butter, and so on. Food processing is one of the earliest forms of manufacturing. So we see the clear distinctions between the three sectors, and we see that the service sector is totally dependent on the first two sectors for creating the wealth that can then be distributed throughout the economy. We see also that the manufacturing sector is dependent on the primary sector for its raw materials.

This essential link between the natural wealth of the earth and the wealth of an economy has become obscured by the financial system, and even by money itself. We confuse economic activity with real wealth creation, because we tend to think of money as wealth, but money is only a representation of real wealth.

To give another example involving our rich landowner/farmer: if he wanted to build a new barn, he might, in the days of barter, pay a builder mostly in food. If he had a large farm, employing dozens of workers, and he wanted several new buildings, the farmer might supply the construction team with enough food to keep them going for weeks. The raw materials – crops and cattle on the one hand, timber and stone on the other – provide the first essential ingredient that enables the exchange to take place. The second essential ingredient is the labor of the farm workers and the builders. In converting the raw materials into something useful, this labor, combined with the knowledge of farming or barn construction, adds value to those materials and results in the creation of real wealth; the food and the buildings. Money isn't necessary; it merely makes the exchange more convenient.

If money is used instead of food in such an exchange, it represents the agreed value of the materials and the labor. The value of the money corresponds to the actual wealth exchanged. Or at least it should do.

But, as I said earlier, this link between money and real wealth was completely severed with the ending of the gold standard, so that over the last four decades the true value of money, relative to the real wealth of the economy, has fallen significantly, to a degree that hasn't yet been absorbed by the markets.

The hard truth of the software revolution

In the modern high-tech economy, the raw-material element in each item produced, along with the labor element, is constantly being reduced. The ideas have become the most important thing. But ideas in themselves don't have real value until they are converted into something solid, using materials and labor. There is no real wealth produced if nothing is taken from the earth.

The computer industry has of course created a great deal of wealth over the last three decades or so – especially for China – but that boom, though far from over, is slowing down for several reasons: a lower rate of growth as markets approach saturation; the rising cost of materials and labor in China, reversing years of falling prices; the rise of cloud computing, which means less hardware bought by businesses (and a reduced requirement for IT support staff) and – the real point I'm making here – the reduction in size of each item produced, which means a reduction in the manufacturing process.

Computers are still dependent on raw materials of course: copper, mercury, lead, iron and aluminum, even gold and other precious metals, plus oil for the plastic casing; in fact a great variety of raw materials goes into each computer and monitor. But, as technology advances and computers become smaller, the quantity of those materials declines and fewer workers are needed to make each unit, and therefore the value added to the economy declines.

This trend has been countered by the increase in sales of laptops, tablets and mobile phones, but, as markets become saturated and as people have less money to spend, sales will ease off and the relative decline in wealth creation will become more evident. I say 'relative decline' because, even if production keeps rising, as it no doubt will in emerging economies for many decades to come, what really matters is wealth creation relative to population.

This point would be disputed by some economists, I suspect, but according to my understanding of the situation,

Figure 63

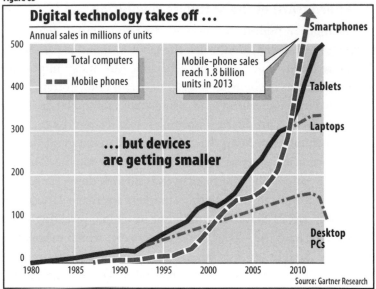

Digital technology takes off …

Annual sales in millions of units

Smartphones

— Total computers

▪▪ Mobile phones

Mobile-phone sales reach 1.8 billion units in 2013

Tablets

Laptops

… but devices are getting smaller

Desktop PCs

1980   1985   1990   1995   2000   2005   2010

Source: Gartner Research

as the software becomes ever more important relative to the hardware, as tends to happen with computers, less wealth will be created. One might assume that the computer programmer creates significant wealth when he or she makes something as useful as a software program that everyone wants to use. But being effectively an idea, requiring no raw materials and no manufacturing process, the intellectual effort that goes into software production – the brain power, as it were – doesn't create any wealth by itself. It is only the production of the hardware that adds real wealth to the economy.

Yes, the software is essential because without software the computer is useless. It is a part of the equation – the idea part, and even some of the labor part because, after all, typing away at a keyboard while sitting in front of a monitor is a form of work – but it still requires the raw materials for the manufacture of the hardware. Without the hardware, the intrinsic value of the idea – the software – cannot be realized.

The whole process of digitization raises new questions about the wealth-creating ability of modern economies, as manufacturing processes use fewer raw materials and less labor. The entertainment industry has been hit particularly hard by this trend, because much of the value added to the economy by entertainers used to involve the sale of manufactured products, but digital entertainment and the internet is changing this.

Free as a bird

I will try to clarify my point with yet another example from history. This takes us back to an even simpler age, say 30,000 years ago; a time when people survived by scavenging, hunting wild animals and gathering fruit and nuts from the trees, as they had been doing since *homo erectus* evolved from the apes two million years previously.

We have a tribe that lives a relatively easy life: comfortable caves in a warm climate, a fast-flowing river that provides plenty of fish, abundant fruit growing on the trees. These people don't make anything because they don't need to, other than sharpening a stick with a piece of flint now and then. They live entirely from the land and from catching fish with stealthy hands, much as their animal ancestors might have done.

At some point however, a young woman of the tribe, while imitating the birds, catches the attention of her fellow tribe members. She can sing. She develops this discovery into an idea – the idea of making up a song and singing it. The song proves very popular with the rest of the tribe, and they encourage her to sing every evening after they've eaten their raw fish. At this stage there is no economy as such – just subsistence, existing from the land. But then, one day, while idly sifting the sands of the riverbed, one of the men finds a little nugget of gold. Having no other use for it, despite admiring its fine color, he offers it to the young woman, on condition that she sings her song for him. She accepts the gold and, being the great innovator that she obviously is, she threads a strand of ivy through the small hole that runs through the center of the nugget, and hangs it round her neck.

Figure 64

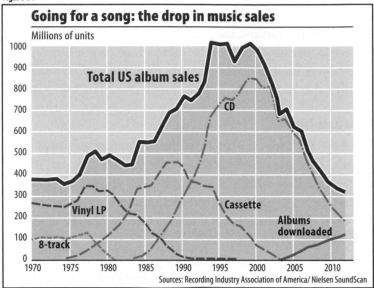

Both her singing and her gold necklace attract great attention in the community. It turns out that both have some value: other members of the tribe desire such things. The girl's idea to sing a song, combined with the man's idea to give her some gold, plus the labor involved in digging the gold from the riverbed, has created wealth. The gold was already there of course, but it had no obvious value until the man offered it to the girl in the hope that she would sing her song again.

The value comes from the combination of natural wealth and human ideas and effort. The exchange of the gold nugget for the song might not seem very different from the bartering of a fish for a rabbit, for example, except for the simple point that a song, in economic terms, is a service rather than a material 'good'; when the girl sang her song for free, there was no economic activity. Now, however, after this fortuitous turn of events, the economy of our tribal community is on the road to riches, with the seeds of an entertainment industry, gold prospecting and a budding jewelry trade.

The young woman could have continued to sing her song for

free, and of course there is a different kind of value in this – such art adds to the quality of life, for sure. But it is only when she sings her song for the reward of gold that she adds to the economy, and it is only because the man is motivated to dig the gold from the riverbed that the wealth is created in the first place. And when the young woman makes jewelry from that gold, turning it into something more desirable than mere nuggets, or even coins, she adds value through her ideas and her labor.

This brings us back to our software developer. Effectively the software developer is the young woman with the song and, even if he could somehow offer his brilliant ideas without the use of computer hardware, he would still be reliant on other people having created some wealth before he could sell his product. The real value of the programmer is that by making the computer more useful – more desirable – he helps to sell more computers and therefore is responsible for increasing the manufacturing element of the process, which is of course dependent on raw materials.

In other words, we cannot create something out of nothing, we cannot create wealth out of thin air, and, in the material world in which we live, an idea by itself is like thin air; it only becomes real when combined with something solid, whether it be computer hardware, a paperback book, or a vinyl or compact disc. And, as all these things are declining, either in material size or in sales volume, so will society's capacity for wealth creation decline.

11 Virtual values

The internet as job killer

Towards the end of 2012, I read an article about a series of new online university courses that were catching on in the US, and were already spreading to Britain. The courses were taught by recognized world experts in various fields, mostly scientific – artificial intelligence, biotechnology, computer science etc – and were based at top universities such as Stanford, Princeton, MIT, Harvard, and now Edinburgh and London. The remarkable thing about these courses was that they were open to anyone, for free. Consequently, they had already attracted hundreds of thousands of students from around the world.

Everyone interviewed for the article was very enthusiastic about this new development. The teachers, in particular, loved the enthusiasm of their online students, some of whom scored higher in exams than the top students who actually attended the universities. What they had done was to tap into some extremely bright and motivated young people in places like China, India, Russia, even Mongolia. The only requirement was to have a reliable internet connection and to understand English. No doubt the drop-out rate will be very high, but that won't matter because nobody will have lost anything, except perhaps hope.

What makes this development possible, besides the spread of the internet, is sophisticated software that ensures that the students really do the work and understand the subject, because, with so many students, there is no way a real live human is going to be marking the papers. If the student qualifies, he or she receives a certificate by email.

What really struck me about this was that nobody mentioned the obvious failings of the system. What gives it value? If hundreds of thousands of students are going to 'qualify' on these online courses, then it seems likely that potential employers will view such qualifications with suspicion, and value them accordingly. No doubt

Figure 65

Rising degrees of graduate unemployment

Percentage of graduates (aged 20-24) unable to find work

EU average

UK

Australia

US

1990 92 94 96 98 2000 02 04 06 08 10 2012

Sources: Eurostat/ EC Eurydice/ US BLS/ Graduate Careers Australia

a lucky few students, perhaps the top 0.01% or so, might find that it helps them to get a good job, but most will be disappointed in that respect, and will have to content themselves with the knowledge that they understand a lot more about biotechnology, or computer science, than most of their colleagues in the office-cleaning or parcel-delivery business, or whichever real-world job they end up in, if any.

Education is a great thing, but it can lead to a higher level of disappointment, as so many more expectations are dashed against the hard reality of the job market. Just ask among the unemployment lines of Greece or Spain, which in recent years have been lengthened by the influx of disillusioned graduates.

These free online university courses are a fine innovation, perhaps, but they will create not a single job in the real world. It is yet another example of how so many people – in this case, very intelligent people – fail to grasp the point that you cannot create something out of nothing. If a lecturer teaches 200,000 students rather than 200 students, then the value of his or her teaching will inevitably be a lot less per student. Not a thousand times less perhaps, but the students won't be getting a real college education; it will be more like reading a book than going to class, and this reduced value will be reflected in the qualification. The lecturers should be much more wary of this new trend, because the next step is that they won't be needed at all. The software will replace them entirely.

What students really need is real training for real jobs, not a virtual education. Yet technological developments such as this will no doubt cut the number of real teaching jobs. The internet is fantastic for spreading information and knowledge, but it is a net destroyer of real jobs.

Falling through the net

There is no reliable data that shows gains and losses in employment due to the growth of the internet, but we can make a few educated guesses based on visible trends. A 2011 report by McKinsey Global Institute, entitled *Internet Matters*, presents an optimistic view of '…the Net's sweeping impact on growth, jobs and prosperity'. The report claims that the internet creates 2.6 jobs for every one it destroys, but the authors make some fundamental errors in their assumptions and give very little real evidence to support their claims.

Take this 'fact', for example: the internet accounted for '21% of GDP growth in the last five years in mature countries'. How do they figure this out? To quote more: 'Internet-related consumption and expenditure is now bigger than agriculture or energy… the internet's total contribution to GDP is bigger than the GDP of Spain or Canada, and is growing faster than Brazil.' They go on to show how the UK 'benefits from online shopping'.

First mistake: To compare the GDP contributions of retail expenditure and online shopping on the one hand, with those of agriculture and energy, two primary producers of real wealth, on the other hand, demonstrates the common failure to distinguish between productive and unproductive GDP that I mentioned earlier. That same failure is responsible for the claim that the internet, in global terms, adds more value than the economy of Canada, a country that produces a great deal of real wealth in the form of commodities, as opposed to 'wealth' that shows up in GDP figures as consumer spending.

Second mistake: This '21% of GDP growth in the last five years...' that they talk about, ran from 2004 to 2009, which covers the last four years of the previous boom, followed by a year of bust. My first chart (Figure 1) showed how the latter part of the boom, from 2004 to 2007, saw exceptional growth due to spending based almost entirely on debt.

Third mistake: When talking about how the UK 'benefits from online shopping', the authors make no mention of the very obvious point that online shopping is merely a replacement for shopping in real stores that actually employ lots of people. The implication here is that, because shoppers find the internet more convenient, they spend more money and therefore make a bigger contribution to the economy. This is absurd. If UK shoppers really spent more money because of online shopping, which I suppose is possible, it still isn't the same as adding more wealth to the economy. UK shoppers certainly haven't been earning more money because of the internet. Quite the opposite, in fact: real wages have been falling, as I showed in Figure 10.

Fourth mistake: The report makes no mention of actual job statistics, probably because it's not possible to distinguish job gains or losses due to the internet. I did, however, come across this little fact from the UK Gambling Commission: the UK online gaming 'industry' employed 6,077 full-time employees in 2011, down from 8,918 in 2008, despite the fact that revenues had increased in this booming business, which apparently 'made' around $2 billion in 2011.

All we can really do is look at the evidence on the ground, but the report's authors don't do that. If they had done, they'd have realized that online shopping is one of many examples of how the internet kills jobs. Think of all the bookshops, travel agents, clothes retailers and so on that have disappeared because we can now shop without the hassle of leaving our homes, plus the post-office workers, bank tellers and supermarket check-out jobs that are no longer needed. Add to that all the stuff that digital technology means you don't need to buy any more: CDs, books, maps, journals, hi-fi equipment, photographic film and its associated development, and so on.

Where has the internet made up for this by creating jobs? Delivery drivers, certainly.

A few more figures might help to give some idea of the internet's likely effect on jobs. The largest company that has evolved purely as a result of the internet is Amazon, which at the end of 2012 employed around 88,000 workers worldwide, many of them part-time. Only around 4,200 of those jobs are based in the UK. Google, the second biggest internet company, employs around 50,000, mostly in the US, while Facebook has created 3,500 jobs worldwide and Twitter only 400. To put this into context, Tesco employs around half a million people worldwide and 300,000 in the UK, while the UK retail sector as a whole employed 4,850,000 people as of September 2012, which was down by 27,000 from March 2012. In other words, the UK retail sector lost far more jobs in six months than all the big internet companies combined employ in the UK, and the trend is rising, with a net loss of 1,800 high-street stores reported in 2012 alone.

According to the McKinsey report, the internet has created thousands of jobs in the telecommunications industry in particular, but this is to ignore the point that we would have been using the telephone anyway, in some form or other, just as we were using phones and computers (and a lot more postal workers) before the internet revolutionized communications.

Yes, the internet has helped sell millions of computers, and that must have created many thousands of jobs around the world, especially in China and the US perhaps, though not that many in Britain. But that initial boom is well and truly over, and the effect now is to kill jobs, as the McKinsey authors unwittingly confirm in their conclusions, with regard to apparent internet-related growth in the service sector: 'This value comes primarily from increased productivity.' This generally means employing fewer workers.

Why more is less

The internet has many uses and undoubtedly makes life a lot more convenient and a lot easier. It offers a great deal: not just shopping, but general communication, research and information gathering; social networking; sharing photographs, music, thoughts, opinions... and in the process it devalues the whole lot. By making all these things available to everyone without the requirement of any real effort or any great skill, the explosion in volume buries the good beneath the mediocre, in much the same way that the explosion in the number of television channels never really added to the number of TV programs worth watching. It is yet another case of quantity over quality, but on a scale never seen before. There is no arbiter of quality and anything of real value gets lost amongst the dross.

There is a fundamental problem here, linked to my earlier observation that real wealth creation requires real work. There is no value to be found in making our lives easier if it doesn't lead to more opportunities for the distribution of the world's wealth through work, as happened in the past.

To return to my point about the free online degree courses, you don't really get anything for nothing. Education is an expensive business and you can only get it for free if someone else is paying. Most of these students would be better off attending a real university in their own country, where they could talk to real lecturers and earn a real qualification that has some recognized value, with the added bonus that they would then have the real student experiences that add so much value to real life. I can't help thinking that the virtual world lacks something. Call it reality.

At the risk of becoming repetitive, the above point brings me back to the idea that you need real workers to add real value to the economic process, not just in industry but in areas such as education too. I have tried to imagine the consequences of a civilization in which all the work was done by machines. This is not such a far-fetched scenario. One of the pioneers in the online university movement mentioned above, a professor of artificial intelligence at Stanford by the name of Sebastian Thrun, built a car, in conjunction with Google's development team, that could get around without a driver. This might not sound particularly impressive in itself – driverless trains have been around for 20 years or more – but this particular car had driven all round California, on real roads, without (as far as I know) crashing into anything.

So it would presumably be quite possible, in the very near future, to have farm tractors harvesting the crops without a farmer in the cab, for example, and robots making the dinner and cleaning the house. And of course we already have aircraft that can fly themselves and robots that can make pretty much anything in the factory.

It appears as if we might be getting close to that future envisioned in 1950s science fiction, when human beings no longer need to do any real work. What happens when even the robots are designed and built by robots?

The Devil finds work...

Would such a world be feasible, in theory at least? Ignoring for now the obvious point that all those idle hands would likely become the Devil's tools, as the old saying goes, let's think what would happen if machines did 90% of the work, while 95% of the people (because only about half the population works anyway) idled away their days doing whatever they felt like doing – playing football, watching movies made by robots, doing free university courses on the internet.

Bearing in mind my earlier equation, in which natural resources are combined with human effort to create real wealth, we find that although the human-labor element has been knocked right down, if there is still a thriving manufacturing industry, where raw materials are converted into things people actually want, and can still afford, then the fact that robots do all the work doesn't stop the wealth-creation process from being valid. The robots are the tools of the laborers; in human terms, there is less actual labor involved, but a higher 'ideas' element. And there is, of course, the labor involved in building the robots, until the robots learn to build themselves.

Such increasing automation would represent a further stage along the road to greater productivity, just another development in a process that began hundreds of years ago, when productivity gains in agriculture and industry helped to make the world a wealthier place.

Ever since the Luddite revolts of the early 19th century, in which skilled textile workers attacked the machinery that was making them redundant during the Industrial Revolution, people have worried that new technology will result in mass unemployment. And each time a new industry evolved that created more work and more wealth, feeding the cycle of economic growth. Why should this time be any different?

Because, as I said earlier, the service sector, which has been employing most of the redundant industrial workers during the last half-century or so, is now becoming more productive itself, in particular thanks to increasingly sophisticated software, as used by the new online university courses and other areas of education, healthcare and all the other recent growth sectors. And this time, unlike in the past, there is no other sector left to become the job creator of the future.

In the real world, as opposed to the optimistic scenarios of

1950s science fiction, the problems begin when the displaced workers can't find new jobs elsewhere. But what if they didn't need to find more work, because the robots were producing enough wealth to go round? If we don't like the idea of all that idleness, perhaps we humans could all be managers, overseeing the robots as they perform all the manual work. Perhaps we could live another of those 1950s fantasies, working a 20-hour week and retiring at 50. This might even be possible, assuming certain conditions:

1 That the profits of industry are distributed evenly among the people, whether they have real jobs or not.
2 That the government still takes in revenue, even though the robots won't be paying income tax or any other tax.
3 That there is still, despite the much-reduced workforce, sufficient demand for the products of all that industry.
4 That the situation is the same throughout the world, so that more competitive economies can't exist.

In other words, such a situation will never happen in a free-market capitalist economy, because none of these conditions would ever apply. In the end, if there's not enough work for real people, the wealth won't be spread evenly, there won't be enough demand and the industry will fail. It turns out that the robots aren't actually making the whole economy more productive, because productivity gains have to apply to society as a whole, not just to certain industries. If you end up with Marx's army of unemployed, then society as a whole becomes very inefficient.

Would it be different if the state controlled the means of production? Well, yes, it would obviously be very different. The state would earn the revenue directly from industry, because it would own the raw materials, the factories and the robots. It would pay the people a certain wage, whether they earned it or not, and it would operate in a closed economy, either because the whole world would operate under the same conditions, or because the state would isolate itself from outside influences.

This sounds suspiciously like we'd be back in the USSR (as the Beatles once sang). We will explore the alternatives to free-market capitalism in the final part of the book, but for now we must return to the real world, whatever its failings.

Getting the balance right

I showed in Figure 40 how, for most of the last half-century, US and UK manufacturing output was falling as a percentage of GDP, while the financial sector was rising. And Figure 52 showed how, after 1980, the industrial workforce began to decline. Although the US and Britain are particularly affected by this trend, the same thing is happening in all advanced economies, even those famed for their manufacturing strength, such as Germany and Japan.

Unlike produced wealth, accumulated wealth doesn't lead to job creation. This is the big dilemma now facing the developed world: how to create more real wealth and real jobs (and to do so without destroying the environment, which is something I'll address in Part Three).

If real industry doesn't create them, where are the new jobs going to come from? An economy based on call-centers and care-homes is an economy destined for decline. As I explained in Chapter 2, the service sector can't grow any more because it relies on the real wealth of industry, but for some years now, at least in the West, there's been a fall in real industrial wealth creation, relative to the economy as a whole. Because of the credit bubble, the service sector has grown beyond the point where there's enough real wealth to feed it, and now it must contract to a sustainable level.

If the decline in manufacturing employment can't be reversed, the problems experienced since the credit crisis will only get worse. But how does a government go about boosting the primary and secondary sectors of the economy?

The ratio of manufacturing to services isn't a result of some carefully thought-out plan; like most aspects of the economy, it is driven by market forces. The wealth created by manufacturing feeds the growth in services, and the growth in services boosts demand for the products of manufacturing. This virtuous cycle only comes to a halt when demand fails to keep up with supply, which it inevitably must do; eventually demand falls because there aren't enough consumers with enough 'need' and enough money to buy the ever-increasing production of the ever-more-efficient factories. And the main reason there aren't enough consumers with money is that the factories aren't employing as many workers, because to be competitive in a global market they have to keep raising productivity levels.

The virtuous cycle turns into a vicious cycle of rising unemployment, lower spending in the shops, lower government tax receipts, more job losses… and on it goes, until confidence returns and demand picks up again. But this time neither confidence nor demand is picking up. Nobody wants to spend money they don't have any more. So a situation develops in which jobs become scarce, wages fall while prices rise, and people buy only the necessities. The middle class is tightening its belt, and the belt is likely to stay tight for a long time.

Figure 54 showed that the job situation is worse now than it's been for a long time, particularly as the official unemployment figures downplay the true picture, excluding anyone who has given up looking for work or those who have taken part-time work, even if they wanted a full-time job (Figure 57). And the younger you are, the tougher it gets.

As I noted earlier, students go to university in the expectation that a degree will give them an advantage in the job market, but they are now finding that the supply of graduates far exceeds the demand for their services. The problem is even worse for school-leavers who don't go to college, who find that even quite menial jobs are snapped up by graduates, as employers take their pick of overqualified job-seekers.

There are few real jobs available, especially for those without

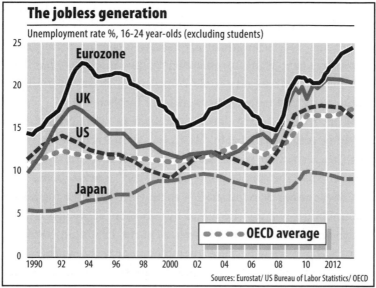

Figure 66

The jobless generation

Unemployment rate %, 16-24 year-olds (excluding students)

Eurozone

UK

US

Japan

● ● ● ● OECD average

Sources: Eurostat/ US Bureau of Labor Statistics/ OECD

experience – and especially for young men, such is the nature of the work that is available (part-time, looking after the sick or the rising number of elderly folk, or other service work where women tend to fit in more easily than men.)

In an unplanned free-market economy – the kind of economy that rules most of the world these days – employment is not guaranteed. Jobs are not a priority of free-market capitalism; the priority is to make a profit. We are at the mercy of global market forces. But what are these forces?

Survival of the fittest

The free-market capitalist system is based primarily on the idea of competition. Private enterprise will provide all needs because of the profit motive; demand will be met by supply; and competition will keep the profit motive, or greed, in check. Competition will ensure that prices are held to reasonable levels. If one producer becomes too greedy, another will undercut them. The system worked well enough for most of the last century, at least for the developed world, because the wealth created by industry was spread via wider employment. Demand-driven growth enriched a growing middle class.

But the great strength of capitalism – the incentive-driven innovation that leads to efficiency of production – has now become its great weakness, as competition drives ever higher productivity and reduces the workforce further.

By its nature, unregulated capitalism is unconcerned with anything other than profit. There is no motivation to create jobs other than to make more profit. Because the system is unplanned – the whole point of the 'free' market being that lack of planning or regulation – there is no thought for future sustainability nor for the equal distribution of wealth. When wealth was spread reasonably well, as in the 1950s and 1960s, it happened primarily because unemployment was low; there was a strong demand for labor and industrialists had little choice but to raise wages.

Unfettered free-market capitalism results in a survival-of-the-fittest situation. Competition drives out the weakest firms and the profit goes to the most efficient producers, who in a global economy are the ones with the cheapest labor and the greatest economies of scale. The combination of unregulated capitalism and globalization is no longer beneficial to the developed economies, even though many of the large transnational corporations are of Western or Japanese origin, and before long it won't benefit developing economies either, because the wealth is no longer spreading to the majority. As shown in Figure 9, only the rich are getting richer.

The reason for this can be found in the financial sector, which, through growth and acquisition, has come to dominate even the productive sectors of industry. The process is linked to the drive for efficiency, as large corporations buy out competitors and expand at the expense of smaller, more local companies.

These transnational corporations have increasing influence over our lives, not only because they are becoming more and more knowledgeable about their customers, thanks to the internet and cellphone technology, but also through political connections: politicians are afraid to confront them because the corporate élite has more power than elected leaders in this global economy. Much of this influence is hidden, as is a lot of the financial activity that goes with it.

Lurking in the shadows

Finance grew with the economic boom of the second half of the last century, as oil money and industrial wealth found its way into pension funds, hedge funds and other investments. After the demise of the gold standard and the subsequent deregulation of banking, the financial sector – in particular the investment-banking side of the business, and the unregulated zone in between, known as shadow banking (as explained in Chapter 6) – then leveraged this wealth by creating credit, and this credit fed the last boom.

Now that this artificial growth has ended, the problem for countries like Britain and some other European nations, and to a lesser extent the US, is that the rebalancing of the economy towards the wealth-creating sectors is going to take place not by the industrial sectors expanding, but by the service sector contracting, as the economy adjusts to the fact that there's less real wealth around than previous growth implied.

The recent growth of the banking sector, and its subsequent influence over the whole economy, is out of all proportion to its real importance. Banking provides a useful service to industry and to individuals – we need banks, just as we need telephone and electricity companies – but a lot of financial services we could do without. More than any other 'industry', finance has conjured up business for itself that is of no benefit to society – that is, in fact, detrimental to society as a whole, being no more use than the betting shop, and just as likely to bring hardship to vulnerable people. For the plain fact is that the more money the banks make for their executives and investors, the more debt they must create.

Figure 67

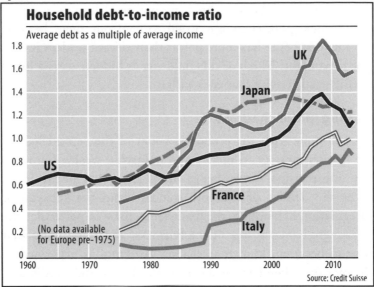

Household debt-to-income ratio

Average debt as a multiple of average income

UK

Japan

US

France

Italy

(No data available for Europe pre-1975)

1960 1970 1980 1990 2000 2010

Source: Credit Suisse

Does debt matter?

Although some aspects of finance have become extremely complicated, the whole system is based on the simple concept of profiting from the lending of money. One person's fortune becomes another person's debt. Usury had a bad name for a good reason: it messed up people's lives.

Debt boosts the economy initially, because the borrower spends the money, but then it becomes a drain on the economy, because the borrower must repay the loan plus interest, which might be an extra 10 or 20%. That interest payment represents money that is no longer available for other things; money that goes to the bank rather than the real economy.

Debt repayment takes money from those who need it, and therefore would have spent it, and gives it to those who don't need it, because debt is nearly always a transfer of wealth from those with little to those with plenty. And because the wealthy don't need that money to spend, having more than enough to meet their needs already, it represents a double blow to society. The bank will then use that money to create more credit, ensuring that the debt-creation cycle goes on, as indeed it must do for the capitalist system to keep on feeding itself, right up until the point when the whole thing collapses.

This is what happened in the credit-fuelled boom years: spending on borrowed money followed by years of debt repayment that sucks real value from the economy, because people are buying less and so less real stuff is made, while the bankers end up even wealthier, despite the crash and the need for bank bail-outs.

Everyone pays

The process of bank deregulation that began in the 1970s led to a massive boom in debt, first private debt and then public debt (public debt is otherwise known as 'national debt' or 'government debt', and sometimes 'sovereign debt', though that can refer more specifically to national debt owed to foreigners). The difference between private debt and public debt is significant. Within reasonable limits, both have their uses. Borrowing money in difficult times can help keep us going until better conditions

Figure 68

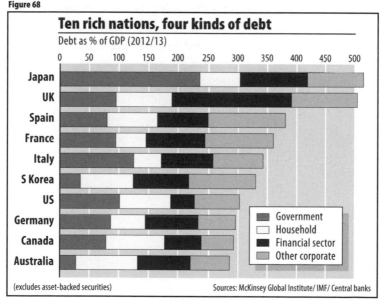

Ten rich nations, four kinds of debt

Debt as % of GDP (2012/13)

Government
Household
Financial sector
Other corporate

(excludes asset-backed securities)   Sources: McKinsey Global Institute/ IMF/ Central banks

return, whether the borrowers are individuals, companies or governments. In particular, borrowing money to invest in real industry is generally beneficial, as it adds to the nation's wealth-creating ability. Such investment generates jobs and future income, some of which can be used to pay off the debt. Borrowing money to buy a house makes sense too, as long as the price isn't over-inflated and repayments are covered by income; in the long term, it should prove a worthwhile investment. The problems occur when we borrow money to 'invest' in already overpriced assets, thus feeding a bubble, or if we borrow purely to fund unproductive consumption, even in the good times, rather than putting money aside for those difficult years that are sure to lie ahead. This applies both to private and public borrowing.

The main difference between private debt and public debt lies in the consequences of borrowing too much. For individuals and private companies, defaulting on debts results in bankruptcy and some form of forced repayment or other punishment. For government or sovereign debt, no such rules apply because there is no higher authority to enforce them. In this case everyone pays the price, because in the end the only possible outcomes are the devaluation of the currency; rising prices, which must eventually result in rising interest rates; and a poorer population.

12 Living in never-never land

Bubble trouble and the debt of nations

For individuals and corporations wanting to borrow money, there are limits to how much the banks will normally lend, based on earnings and assets. These limits were set too high in the credit boom because assets, especially US houses, were overvalued by banks. This overvaluation of US housing was the main cause of the crash of 2008, though one could argue that the overvaluation itself was caused by the availability of too much cheap credit.

The cycle was self-sustaining for a few years, as the housing and credit bubbles combined, feeding each other on the promise of higher returns. Bankers developed increasingly complex packages of debt and began a process of disconnection from the real events on the ground, so that the big international banks that ultimately took on the debt hadn't a clue what the risks were.

This huge bubble was linked to the growth of the poorly regulated shadow-banking sector, which in turn was linked to the growth of accumulated wealth and the search for returns on that wealth. The banks were so eager to lend as much as possible that they lowered their lending standards to the point where people with low incomes, insecure jobs and few assets were being offered loans to buy houses that weren't really worth the inflated prices.

These 'sub-prime' mortgages were offered at low initial rates of interest that soon jumped to much higher rates. The result was that many borrowers couldn't afford the repayments and therefore defaulted. Banks ended up with houses they couldn't sell and prices began to fall, as shown in Figure 69.

But this was only the start of the problem. Once banks realized there was an issue with loans connected to US housing, they stopped lending, even to each other. Some banks were in deep trouble, but it wasn't obvious at first which ones, so the whole inter-bank lending market suddenly dried up. Because the governments

Figure 69

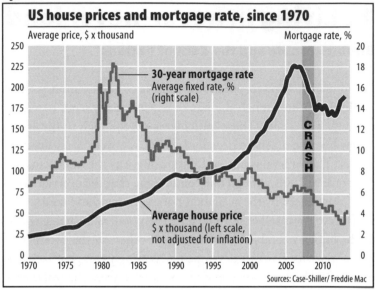

US house prices and mortgage rate, since 1970

Average price, $ x thousand   Mortgage rate, %

30-year mortgage rate
Average fixed rate, %
(right scale)

CRASH

Average house price
$ x thousand (left scale,
not adjusted for inflation)

Sources: Case-Shiller/ Freddie Mac

of most advanced countries guarantee their citizens' bank savings, and because bank failures are bad for the whole monetary system, which relies on public trust in the banks, governments can't afford to let them fail, especially big banks. They have little option but to support the financial system. So with banks in danger of failing, both in the US and Europe, governments put public money into the banks, either buying their shares, buying up 'toxic assets' (debts that are unlikely to be paid) or using a process known as quantitative easing, which involves the central bank buying government bonds (public debt, in other words) from the banks, or from other financial institutions.

As the crisis dragged on and the idea took hold that there was a shortage of 'liquidity', or cash, in the banking system, the process of quantitative easing was stepped up. If the banks had more funds available to lend out, so the theory went, it would 'stimulate' the economy.

But even before the crisis, most governments were already deep into debt, so where had all this public money come from? The answer is that it involved more debt: it either had to be borrowed by issuing more bonds, or simply conjured out of thin air. The process of quantitative easing effectively amounts to the government printing money – in order to buy those bonds from the banks, the central bank creates credit (though not actual money) out of nothing.

By mid-2012, all that buying of government bonds meant that central banks globally held $18 trillion in public debt, according to the Bank for International Settlements. This figure is remarkably close to the $19-trillion estimated 'cost' of the crisis, a cost that fell mostly on rich investors.

In other words, the government has been paying off private debt (in the banking system) by creating more public debt. And who will have to pay this public debt? The short answer to that question is, not surprisingly, 'the public'. All the citizens of all the indebted nations will pay, through higher taxes and higher prices. So the process of saving the banks is effectively a transfer of wealth from the general public, including the poor (because even if the poor don't pay income tax, the cost of food and fuel will rise and benefits will be cut), to the wealthy (bank executives, who will benefit twice over from this new flow of public money, because not only are their banks saved from collapse, despite their own failings, but also the injection of funds brings new business opportunities).

But there is a longer, more complicated answer to this big question of who pays the debts, because, in the end, while it is certainly true that everyone pays, it might turn out that the rich will have to pay more after all – a lot more.

Debt and hyperinflation

Governments are of course well aware that printing too much money can result in rising prices. One reason Germany has been so cautious about stimulating the European economy by injecting new money is because of its experience after the First World War, when the printing of marks to pay off war debts resulted in the rapid devaluation of the currency, to the point

Figure 70

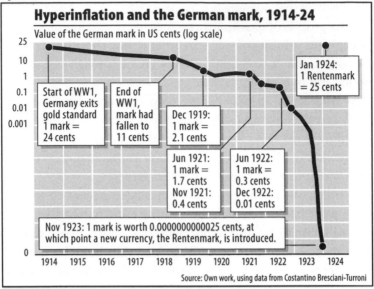

Hyperinflation and the German mark, 1914-24

Value of the German mark in US cents (log scale)

Start of WW1, Germany exits gold standard
1 mark = 24 cents

End of WW1, mark had fallen to 11 cents

Dec 1919: 1 mark = 2.1 cents

Jan 1924: 1 Rentenmark = 25 cents

Jun 1921: 1 mark = 1.7 cents
Nov 1921: 0.4 cents

Jun 1922: 1 mark = 0.3 cents
Dec 1922: 0.01 cents

Nov 1923: 1 mark is worth 0.0000000000025 cents, at which point a new currency, the Rentenmark, is introduced.

Source: Own work, using data from Costantino Bresciani-Turroni

where a thousand-mark note (or even a billion-mark note, by the end of the Reichsbank mark's life) wasn't worth the paper it was printed on. Other nations have suffered similar bouts of hyperinflation after trying to print their way out of debt, including Hungary in 1946, Argentina in the 1980s and Zimbabwe in the first decade of this century.

These are extreme cases, and for now there is little danger of hyperinflation in the economies of the developed world. Some economists and politicians have been more concerned about the risk of deflation (falling prices), as happened to Japan during the 1990s. In the following chapter I take a brief look at the Japanese experience, but my main point here is that falling prices seem unlikely, bearing in mind all the money that's been pumped into the financial system in recent years, and the general devaluation of money relative to real wealth, the effect of which has yet to feed into the real economy.

Figure 71 shows the effects of all this quantitative easing on the monetary base, which is a measure of the amount of cash in circulation, though in fact the new money isn't really circulating

Figure 71

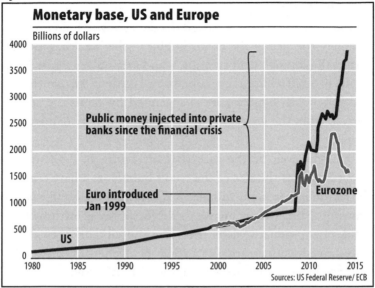

yet because banks are hanging on to most of it.

Regardless of whether quantitative easing is really the same as printing money (it's a debatable point, because there are differences), it seems quite clear that the money-creation process has far exceeded the wealth-creation process in recent years, with the result that money must have lost value against real stuff such as food and energy and all other commodities. At some point in the not-too-distant future, commodity prices are bound to rise, because they are currently undervalued in real terms, mainly due to suppressed demand.

A correction seems inevitable: there's a fundamental principle of economics involved here, a kind of natural law. An economy boosted by spending based on unproductive debt is unsustainable. The resulting growth in GDP is artificial and therefore, as I explained in the first part of this book, we now face an adjustment down to the level at which real economic activity – meaning activity based on productive industry, including service-sector activity that results from genuine wealth creation – would have taken us.

Bubble trouble

At the start of Chapter 4, I used the data shown in Figure 13 to calculate the size of the credit bubble – the 'wealth' produced artificially through debt creation – and arrived at a figure in the region of $200 trillion. I explained how I came to this conclusion, and how GDP figures were exaggerated by economic activity derived from the leveraging of old wealth, rather than genuine output.

It might even be the case that my figure of $200 trillion underestimates the size of the credit bubble, as I have erred on the cautious side in my calculations, and also the bubble is now growing again, even as I write this. Not all the growth will be a result of unproductive debt; there has undoubtedly been a boost to genuine wealth creation as a result of all this easy money, but this production, like the artificial wealth, has been 'borrowed' from the future. Whichever way we look at it, the resulting recession and the tough times to come are a consequence of having to pay back the unearned prosperity of the last few decades.

If we look at recent estimates for the total amount of debt in the world, we get a figure somewhere between $120 trillion and $200 trillion, depending which criteria are used for defining debt (some debts cancel each other out, others get counted twice; it's all rather complicated). Figure 72 shows an average of the various estimates for total debt, and the relationship of this debt to global GDP.

So my figure of $200 trillion begins to seem quite feasible, as it ought to correspond quite closely to present total debt levels, which, despite the bursting of the credit bubble, are still rising. Actually I shouldn't say the 'bursting' of the credit bubble, because it never really burst, but rather deflated somewhat. Although consumers are spending less as they pay off their debts, governments have taken over as the really big spenders, trying in vain to stimulate the economy with more credit. This fails to recognize that it is not a difficulty in

Figure 72

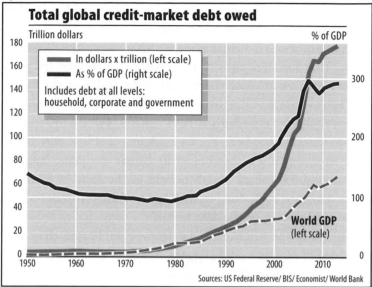

Total global credit-market debt owed

Trillion dollars | % of GDP

In dollars x trillion (left scale)
As % of GDP (right scale)
Includes debt at all levels: household, corporate and government

World GDP (left scale)

Sources: US Federal Reserve/ BIS/ Economist/ World Bank

obtaining credit that is stopping people and businesses from borrowing but rather a shortage of real wealth and real jobs, and a lack of confidence in the ability of governments to tackle the big issues.

Phantom fortunes

It seems clear enough that there's a lot less genuine wealth around than the figures from Credit Suisse et al would suggest, simply because money has lost so much value compared to the real wealth of industry. Even if we take the lower debt estimate of $120 trillion, what does all this debt actually mean? To whom is it owed? What is the relationship between that $120 trillion in debt and the $240 trillion or so of private wealth that, according to Credit Suisse, exists in the world?

Estimates of total private wealth are obviously net figures (in other words, they subtract personal debts). But in reality, some debts are counted as being other people's assets, and will therefore end up as part of that $240 trillion. There are so many different components of debt, and such a complex inter-relationship between banks and investment funds, that it's impossible to make sense of it all.

A pattern seems to be emerging in this investigation, however, in that this one-third-debt to two-thirds-wealth ratio fits with the evidence of my first chart, which showed that the credit bubble had boosted GDP by around a third in recent years.

One thing we can be fairly sure of – much of that $240 trillion of private wealth has been put to work by being lent out. That's what investing is all about. Credit Suisse estimates suggest that around 55% of all wealth is held in the form of financial assets, giving us something in the region of $130 trillion, which corresponds closely to the debt figure.

But again, the situation is far more complicated than this matching of figures would suggest. Much of that $120 trillion of debt, or $200-trillion or whatever it might be, is either government debt or inter-bank lending. Much of it has gone into the creation of new money. This brings us back to the relationship between money and real wealth. If around a third of all the money in the world is credit based on the leveraging of existing wealth, then money is overvalued relative to the real wealth of the world by a factor of one third.

In other words, there might well be $240 trillion worth of wealth in existence, measured in dollar terms, but, when measured in terms of the real wealth produced by industry, this would equate to something like $160 trillion. The $80-trillion difference represents the amount lost through the devaluation of money relative to real wealth, in much the same way that $19 trillion was 'lost' in the financial crash. We might note also that US house prices fell by a third after the crash, returning to the long-term trend (though they have recently been rising again).

It might also be significant that the world's central banks currently hold about $18 trillion in government debt, which is not far off a third of global GDP. As I mentioned in Chapter 6 (when comparing the derivatives trade to real trade) this ratio of one-third phantom wealth to two-thirds real wealth keeps coming up, albeit in different guises.

If we take another look at the chart showing GDP relative to the natural wealth extracted from the earth (which I reproduce in Figure 73), taking the trend line for GDP as it would have been if it followed the pre-1971 trajectory (real output without the boost from credit) we can actually see that missing $80 trillion in relation to the $200-trillion credit bubble. We can also see how it fits the scale of the blip caused when $19 trillion disappeared in the financial crash (according to the US Treasury Department). And we see also that the credit bubble appears to have been re-inflated by all the new debt that's been created since the crash – debt that has presumably been boosted by the injection of $5 trillion or so of central-bank credit into the system.

In Chapter 8 I explained how, when I was attempting to work out how much 'produced' wealth there might be in the world, I knocked off $60 trillion of private wealth compared to the Credit Suisse estimation, because I considered that money was overvalued relative to real wealth. It now appears that I might have been a bit generous with that figure, and really I should have knocked off $80 trillion.

Although these figures are educated guesses at best, I feel reasonably certain that there is something in the region of one-third less real wealth in the world than most estimates suggest, thanks to the creation of $200 trillion in credit over the last decade or two. I keep coming to the same conclusion after analyzing different sets of data. I explained in Chapter 4 how I came across my first chart in a United Nations report from 2011, in which the authors couldn't understand why the world economy apparently grew faster than the rate of natural resource use would suggest it should have done. I also read a 2012 report by the US Energy Information Administration (as explained in Chapter 8) in which the authors were puzzled by a sharp increase in GDP that somehow occurred without

Figure 73

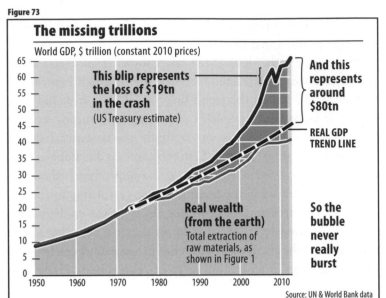

The missing trillions

World GDP, $ trillion (constant 2010 prices)

This blip represents the loss of $19tn in the crash
(US Treasury estimate)

And this represents around $80tn

REAL GDP TREND LINE

Real wealth (from the earth)
Total extraction of raw materials, as shown in Figure 1

So the bubble never really burst

Source: UN & World Bank data

a corresponding rise in energy use (as shown in Figures 48 and 49).

In the following graphic (Figure 74) I put these two results together to show more clearly how they are telling us the same story: the growth of GDP, global in one case and US in the other, without the use of resources. This 'decoupling' of growth can't be attributed to dramatic improvements in energy efficiency or mineral recycling; such an effect is relatively small, as I said, and has anyway been taken into account. The boost in economic activity can only be accounted for by the credit bubble, and this artificial growth accounts for somewhere in the region of a third of the total growth; a bit more in the US, a bit less elsewhere perhaps, which is what one might expect, given the dominance of Wall Street in global finance.

Looked at another way, of the $200-trillion credit bubble, $80 trillion is debt that is not backed by real wealth of any kind; debt that will have to be repaid from future earnings. Of all the reasons why the rich world is going to get poorer, this is perhaps the most significant in terms of likely effect. Perhaps it will also

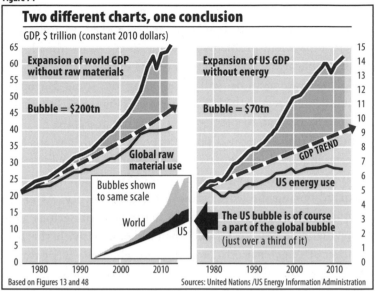

Figure 74

Two different charts, one conclusion

GDP, $ trillion (constant 2010 dollars)

Expansion of world GDP without raw materials

Bubble = $200tn

Global raw material use

Bubbles shown to same scale

World

US

Expansion of US GDP without energy

Bubble = $70tn

GDP TREND

US energy use

The US bubble is of course a part of the global bubble (just over a third of it)

Based on Figures 13 and 48　　Sources: United Nations /US Energy Information Administration

be the simplest to put right. After all, wiping out debts ought to be easier than creating more jobs, though of course the latter is made more difficult by the debt burden in the first place. All the major economic problems are interrelated. But what does all this debt actually mean for the future of the world economy?

The debt of nations

Private debt has been around for as long as civilization itself, at least since those Babylonian IOUs from 5,000 years ago, which I mentioned in Chapter 5. The scale might have grown, but, as a percentage of total wealth, private debt is still just about manageable. It might hurt the economy, but it isn't going to wreck it totally. Some countries – the US for example – have begun to reduce overall levels of private debt from the credit-bubble peak, though there are problems ahead concerning student debt, which recently passed the one-trillion-dollar mark and is increasing rapidly (Figure 75), and which represents a reduction in future economic activity, because all these graduates, even if they get good jobs, will have lower disposable incomes until they've paid off their debts. Another source of potential trouble is the default rate on student loans, at 11% and rising, indicating serious repayment problems for many in the years ahead, plus all the implications that go with a record of bad debt.

And private debt is still a big drag on some European economies, especially the UK, as we saw in Figure 67, but also in Ireland, Spain and, to a lesser extent, France and Italy.

But the real problem is public debt. Although nations have become indebted in the past, the scale of sovereign debt that we are seeing now is greater than ever before; greater even than occurred during the world wars of the last century. After the Second World War, for example, nations with serious debt problems were able to rebuild their economies with the help of other stronger nations, as happened when the US gave aid to Europe. But the situation is very different now. Most of the developed world is mired in debt, became that way even though our economies, far from being devastated by war, were supposedly booming. The whole debt problem was brought about by a prolonged and sustained failure by rich-world

Figure 75

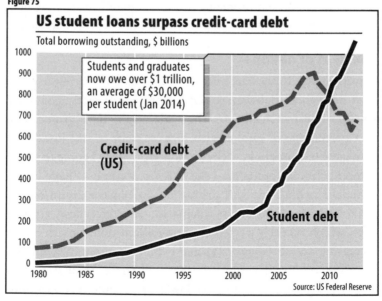

US student loans surpass credit-card debt

Total borrowing outstanding, $ billions

Students and graduates now owe over $1 trillion, an average of $30,000 per student (Jan 2014)

Credit-card debt (US)

Student debt

Source: US Federal Reserve

governments to balance the books when times were good, in conjunction with a financial sector all too willing to lend. Our leaders acted like shopaholics let loose with a stack of credit cards, safe in the knowledge that the debts wouldn't have to be paid until well after their retirement from public life. They could reap the rewards of their own generosity, and leave the consequences to their successors. Either that or they genuinely believed that the economy could keep on growing forever, powered by the phantom fuel of never-ending credit.

Figure 76 shows the deterioration in US finances in recent decades, especially this century, while the inset chart shows how the largest five of the G7 advanced economies have been getting further into the red in recent years, with governments spending more than they've been earning in tax receipts. In many cases debt repayments are taking up over 20% of national income; 50% in Japan's case. And ultimately these repayments must come from the people, from incomes that are already declining relative to prices. These debt levels are obviously unsustainable, as the Bank for International Settlements noted in its 2012

Figure 76

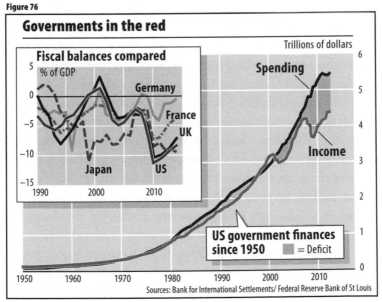

179

Annual Report: 'In most advanced economies, the fiscal budget, excluding interest payments, would need 20 consecutive years of surpluses exceeding 2% of GDP – starting now – just to bring the debt-to-GDP ratio back to its pre-crisis level. And every additional year that budgets continue in deficit makes the recovery period longer.'

Although the report doesn't spell it out, such a recovery is not going to happen: there is no solution to this problem that does not involve some kind of default.

Who owes whom?

Nobody understands fully what such huge debts mean for the global economy. One might ask, taking in the overall picture, how is it even possible for the whole world to be in debt? It isn't, of course. On a global level, the books must balance; borrowing and lending must be equal. So who owes whom?

One answer is that some developed economies of the world, in particular the US (but also some European countries, including the UK), owe some developing economies, in particular China (but also some developed economies, such as Japan[1]). This is because the countries that make lots of real stuff have invested their profits in the countries that have the most trusted governments.

In other words, nations such as China and Japan, which have thriving manufacturing industries, along with oil-rich nations such as Saudi Arabia and Russia, have used the earth's natural wealth to make more money than they want to spend right now. They have therefore chosen to invest that money in the US, UK, Switzerland and other European countries. This is partly because these nations have sound currencies and can be trusted not to default on their debts, and partly because they are the dominant consumers of the investor countries' products, so some of that money is returned in the form of more trade.

A situation has developed where the Eastern producer nations lend money to the Western consumer nations so that they can keep buying more products. More specifically, American money initially created jobs in China, which helped China grow wealthier, and now the Chinese are lending the Americans more money to maintain those jobs. Looked at on a global scale, it might not seem like a bad deal. Doesn't everyone benefit?

If the global economy was like one great nation, it might not matter too much. But because we are talking about individual sovereign states, it means that potential conflict is building up. The US (like several other rich nations) is living beyond its means, encouraged by cheap credit. If the Chinese and Japanese decided to stop lending to the US (in other words, they sold all their US government bonds), it would raise America's cost of borrowing, worsening the already-dire budget situation at the very least, and potentially sending the global economy into meltdown – which is why they are unlikely to do so. But even though they hold over $2 trillion between them, China and Japan are by no means the biggest holders of US debt, as my next chart shows (Figure 77).

We can see that Chinese and Japanese holdings amount to around 14% of the $17 trillion US debt, as of December 2013, and all non-US holdings come to 34%, the rest being held by Americans, in various forms. The biggest holders of US debt are in fact the nation's own welfare trust funds, and this highlights a more general point about all this build-up of debt in the developed world: if a nation borrows from its own social-security, health and pension funds, what are the long-term consequences?

This brings us back to the question: Who owes whom?

The real answer is that present generations of adults, in particular the older half of the population, which includes those currently in charge of most governments and businesses throughout the rich world, are borrowing money from future generations. Or at least, we would be borrowing money from future generations if it were not for one minor point: we won't be paying it back, because there's no way that the US (along with much of Europe) will ever be in a position to honor these future

Figure 77

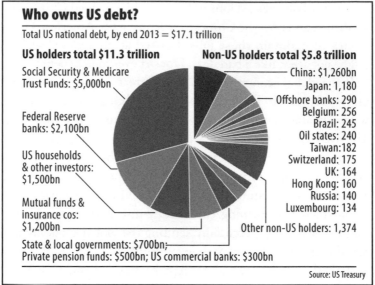

Who owns US debt?

Total US national debt, by end 2013 = $17.1 trillion

US holders total $11.3 trillion

Non-US holders total $5.8 trillion

Social Security & Medicare
Trust Funds: $5,000bn

Federal Reserve
banks: $2,100bn

US households
& other investors:
$1,500bn

Mutual funds &
insurance cos:
$1,200bn

State & local governments: $700bn;
Private pension funds: $500bn; US commercial banks: $300bn

China: $1,260bn
Japan: 1,180
Offshore banks: 290
Belgium: 256
Brazil: 245
Oil states: 240
Taiwan:182
Switzerland: 175
UK: 164
Hong Kong: 160
Russia: 140
Luxembourg: 134

Other non-US holders: 1,374

Source: US Treasury

welfare commitments.

So, in effect, the current generation with the most influence in the world – the post-War generation of 'baby-boomers', the richest generation ever to walk the earth, whose expectations grew to include generous pensions and healthcare provisions – is plundering the wealth of its own children and grandchildren.

Our children and grandchildren will be paying these debts, one way or another, for decades to come. Besides having to pay off their student loans, they will be earning lower wages, paying higher taxes, paying higher prices for food and fuel, and higher interest rates on loans. Why? Because we baby-boomers didn't want to pay higher taxes ourselves. We didn't want to pay the full costs of all those generous entitlements, even though we were quite happy to vote for the governments that promised them to us.

We thought that the good times would keep on rolling forever, and even after it became obvious that they wouldn't, we fooled ourselves into thinking things would soon return to 'normal'. Yet what we thought of as normal was in fact a mere blip of prosperity – genuine prosperity for a couple of decades, and then an illusion of prosperity that we managed to sustain until the crash of 2008 offered us a glimpse of reality. And now the debts will pass to future generations, in one way or another, even if they are never paid.

What would default really mean?

Although we can never really be sure about anything, especially concerning the future, we can be fairly certain that some nations will default on their sovereign debts to some extent, simply because it will be impossible to pay them in full.

We have heard a lot about the Eurozone crisis, and the problems of Greek and Spanish debt in particular, but, as my next chart shows, total Greek debt is actually less than German debt, and way below UK and Japanese borrowing levels.

The reason it's more of a problem for some Eurozone nations is due to the nature of the debt. In the case of Greece, it's mostly sovereign debt, and government revenues are nowhere near enough to make the repayments, which pushes up the cost of borrowing, because investors don't want to buy such risky debts

Figure 78

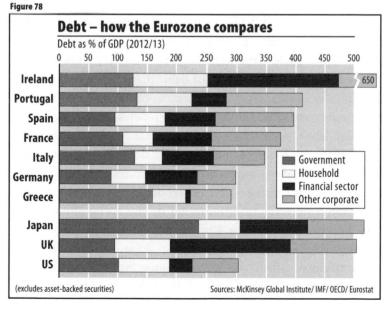

183

unless the yields are high. A big chunk of UK debt is owed by private banks, and much of this is offset by assets (mostly loans to other banks). And although the UK government is also highly indebted, it is seen as a much safer bet than Greece because the economy is struggling less and the UK has a good record of paying its debts, which in turn means lower borrowing costs. The same applies to Germany, which has the added advantage of a thriving manufacturing sector that creates real wealth.

But, there again, the US is also seen as a safe bet, possibly the safest of all, with its huge economic power and its dominant position in the world. Yet the US is struggling almost as much as Greece under its massive debt load.

For most nations, there are only two ways out of the debt trap. A government can attempt to pay off its debts by increasing revenue relative to repayments, through some combination of tax rises and spending cuts, as most of the struggling Eurozone nations are attempting to do. Or they can default – just refuse to pay up. For the time being, this option is not realistically open to the Eurozone countries, simply because the club of which they are members won't allow it.

The US, however, has another option that the rest of the world lacks. Because it issues the currency that dominates international trade – the default global currency – the US can theoretically print its way out of debt. If any other nation were to print a lot more money than its economy warranted, it would devalue its currency against other currencies, and therefore its external debt repayments would rise to reflect this devaluation. But the US pays its debts in dollars, so it doesn't have that worry. If the dollar weakens against other currencies, it actually helps the US economy because US exports become more competitive.

So for Americans, a devaluation of the dollar should help to reduce the debt burden. Only when commodity prices start to rise – commodities being priced in dollars – does a weaker dollar begin to affect the US economy. And this will surely happen. Eventually, the fact that the US keeps printing more dollars must lead to further devaluation.

It seems inevitable that creditor nations such as China will lose out one way or another, as their dollar holdings are reduced in value, industry is hit by higher commodity prices and consumer spending declines because of reduced wealth. In the end, we will all pay the price for all this debt. It simply isn't possible to live off debt indefinitely; to be forever buying now and paying later, in the hope that 'later' never arrives. Although governments can kick the day of reckoning much further down the road than individuals can, they can't kick it into oblivion. At some point we'd get hyperinflation, and everyone would realize how much poorer they'd become.

Perhaps eventually the rich nations will reduce their debts to sustainable levels, even if they do so through inflation. But some poorer nations won't be able to do this. And why should they? History abounds with cases of poor nations refusing to repay loans to the rich world; loans that were often given with unreasonable and damaging strings attached, arranged between banks looking for high returns and corrupt leaders who didn't give a damn about the people.

There is no international law that can enforce such repayments. All that the creditor countries can do is to stop trading with the defaulter and make life difficult for them. But in many cases of such defaulting, the poor country has recovered after a few years because its economy has been released from the choking grip of debt. The list of nations that have defaulted on sovereign debt is a long one, going back to 16th-century Spain. More recent examples include Russia in 1998 and Argentina in 2001.

Sovereign debts have resulted in revolutions – the French Revolution was partly a result of Louis XVI trying to raise taxes to pay for the ongoing conflict with Britain over the American colonies (most sovereign debts were due to wars, until very recently) – and revolutions have often resulted in default, as with Russia in 1918. Incoming leaders feel no obligation to pay a debt agreed by the previous administration, which they've just kicked out for being inept and corrupt. The most recent example is Ecuador, which defaulted on $3 billion of government bonds in 2008, only to buy them back at a good discount after the price fell. The lessons are clear enough; when it comes to sovereign debt, default is always an option.

It is essential that we break this cycle of debt creation; to stop spending money we don't have and reduce debts sooner rather than later. The price of real stuff is going to rise anyway, and the longer we leave it, the more disruptive the adjustment will be, especially for future generations. Because the more we 'borrow' from the future, knowing full well that we won't be repaying the loan, the poorer those future generations are going be.

1 It might seem odd that the Japanese government is a massive borrower from its own people (owing over $6 trillion) and a big lender ($1.2 trillion) to the US. But if it sold its US bonds to pay off some Japanese creditors, the yen would appreciate strongly against the dollar and its exports to the US, which earn the dollars in the first place, would be hit hard, and also there would be nothing left in reserve. It's a bit like a householder having a large mortgage but keeping some savings in a different account.

13 The decline of Europe

What can the Eurozone learn from Japan?

For Europe in particular, prolonged recession – the end of growth – seems inevitable. There is no new industry to kick-start the growth process, no major oil finds or new technology boom, as helped between the 1970s and the 1990s, and of course there's no chance of repeating the credit-fuelled construction and consumer-spending spree of the last decade.

It had to happen some time: as I pointed out at the beginning of this book, continuous economic growth is ultimately impossible, as well as being ecologically undesirable. And perhaps it isn't surprising that Europe, the first developed region of the modern world, should be the first to experience decline. Europe is showing the symptoms of malaise that one might expect of an advanced economy that has reached the limits of growth, with many of its natural resources close to depletion, falling industrial output, rising unemployment and declining populations in many nations.

A decline in population is a good thing in terms of a sustainable future, but it raises questions with regard to the strength of the economy. How will a smaller workforce provide for an ageing population? Will there be enough workers and enough real wealth production to fund pensions, healthcare and other future government obligations? It is almost certainly the case that there will not be – at least not while expectations are based on the boom years of the last half-century.

One might argue that European nations are not the first to experience such problems, and that Japan has been in a similar situation for a decade or more. This is perhaps true, but Japan is a bit different in that it is one stalled economy in a generally buoyant region. And Japan has managed to avoid the real killer of high unemployment, partly because it still has a strong manufacturing base with a large export market. In this respect

Figure 79

Europe's falling share of global wealth

% share of world GDP

EU = total of 27 member states as of 2012, even though many weren't actually members until recently

Forecast based on HM Treasury estimates

EU

US

Japan

Latin America

China

Sources: World Bank data/ US Department of Agriculture/ HM Treasury

Japan is more akin to Germany than to the rest of Europe. It does, however, provide some interesting clues as to what Europe might expect in the near future, suggesting that, if expectations are lowered until they meet with reality, prospects don't have to be as bad as they seem right now.

Lessons from Japan

The strong economic growth that marked Japan's post-War recovery came to a sudden halt in 1991. Growth from 1960 to 1990 averaged over 6% per year, while in the 1990s it fell below 1%. Part of the reason for this was that the strong post-War growth was from a low base: Japan was simply catching up with the West, aided by good industrial practices and the advantage of being able to copy, and in the process improve on, Western manufacturing methods.

By the 1980s, however, Japanese industry was beginning to lose its cost advantage, as wages reached Western levels and even surpassed them. Other developing countries – South Korea in particular, and then China – were becoming serious rivals to

Figure 80

The Japanese bubble experience

Nikkei stock index (x1000) — Urban land price index

Urban land prices (Japan)

Tokyo stock market

Sources: Bloomberg/ Japan Real Estate Institute

Japanese industry.

What happened to Japan in the 1980s was a prelude in some respects to the years leading up to the credit crunch in the US and Europe. Asset prices shot up and bank lending grew as people borrowed heavily to invest in stocks and property, confident that the boom would continue. They had some reason for confidence in the sense that the Japanese economic miracle was real, being based on genuine industrial strength. But the problems began when the bubble burst.

Both corporations and individuals found themselves burdened with huge debts against assets that were rapidly falling in value, plunging the banking system and business generally into a long period of stagnation, in which debt repayment soaked up earnings and left little over for real investment or consumption. The government countered the slump by spending on massive infrastructure projects, which prevented unemployment levels from rising too much (Figure 81), but the borrowing required for these public works, combined with falling tax revenues, resulted in the huge national debt with which Japan is still saddled.

Figure 81

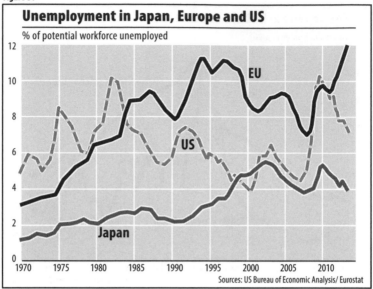

The causes of Japan's banking crisis, which began in 1991, now look very familiar: deregulation and lax governance resulted in excessive lending during the boom, creating an unsustainable asset bubble that eventually burst.

It is worth noting, however, that Japan's situation is rather different from other heavily indebted nations for several reasons. Nearly all its government debt is held by Japanese savers rather than foreigners, and it also holds over $3 trillion in overseas assets (including those US Treasury bonds). And because Japan has a positive trade balance, being a net exporter, it can still fund its own debt, unlike the struggling Eurozone nations.

Japan was able to keep its economy going by exporting products such as cars to the rest of the world – a world that was booming on the back of the technology industry. Even so, there have been some pretty dire forecasts by the IMF and others concerning Japan's future ability to keep paying its debts. Nations everywhere face unprecedented challenges, and Europe faces some of the toughest.

The Eurozone debt problem

Why have some European countries, such as Greece and Spain, been hit so hard by the debt crisis? Because, in the artificial boom of the credit bubble, they borrowed too much money relative to the size of their economies. They cannot produce enough real wealth to pay the interest on their debts. And, because they are members of the Eurozone, their ability to restructure their economies is severely limited. They can't devalue their own currencies or set their own interest rates, for example.

It is certainly the case that even the worst-hit countries of Europe don't, for the most part, have debt levels any higher than several other nations, in particular the UK, US and Japan. The difference lies in the limited options that these smaller Eurozone countries have for raising revenue and cutting costs, which results in their paying a higher rate of interest on loans, because their government bonds are considered by investors to carry a higher risk.

Each country borrowed money for different reasons and on

Figure 82

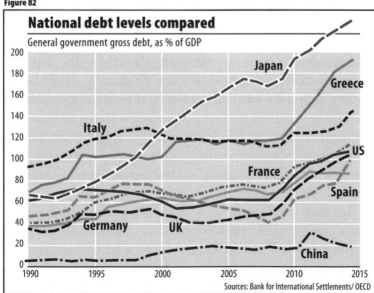

National debt levels compared

General government gross debt, as % of GDP

Sources: Bank for International Settlements/ OECD

191

different terms, but the solution ought to be the same for all: raise more income through taxation and cut public spending. Unfortunately, this strategy is next to impossible. Raising more income would require economic growth, which would require an increase in demand for industrial products, which in turn would require consumers to earn more money, or at least to spend more. And at a time of rising unemployment when the majority of people throughout Europe, especially in the hardest-hit nations, are becoming poorer, few people are spending money on anything but essentials. And, as Figure 83 shows, there will soon be fewer taxpayers in many European countries, as the EU follows Japan's example of a shrinking, and therefore ageing, population.

For the same reasons, governments are severely limited in their scope for public-spending cuts, which inevitably lead to greater poverty. As the number of people in work continues to fall, this problem can only get worse. The situation appears to be hopeless; Europe faces a future of economic decline.

So the real issue facing Europe – an issue that needs to be recognized and addressed – is how to manage this decline. A default on debt by some Eurozone nations seems inevitable, and is probably the best solution. The break-up of the Eurozone itself is also a possibility. This would give individual nations more options when it comes to managing the crisis. The financial sector generally, and individual investors globally, would be hit hard by such debt defaults, but the banks were responsible for lending the money in the first place, often with the same lack of caution that led to the sub-prime crisis. Wealthy investors make their money from speculation, unlike the majority of people who have to work for a living, so they should expect to lose out now and then.

This time, unlike in the previous crash, governments will not be in a position to prevent bank failures by further indebting the taxpaying public. And, as it's mostly the wealthy who will lose out, simply because the poor have less to lose, such action will have the effect of reducing inequality. A harsh method, perhaps,

Figure 83

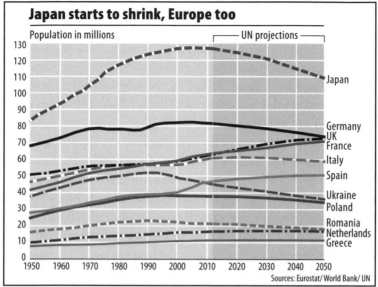

Japan starts to shrink, Europe too

Population in millions — UN projections

Japan
Germany
UK
France
Italy
Spain
Ukraine
Poland
Romania
Netherlands
Greece

Sources: Eurostat/ World Bank/ UN

but as I made clear in previous chapters, no real wealth will be lost if nations default on their debts; all those billions of euros never really existed in the first place.

What the banks will lose is the future gains they'd been hoping to make from the taxpayers of the nations of southern Europe. As with most debts, the repayments represent a transfer of wealth from the lower and middle classes to the rich, so perhaps we shouldn't worry too much if those poorer nations default.

Another option for Europe would be closer integration – instead of the Eurozone being broken up, it could be strengthened by creating a real, democratically elected European government, with a corresponding reduction in the power of national governments. It was the half-hearted nature of the Eurozone's unity – a single currency but lots of individual and unrelated government policies – that exacerbated the debt problem in the first place.

In a way this would reflect the reality of what is happening in this ever-more-connected world: national governments are becoming less influential as market forces and transnational corporations, especially banks, wield more power.

Globalization requires better regulation from a higher level than national governments can provide, so a stronger European Union would be a good thing, in conjunction with increased representation at a local or regional level. I look at this idea more closely in Part Three.

Whether Europe opts for looser or closer integration, a dark cloud of economic decline looms over the continent, denser in the south perhaps, but casting its shadow across the north too, apart from the sunny spot that falls on oil-rich Norway. But Norway is the exception: a small population with lots of natural wealth. For most small nations in Europe, and the larger ones too, closer integration is probably the best option. Only together can the people of Europe hope to make their voices heard in the new world order, in a global marketplace otherwise dominated by the US and the rising eastern powers of China, India and, to a lesser extent, Russia.

What the economies of the West really need, and what they

Figure 84

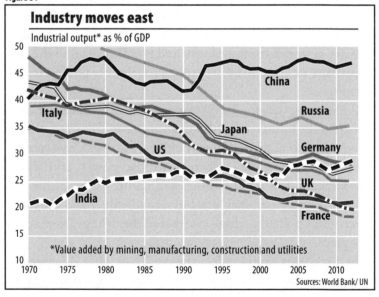

Industry moves east

Industrial output* as % of GDP

China
Russia
Italy
Japan
US
Germany
India
UK
France

*Value added by mining, manufacturing, construction and utilities

1970　1975　1980　1985　1990　1995　2000　2005　2010

Sources: World Bank/ UN

will find hardest of all, is to reverse the trend of declining real industry, as shown in Figure 84.

Europe in particular needs to rebalance its economies away from services, especially finance, and back towards the production of genuine wealth. The chances of this happening are remote indeed, as long as half the world is competing with lower wages and lower costs. Unless this competitive advantage for the rest of the world can be reduced, Europe faces a shrinking service sector with little prospect of a revival in manufacturing.

Even Germany, Europe's industrial powerhouse, will probably find that the demand for its niche goods – machine tools and luxury cars, for example – falls away, as the developing nations of the east adapt to lower growth themselves, and as these nations – China and India in particular – make more of their own cars and machine tools.

But this is not to say that Europe necessarily faces as bleak a future as might be implied by the picture I've just painted. If the leaders and the people of Europe can accept the reality of their situation – and this includes Britain, because Britain faces the same problems of declining real industry, dwindling resources and an over-reliance on other people's wealth – then there is no reason why the problems can't be overcome. What is needed is a recognition that economic growth is no longer possible or even desirable, and to work from there. Europe can, and should, lead the way in changing to a more sustainable economic system – to a system that puts employment and the environment before profit and material wealth.

It is clearly absurd for politicians and economists to keep going on about a return to growth, becoming more competitive and raising productivity yet further, as if such things could go on forever, even as the dole lines keep growing. Those days are gone, and the sooner we accept it the better.

The 21st century will be very different from the last one. In what way it is impossible to predict, of course, but the

Figure 85

Europe's unfolding job crisis

Youth unemployment rate %, (16-24 year-olds, excluding students)

Source: Eurostat

focus of government action, especially in Europe, will have to be jobs, because the trend shown in Figure 85 represents potentially the biggest crisis facing Europe since the Second World War.

Labor is not a commodity

One reason for the current failure of free-market capitalism is the way it tends to treat labor as just another commodity, to be bought and sold in the marketplace, its value purely a function of supply and demand. Human labor is, of course, much more than a commodity: work is the essential component that transforms the earth's natural wealth into something useful; the source of all economic value. But work is even more than this. It is the source of all spiritual value too, of self-respect and dignity. Without work, leisure time loses its meaning; life loses all meaning.

We humans have developed the concept of employment into an elaborate system, complete with rituals, rules and hierarchies – an element of civilized society – but in the end it is still a function of the struggle for survival. If we don't work, we don't eat. Even the cave dwellers had to work, because even the act of catching a grub or picking a berry from a bush is a form of work. The hunter-gatherers would have spent a lot of their time working; trying to collect enough food to fend off hunger, enough wood to fuel their fires. And obviously parenthood is also a form of work – in some respects the most valuable work of all.

Perhaps it is the sense of purpose that employment provides that makes it so vital, even in the modern service-dominated economy, where most of us don't need to do the really important stuff any more, such as growing food or building shelters or making tools.

I made the point earlier that the service sector does not create wealth, being one or two steps removed from the industrial processes of extracting and transforming the natural wealth of the earth, but that doesn't mean that service-sector jobs lack value. There is clearly a great deal of value in the work of a teacher, to use the most obvious example. As I mentioned in Chapter 2, a teacher adds 'intangible' wealth to the economy, a kind of wealth that can't be measured in physical units because its quality is not a material thing, but consists rather in the value that education adds to society, in what is sometimes referred to as 'human capital'. Without a good education system, society would undoubtedly be poorer, in terms of both spiritual wealth and tangible wealth; industry would be less advanced and less real wealth would be produced.

The same can be said about policing, law, healthcare and, to varying degrees, many other service-sector jobs. So, in a modern economy at least, the wealth-creation process is to some extent reliant on the service sector. All real work adds a kind of value – even if it isn't actually creating material wealth directly, it still leads to greater wealth creation. Even bankers have their uses, just as long as they stick to the business of productive investment, rather than speculation.

Zen and the curse of unemployment

In his book *Zen and The Art of Motorcycle Maintenance*, Robert Pirsig describes how, as a lecturer in philosophy, he asks his students to define 'Quality'. None of them can, and the lecturer finds that he can't either. 'You know Quality when you see it,' he says, even if nobody can describe it. But in his book Pirsig shows us what 'Quality' is, even if he doesn't spell it out. Quality is the material or visible representation of good work. It is good work made tangible, and this is why I said in Chapter 11 (with regard to the internet) that there is no value to be found in making our lives easier or more convenient if it doesn't lead to more productive industry. Good work is rarely easy work.

'Quality' is what you get when you add a lot of value to whatever raw materials you might be using. Perhaps they should be high-quality raw materials, or perhaps you turn something quite ordinary into a high-quality product purely through the application of human skill. Or perhaps the only materials are ideas – the creative abilities of an artist. A song can have quality, as can all art.

This brings us back to my assertion that the source of all value is in work, in the effort we put into our lives. Although the majority of people might not be able to earn a living doing what we might call a 'quality' job, this doesn't prevent anyone from adding quality to their work. Most jobs can be done well or badly, depending on the approach taken. Most jobs can give a certain kind of satisfaction and self-respect, even if it's only the feeling that one has worked hard and earned one's pay or deserved a drink at the end of the day.

If your job is tedious and apparently lacking in any reward other than the paycheck, there is still a kind of satisfaction to be had from knowing you've got through another shift – you've 'endured' that tedium, which is in itself a form of hard work. Obviously this reward is very small with a lousy job; barely noticeable, perhaps. But it's there, nonetheless. Surely any work contains the potential satisfaction that comes from doing a good job.

This is the curse of unemployment. If we don't have a job to do, we lose the means to achieve this self-respect. We are deprived of this satisfaction; we don't get to feel that dignity. Idleness is destructive because life isn't supposed to be easy; we are genetically programmed to fight for survival in a harsh environment. If we don't have work to keep us occupied, this survival instinct finds other outlets, usually to the detriment of society.

It seems clear to me that jobs are a vital element of society, that aiming for full employment, or as close to full employment as possible, should be the top priority of any government policy. I return to this topic in Chapter 15, but first I think we need to look more closely at the reasons for the current decline in real employment.

14 A race with no winners

The high price of cheap goods

I have made the point in previous chapters that the focus on productivity, which is seen by industrialists and economists as being vital for growth and prosperity, is a function of competition between corporations, and also between nations, for market share. The 'winner' of this competition is the company or country that produces the most goods with the fewest workers. Even though the rules might be altered when a nation such as China enters the game – with a hundred million or more low-paid farmhands heading for the factories – in the end, as China is finding now, there's no escaping the race for productivity.

The problem with this competitive element is that, as with most competitions, there are more losers than winners, and in this case the trend is for more and more losers to the point where, in the end, there will be no winners at all. The whole world will have lost.

The key to productivity is technological innovation. During the 20th century, as the focus on productivity grew sharper, the US gained a lead over the rest of the world, a lead that lengthened with the Second World War, by the end of which the US had no significant rivals for industrial supremacy.

With a certain irony, it was the losing nations of the war, Japan and Germany, which, after rebuilding their industrial bases from scratch with US help, eventually challenged this US supremacy, and, since the 1970s, other nations have joined the race. South Korea is a recent winner, having focused on real industry rather than finance and services; besides making cars and high-tech electronics, Korea now builds over a third of all the world's new ships, and industry doesn't get more real than shipbuilding.

Even the communist leaders of the Soviet Union couldn't resist entering this competition between nations, a competition that ended up playing a major role in the Soviet empire's downfall. For the duration of the Cold War, from 1946 until 1991, the USSR tried to prove that it could beat the US in all fields: industry and agriculture; science and space exploration; even sport. In the end it lost the race, a race it should never have entered in the first place. I can't help thinking that the Soviet Union would have stood a much better chance of success if it had allowed a bit of small-scale competition in the local marketplace, rather than trying to compete with the US in areas that didn't really matter. It might then have stuck to its ideals and concentrated on building a better, more equal society, based on its huge land area and its generous share of the earth's natural wealth.

Competition can be damaging in other ways too. Why should it cost three times as much to take the train from London to Glasgow, for example, than it does to fly? It is bad for the environment and we want people to use trains more and to fly less, yet because of the nature of the transport market, the opposite happens. The reason is that competition doesn't work very well for railways, but it does for airlines. Privatization of the UK railways never really made any sense, but it went ahead anyway because at the time, in the 1990s, free-market competition was seen as the answer to all the world's problems.

Work for work's sake

Perhaps the time has come to question the idea that all this competition is a good thing. To remain competitive in a global marketplace, businesses have had to become 'leaner' and 'fitter'. In other words, they've been cutting costs to the absolute minimum: shedding jobs, outsourcing to low-wage countries, avoiding corporate taxes wherever possible.

The capitalist argument is that everyone wins because we get better goods at lower prices, but the price is really very high: fewer and fewer jobs, not just in the rich West, but eventually everywhere, because the need to be competitive never ends as long as the system demands it.

Figure 86

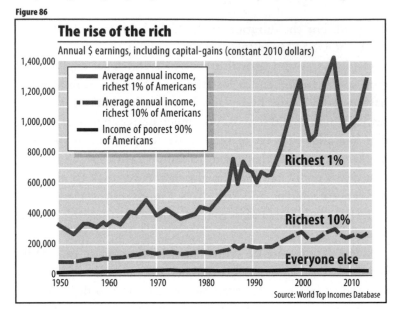

The rise of the rich

Annual $ earnings, including capital-gains (constant 2010 dollars)

- Average annual income, richest 1% of Americans
- Average annual income, richest 10% of Americans
- Income of poorest 90% of Americans

Richest 1%

Richest 10%

Everyone else

1,400,000
1,200,000
1,000,000
800,000
600,000
400,000
200,000
0

1950　1960　1970　1980　1990　2000　2010

Source: World Top Incomes Database

Would it not make more sense to have everyone employed and pay a higher price for the products?

One problem with capitalism is that it doesn't value work for its own sake. There is no obvious financial benefit to a business employing more workers if it can produce the goods without them. The market, being governed only by the relationship between supply and demand, has no way of responding to anything that isn't immediately obvious, such as the long-term benefit of employing more people, or the fact that resources will become scarce in the future, even if they seem abundant right now. This accounts for the wild fluctuations in commodity prices, which don't reflect the underlying reality, but are driven instead by the herd mentality of the market players.

The real winners in the productivity race are the owners and financiers of global businesses. The process leads to a concentration of production in a relatively small number of very large corporations because, when it comes down to survival of the fittest, it is these transnationals that have bought out or forced out the weaker competition. As with evolution, the losers

Figure 87

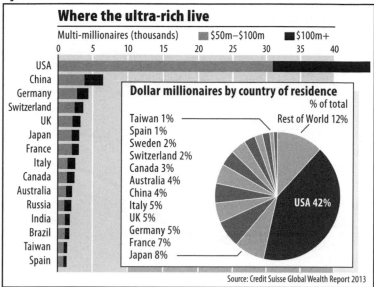

get swallowed up or left to die.

The result is an increasing concentration of wealth in the hands of the corporate élite – in the hands of those executives and bankers who control the large corporations and investment funds. This trend can be seen in the growing disparity between the highest earners and everyone else, as I showed in Figure 9. An even starker example can be seen in Figure 86, which shows how the incomes of the corporate élite – the top 1% – have shot up in recent years, while those at the lowest end of the pay-scale have seen a fall in real earnings.

Although the same thing is happening globally to varying degrees, the US represents by far the largest share of this extreme concentration of wealth, owing to the dominance of US industry over the last half-century or more. I mentioned in Chapter 3 that, according to data from Credit Suisse, the US has 30% of all the world's wealth and over 40% of all individuals with $50 million or more, even though it accounts for only 4% of global population. Because so many of the world's largest corporations are American-owned, and because this has been the case for the

Figure 88

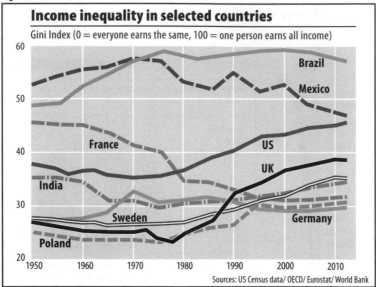

Income inequality in selected countries

Gini Index (0 = everyone earns the same, 100 = one person earns all income)

Sources: US Census data/ OECD/ Eurostat/ World Bank

past 60 years or more, a disproportionate share of global wealth has gone to US companies, and therefore to their executives and shareholders. Even when the products are manufactured in China or some other low-wage country, the US élite still rakes in a hefty share of the profits. Figure 87 shows this disparity very clearly.

The majority of US citizens, on the other hand, see very little of this wealth. Whereas in the post-War boom years Americans benefited from the creation of both industrial and service jobs, the focus on productivity, combined with global competition, has led to a situation where far fewer well-paid jobs are created now, even as US corporations continue their world domination.

The old industrial cities that once thrived on making the goods that fed America's prosperity, and which had full employment well into the 1970s, now resemble wastelands, deprived of all wealth after the middle classes moved out to the leafier suburbs, leaving the inner cities to decay and the factories to crumble around them. The jobs and the money went elsewhere and the poor were abandoned, right in the very heart of the wealthiest nation in the world. The system failed them.

The damage done by inequality

Although the contrast between rich and poor is starkest in the US and Latin America, it is not only Americans who suffer from this problem. The UK, for example, which, like the US, has a disproportionate share of the world's large banks, has also seen rising inequality in recent decades. Figure 88 shows an index of inequality known as the Gini coefficient, which is a measure of the proportion of wealth that goes to the rich minority.

Another way of showing this difference between the very wealthy and the majority is to compare the average wealth (or mean wealth, as in total wealth divided by population) with the median wealth, which represents the middle number if one were to list every person's wealth in order of value. Whereas the mean can be distorted by the presence of a small number of exceptionally high values – in this case very rich people – the median takes into account the large proportion of very poor people. Consequently the difference between the mean and the median figures gives a good indication of the degree of inequality in a society.

Figure 89 shows various nations in order of per-capita GDP (actually measured per adult, for 2012), plus the mean wealth and the median wealth, as explained above. So the first bar gives an indication of average annual income, while the other two bars show the distribution of total wealth. The difference between the figures reveals a lot about each country.

For example, Australia has the highest median wealth level by far of the nations shown here (the highest in the world in fact, though several small nations have a higher per-capita GDP), and this suggests that Australia's wealth is spread more evenly than in most rich societies. Australia has a relatively small population blessed with an abundance of natural wealth in the form of minerals, the majority of which are exported. The result is that most Australians are now considerably wealthier than most Americans, a situation that is unlikely to change because it is partly this even distribution of wealth that keeps

Figure 89

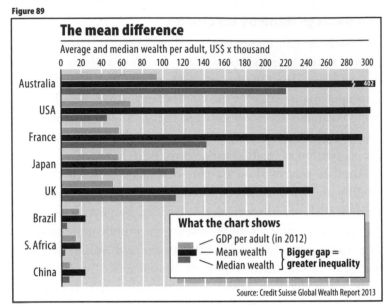

The mean difference

Average and median wealth per adult, US$ x thousand

Source: Credit Suisse Global Wealth Report 2013

the economy strong. This is America's greatest failing: the huge gulf between its mean and median wealth levels indicates a high concentration of wealth at the top and a lot of very poor people at the bottom. It would be in the interest of the whole nation – the wealthy just as much as the poor – to spread that wealth much more evenly. A fairer society works better for everyone, and in the end it is the rich who have the most to lose when the system breaks down.

Another interesting point is that the Japanese also have a high level of wealth, quite evenly spread, but their income is now lower because of their heavy debt burden, which eats into earnings.

These wealth figures tend to fluctuate significantly from one year to the next because of variations in exchange rates and also in valuations of assets such as property. The wealth of Britain, for example, appeared to drop much more than that of France in recent years, as house prices fell from their inflated peak. And this highlights one of the problems with looking at wealth in this way: a house is primarily a home, not a store of wealth. It is this kind of 'wealth' that's likely to disappear when house prices fall

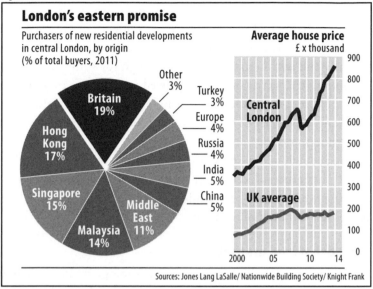

Figure 90

London's eastern promise

Purchasers of new residential developments in central London, by origin (% of total buyers, 2011)

Other 3%
Turkey 3%
Europe 4%
Russia 4%
India 5%
China 5%

Britain 19%
Hong Kong 17%
Singapore 15%
Middle East 11%
Malaysia 14%

Average house price
£ x thousand

Central London

UK average

2000   05   10   14

Sources: Jones Lang LaSalle/ Nationwide Building Society/ Knight Frank

to their true value, something that Britain should still be wary of, bearing in mind that, as Figure 29 showed, average UK house prices are still very high compared to the long-term trend (and especially to wages). This is partly because the average is skewed by London prices, which are inflated by wealthy foreigners buying into the world's financial capital. As Figure 90 shows, central London is popular with investors from the east, with new wealth in search of good returns in an uncertain world.

High property prices widen the gulf between the rich and everyone else. For the majority they can be a real burden, raising the cost of living, severely cutting disposable income and in many cases, in the southeast of England for example, making it impossible for people with average incomes to reach the first rung of the property ladder and difficult even to find affordable accommodation to rent.

This rapid growth in the wealth of the very rich at the expense of the majority, as I demonstrated in previous chapters, is a result of the accumulated wealth of past industry ending up in bank accounts and investment funds (including property), rather than going to the majority in the form of wages, as happened in the post-War 'golden age'. The natural wealth of the earth has been very poorly distributed, both globally and within nations, and although for some developing economies the situation has improved in recent years – as the poor of China and India, for example, find work in industry – for many, especially in the West, the situation is getting worse, as earnings and jobs decline.

Are the rich world's poor any better off than the poor world's poor? They are less likely to starve to death, perhaps, but to have nothing while being surrounded by the abundance of others brings its own kind of torment.

Not such a free market

I mentioned in Chapter 11 how, as technology makes industry more productive, humans must compete with machines for jobs. We know that machines always win this centuries-old contest, of course, because they work harder for less pay. But in the global marketplace workers also face competition of a different kind. Even when the work can't be done by machines, nations compete to offer the highest levels of output relative to wages, yet this competition is not fair because workers are not free to move around the globe in search of jobs. The global marketplace is only really 'free' for goods and money, not for people.

I would suggest that competition and productivity are, like a lot of things, good in moderation but not when taken to excess. The inevitable consequence of ever-increasing productivity is a world with few jobs. We need to rethink the system, putting jobs first.

Why should industry be as efficient as we can possibly make it? Just so goods can be made as cheaply as possible? Not only does increasing productivity result in fewer jobs, it also means that consumers end up buying more stuff than they really need, and that more resources are wasted on the production of consumer items that add nothing to the overall well-being of humankind.

As society becomes wealthier, the benefits of new and ever-cheaper products become less and less significant. In the 1950s and 1960s, people in the West were able to buy cars, washing-machines and televisions for the first time. Life became easier and, for a few decades, the boom in consumer items led to massive growth in the economies of the West and Japan. The boom times were self-perpetuating: as the price of goods fell relative to wages, more people could afford them, more goods were produced, and so on.

But during the last decades of the 20th century, as markets became saturated, companies had to resort to aggressive advertising and price competition to keep selling more and more goods that people didn't really need. Products became less and less useful, geared only to making life a little easier, at best. But how easy does life need to become? Advertisers had to create the desire for things by appealing to the baser instincts of greed and envy. You might not need a four-wheel-drive gas-guzzler or a massive TV, but you'll surely want such luxuries, especially as the neighbors are bound to buy them. And don't worry if you can't afford it right now, because it's never been easier to borrow money.

But, long before the crash of 2008, it was becoming obvious, at least to those who thought about such things, that an economic system based on greed and envy was not only shallow and ethically bankrupt, it was also unsustainable. Even if consumers could be persuaded to keep buying stuff they didn't need, the waste of natural resources and the environmental destruction couldn't go on forever, not without serious consequences for the planet and for all life on it.

The advanced economies of the West were becoming increasingly dependent on a combination of unsustainable trends: competition and technology-led productivity driving prices ever lower in the global marketplace; banks awash with oil wealth and new money created out of nothing (money that needed to be lent out so the banks could make more profit); rising house prices that gave consumers a feeling of wealth and confidence as well as a source of equity against which they could borrow more, even though most people's incomes had in fact stopped rising and had even begun to fall.

This was turning out to be the biggest failing of the free-market capitalist system: the benefits of the productivity gains in industry went only to the wealthy owners and executives of the large corporations. Combined with global competition, all this increasing productivity means fewer and fewer jobs in Western industry, and is bound to lead to fewer jobs everywhere, because this particular race never ends.

Another related outcome of productivity gains, and of the capitalist system in general, is a trend towards productive capacity in excess of real consumer demand, as the income of the majority falls due to lower wages and rising unemployment. The system destroys itself, because its only mission is to profit from producing as much stuff as possible as cheaply as possible. There are no higher goals and no plan, just an unquestioning belief in competition and the free market.

The consumer demand on which the system is so reliant, and which in recent years was fuelled by debt, must inevitably fall, as people adjust to the reality of being poorer. And because so much consumer spending went on things people didn't really need, there is large potential for cutting back when times get tougher, as Figure 91 shows with regard to US output this century.

But industry is slow to respond to this fall in demand because capacity is not an easy thing to adjust. Workers might be laid off but the capital is still there – the factories and the warehouses and shops and so on – and there it stays as long as the owners have faith that demand will return. Investment will fall, certainly, but what if demand remains below the recent trend because consumers have less money to spend? In the longer

Figure 91

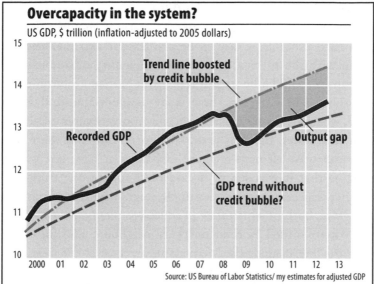

Overcapacity in the system?

US GDP, $ trillion (inflation-adjusted to 2005 dollars)

Trend line boosted by credit bubble

Recorded GDP

Output gap

GDP trend without credit bubble?

Source: US Bureau of Labor Statistics/ my estimates for adjusted GDP

term, supply will fall to match the reality of lower demand and, when it does, prices will rise to a more realistic level. So in one sense Figure 91 is showing us why price inflation hasn't taken off yet, despite the devaluation of money.

All these trends are linked to the rise of the financial sector relative to real industry:

+ The surplus of easy money looking for returns, which not only leads to more borrowing and speculation but also inflates stock markets and property prices, making housing more expensive;

+ The concentration of production in the hands of transnational corporations that use globalization as a way of avoiding national regulation;

+ The declining industrial workforce that results from the focus on productivity rather than employment;

+ The rise in inequality that is the inevitable result of falling wages and fewer real jobs, with the corporate élite reaping the rewards and investing their wealth in the offshore financial system instead of in job creation.

From running track to battlefield

Where did this idea come from, that nations should compete with each other in a race to be the leanest and meanest? It fits in with the survival-of-the-fittest mentality of free-market capitalism. Could it be a natural phase of human evolution?

I showed in Part One how trade developed around 3000 BCE, when the people of the first civilizations began interacting with each other. It seems reasonable to assume that there was no competitive element to these exchanges at first; one would imagine that it was simply a case of swapping one thing for another. The Sumerians, for example, might have traded pottery and grain, both of which they produced in plenty, for the silver and copper mined by their northern neighbors, and for cedar from the forests along the Mediterranean coast to the west.

As long as everyone seemed to benefit and times were good, we might assume that this trade went on amicably. But at some point there came the inevitable downturn in the economy. Archeological records from the region suggest that, during a period of drought and crop failure, armies of the allied kings of the Sumerian and Akkadian empires invaded the civilizations to the north and west and took control of the mines and the cedar forests. And ever since this time, to cut a long story short, there have been wars fought over precious resources. Most wars in fact, in the last 5,000 years or so at least, have been linked to land and resources in one way or another.

The combination of technology and competition brought great wealth to many people in the last century, at least in the more developed parts of the world – to the winners, as it were. It also brought terrible destruction and the worst atrocities ever committed in the history of so-called civilization, followed by a period in which the possibility of nuclear annihilation seemed high.

Perhaps it is time to rethink this idea that success is all about winning the race for profit.

15 The case for public enterprise
Socialism is not a dirty word

So what happens when we've become so productive that there's no longer enough work to go round? I've already suggested that the service sector has passed the limit where the industrial base can support it. Now that the consumer credit boom is over, there'll be no more jobs created in the non-productive sectors of the economy as long as industry keeps cutting employment relative to output. The only solution is to create more jobs in the primary and secondary sectors of the economy, and, if private enterprise isn't going to do this, then the government must take over. There is no other option.

Once we take out the free-market element of competition, we can focus on the real long-term values – jobs and sustainability – rather than short-term shareholder profit. If everyone has work, then it matters less if the prices of goods rise to levels that reflect their true value. We must accept that the 'easy' times have gone forever, that the dream of ever greater prosperity and ever more leisure time was just that: a dream. In the real world, we need to work, because work is the source of all value.

The fact that the easy times turned out to be an illusion, however, doesn't necessarily mean that the majority have to be worse off. If the natural wealth of the earth can be spread more evenly, preferably through employment, most people will at least earn enough to live in reasonable comfort. In a more equal world, although food and fuel prices will rise – a reflection of the fact that costs have been driven down over the past century by the market's distortion of values – housing should become more affordable because it will be valued for what it is, not as a way of making more money.

In a more equal society, success will not be measured by the size of one's house or car but by the quality of the environment, both literally and in a social sense. But how do we bring about this more equal society?

Why we should look again at socialism

The West derided the communist states of the East for their inefficiency, and there were undoubtedly some very serious failings with the system of the USSR, for example. There was a combination of over-centralization, excessive bureaucracy, corruption and poor management; a failure to acknowledge the importance of incentives, of rewarding hard work; and the whole thing was too cumbersome to be run properly. Despite my criticism of the current free-market system, there is no better way of fixing prices than letting the market decide. The important thing is to ensure that market prices aren't distorted by excessive speculation. And we need sound money that has a value linked to genuine wealth creation.

So we can definitely rule out a return to Soviet-style communism. That doesn't mean all socialist ideas are without merit, however, as I've tried to show with regard to Marx's theories. Perhaps the current Chinese system offers more useful pointers as to what works and what doesn't. Although China is officially one of the few remaining communist nations and has an authoritarian system of government (it is highly centralized and undemocratic), in recent years it has become more open to the idea of democracy, at least at a local level. Following the death of Chairman Mao in 1976, the new leadership gradually embraced certain aspects of capitalism, such as the privatization of agriculture and small-scale business enterprises. But they retained state control of most large-scale industry, while at the same time adopting Western-style management ideas to improve efficiency.

Figure 92 shows the rise of manufacturing employment in China, and the corresponding decline in farm work as the nation adopts a more efficient agricultural system. We see also that the service sector begins to expand as the economy develops.

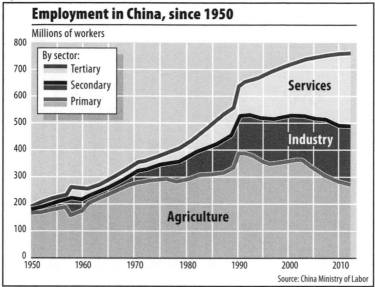

Figure 92

Employment in China, since 1950

Millions of workers

By sector:
- Tertiary
- Secondary
- Primary

Services

Industry

Agriculture

Source: China Ministry of Labor

These reforms resulted in sustained economic growth from the early 1980s onwards, partly supported by foreign investment in the new Special Economic Zones that the government set up along the coast, and which became a magnet for young job-seekers from the poor agricultural communities further inland. Millions migrated from the rural heartlands to the coastal zones, where they worked 12-hour shifts and slept in cramped accommodation provided by the new factories.

The government embarked on a massive program of improvements to infrastructure, building new ports, highways, railways, and also office and apartment complexes. It also created new cities out of small towns and even villages, the first and biggest of which is Shenzhen, just across the border from Hong Kong.

As a consequence of this policy of industrialization, China underwent a period of concentrated wealth creation on a scale never seen before anywhere in the world – and never likely to be seen again either – in which tens of millions of workers added value to vast quantities of the earth's natural resources, much

Figure 93

From village to megacity – the growth of Shenzhen

Source: Shenzhen Statistical Bureau

of which were imported from Africa and Australia. This was real wealth creation of the kind that began in Britain with the Industrial Revolution, and which subsequently made the US the world's richest nation. The main difference here was the speed: what the West achieved in more than a century of growth, China packed into two decades of frenzied activity.

Such rapid growth is only possible from a very low base and is already slowing down, thanks in part to the global reach of the financial crisis. As the developed world becomes poorer, China will rely less on exports and more on its own expanding middle class to sustain economic growth. In 2009, for example, as domestic sales began to take off, China overtook the US to become the world's biggest car manufacturer.

This transformation of the world's most populous nation, from poor agricultural society to middle-income industrial superpower, has been a terrific success from an economic point of view. From an ecological viewpoint, however, it's a very different story; one that I'll return to in the final part of the book.

As far as the Chinese people are concerned, although the

Figure 94

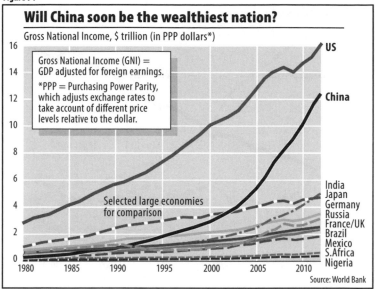

Will China soon be the wealthiest nation?

Gross National Income, $ trillion (in PPP dollars*)

Gross National Income (GNI) = GDP adjusted for foreign earnings.

*PPP = Purchasing Power Parity, which adjusts exchange rates to take account of different price levels relative to the dollar.

US

China

Selected large economies for comparison

India
Japan
Germany
Russia
France/UK
Brazil
Mexico
S.Africa
Nigeria

Source: World Bank

government is undemocratic and has often bulldozed its policies through with little regard to local opposition, it appears to be broadly popular because it has been successful in making the majority more prosperous, and it did this, initially at least, without letting inequality get out of hand, as recently happened in Russia. China today has something in common with the US of the 1950s and 1960s, in that the economy has grown from a relatively low base through genuine wealth-creating industry, spreading wealth through job creation. The actual base was much lower, of course, as were people's expectations, so perhaps it isn't surprising that the government is generally popular.

Figure 94 shows how China is on target to overtake the US as the world's biggest economy in terms of overall output. Figure 95, meanwhile, shows GDP per person, and obviously China has a long way to go before it gets anywhere near US levels of average individual wealth, because although the GDP figure for the nation as a whole is set to pass that of the US in the next decade or two, that wealth is distributed among four times as many people. The chart also shows the percentage of

Figure 95

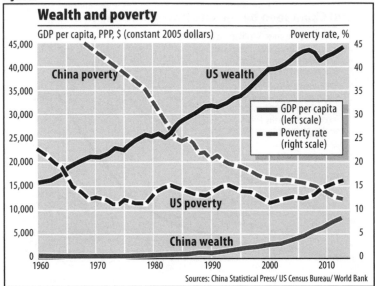

Wealth and poverty

GDP per capita, PPP, $ (constant 2005 dollars) — Poverty rate, %

Sources: China Statistical Press/ US Census Bureau/ World Bank

the population that is officially below the poverty level in each country, and on this measure China is apparently doing better than the US, where poverty is on the increase, though obviously the two countries measure poverty differently.

It is highly unlikely that China or any other developing nation will come close to the levels of individual wealth seen in the richest nations and, for the sake of the planet as a whole, it is far better that they don't. The gap will close, for sure, but this convergence must come as much from the rich world becoming poorer as from the poor world getting wealthier, at least when measured in GDP terms. I will return to this theme later, but first, a brief philosophical interlude.

Can freedom ever be free?

While we should be wary of reading too much into China's recent success, there ought to be some lessons we can learn regarding the mix of state control at the higher levels and free-market incentives at the lower levels – on the ground, where people go about the business of survival. There is, after all, something to be said for government planning, as opposed to having no plan at all, just as long as the government knows what it's doing and the people remain reasonably free.

I say 'reasonably' free because people aren't really free to do anything they want, even in the least regulated societies. You can't, in the US for example, just go into a forest and cut down a few trees, build yourself a cabin on a nice plot of land near a stream, plough the nearest field and put your cows to graze on the adjacent pasture. Perhaps there was a time when you could have done such things, but these days, if you don't 'own' the land, and quite likely even if you do own the land, you'll have broken some law or other.

Even Enlightenment thinkers such as John Locke, the 'father of classical liberalism', and an important influence on Thomas Jefferson and other US Founding Fathers, acknowledged that to be a citizen of a state inevitably requires that one give up a certain degree of freedom. There's an unwritten 'social contract' between the citizen and the state, whereby the state provides protection to its people on condition that they respect certain laws. Americans might look back fondly to the pioneer days of the Wild West, but not many would choose to live without the protection of the state. Without the state there would be no law, no infrastructure, no real civilization, and therefore no opportunity to earn much wealth in the first place.

The argument these days concerns the degree of state intervention. Most people accept that the state should provide security and a legal system, plus the infrastructure on which the economy depends – roads, water supplies, sewers and so on. Wasn't that why the original city states came into being in the first place? Because people couldn't provide these things on an individual basis, they found it beneficial to gather together in a community, to pool resources and help each other out. They chose not to live in the wilderness, where life was 'nasty, brutish and short', to quote Thomas Hobbes, another founding philosopher of social-contract theory.

So, if the main purpose of the state is security – meaning protection from invading armies, from rogues, criminals, psychopaths and anyone else who has a mind to go around raping and pillaging – it follows that the state is expected to protect the more vulnerable members of society against the unruly, meaning the less charitably inclined of the strong. Civilization therefore progresses beyond the survival-of-the-fittest mentality that has previously guided our evolutionary development, and which still appears to be the guiding rule for free-market capitalism. Perhaps the time has come for our economic system to catch up with this Enlightenment thinking.

I'll examine these ideas more closely in the final part of the book, but first there's another aspect of the competitive element of capitalism that I want to touch on briefly.

Secretive banks and stolen wealth

It is not just in industry that competition brings questionable rewards. One of the main reasons why so many governments are borrowing so much and failing to balance the books is that competition between nations to attract global business has resulted in a lowering of tax rates in much of the world. And this competition is not just between nations, but also within nations, as regions with strong autonomy – US states for example – compete with each other to attract investment.

One reason Switzerland became such an important banking center was that competition between the self-governing cantons to attract wealth from abroad led to very low tax rates. Isolated in their Alpine valleys, the Swiss made the most of their neutrality over the centuries, always willing to shelter the wealthy during wars between European powers. The bankers of Geneva and Zurich soon realized that discretion was good for business. As income taxes became more widespread in the early 20th century, especially after the First World War, wealthy individuals from France and Germany and other nations knew that the Swiss banks could be trusted to protect their money from prying governments back home. During the Second World War, the Nazis stashed more and more of their wealth, much of it stolen from Jewish citizens, in Swiss banks, and there has been much controversy ever since regarding the Swiss reluctance to allow investigation of bank accounts, even when the wealth stashed away is most likely the result of criminal activity.

But it wasn't just the Swiss that feared investigation. After the Second World War, British officials fought US attempts to probe further into Swiss banks for Nazi loot, fearing revelations about their own secret stashes of wealth. Switzerland had become a tax haven for all wealthy Europeans. Swiss central bank estimates suggest that over $2 trillion of non-Swiss money is invested in the country, safely hidden from the depositors' tax inspectors. Switzerland has done very well out of other people's money, but other nations have lost out in reduced tax revenues, in wealth that should have been spread among their own population.

Investment and taxation have become additional elements in the competitive market, as banks and nations vie to attract global wealth, whether it be from industry past or present. Yet this competition is even more damaging than the race for productivity; it increases inequality without creating a penny of real wealth.

Figure 96 shows how tax revenues in the rich world have tended to decline slightly this century, while government spending has of course been rising, leading to the current sovereign-debt crisis. The chart also shows one reason why the US is such an unequal society compared to Europe.

The wrong kind of trade

John Maynard Keynes, probably the most influential (and many would say the most brilliant) economist of the 20th century, who was far from being a radical socialist, said in 1944: 'The decadent international but individualistic capitalism, in the hands of which we find ourselves... is not a success. It is not

Figure 96

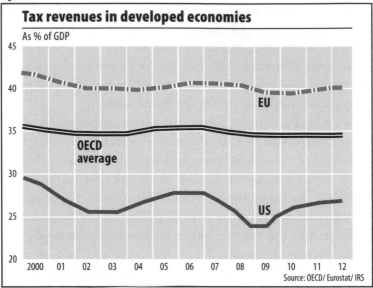

intelligent, it is not beautiful, it is not just, it is not virtuous, and it doesn't deliver the goods.'

Keynes helped to improve things at the time, with his involvement in the Bretton Woods system of monetary controls, but following the end of that system his comment has become more pertinent than ever. He was greatly influenced by another famous English economist, Alfred Marshall, whose ethical approach to the subject led him to focus on the elimination of poverty and the reduction of inequality.

Keynes had some success in working towards this goal, for he was able to exert considerable influence on the post-War rulers of Britain and the US, and even on some European governments. It is only since Keynes' views lost favor in the 1970s and 1980s, with the corresponding rise of the free-market economist Milton Friedman's 'monetarist' theory – the minimal-intervention approach adopted by Ronald Reagan and Margaret Thatcher – that these gains in social equality have been reversed.

Keynes also made the point that free trade in goods is generally beneficial, but financial trade is different. Industrial capitalists become subservient to financial capitalists, as do governments.

Financial speculation limits the ability of governments to boost national economies, because if interest rates are reduced, capital will flow abroad in search of greater returns. There is a basic conflict between producers, for whom high interest rates are a burden, and investors, for whom they are a bonus. As bankers gain ever greater influence over the global economy, non-productive financial investment takes precedence over production. Unproductive speculators reap the rewards, while the real workers lose out.

Although Keynes' point about interest rates might seem less applicable when rates are effectively down to zero anyway, there is always a tricky balancing act between controlling inflation, encouraging investment and maintaining a favorable exchange rate. Excessive flows of investment between nations – 'hot money' in search of the highest returns – can be very damaging to emerging economies in particular, and is closely linked with debt creation and asset bubbles, as happened to the Far East in the 1990s, when high interest rates and a promising economic outlook attracted half the world's foreign investment at the time.

The economies of South Korea, Thailand, Malaysia and Indonesia experienced rapid growth that led to unsustainable asset bubbles – similar to Japan's experience the previous decade. When these burst, in 1997, the 'Asian economic miracle' turned into a debt crisis. International investors, having made a quick profit, withdrew their money, while at the same time speculators gambled on certain currencies falling. In a bid to prevent these currencies from collapsing, which would lead to excessive inflation and further capital flight, the affected governments raised interest rates to high levels, which in turn worsened the crisis.

China avoided the problem because it had looked to the long term, directing inward investment into real industry rather than financial assets. Investors couldn't withdraw their money even if they wanted to, as it had gone into the construction of factories.

Not being constrained by having to satisfy the markets, China kept its currency pegged to the dollar and was largely unaffected by the crisis that crippled the rest of the region.

Bad investment

Non-financial business investment is generally productive but, as we saw in Figures 26 and 27 (in Chapter 5), over 75% of lending these days goes either to households or governments, or remains within the financial sector, where the only purpose it serves is to enrich the bankers themselves while sucking wealth from the real economy. Because banking can't create wealth, all its profit must come from somewhere else: from real industry, pension funds and other investors, house-buyers, credit-card holders, student loans and so on.

I came across the following chart (Figure 97) while researching this book. It comes from a 2009 report entitled *Credit and Crisis in Historical Perspective*, by Professor Dirk Bezemer, of Groningen University in the Netherlands.

Using data from the US Federal Reserve flow-of-funds accounting ledger, the chart shows how bank credit to the real economy corresponds to real growth, while credit to the financial sector corresponds to the build-up of debt. During the quarter-century credit boom that preceded the financial crisis, banks profited more and more from financial speculation and unproductive debt creation instead of real investment in the economy. In other words, the growth of the financial sector became increasingly detrimental to the US economy, and much the same thing was happening throughout the developed world.

As I said earlier, this is the consequence of banks profiting from the build-up of accumulated wealth relative to actual production. And as Professor Bezemer notes: '…bank credit creation bears no link to real economic growth patterns at all during the era of financial liberalization.'

Although it isn't showing exactly the same thing (because this is growth in credit relative to GDP), this chart's data reinforces

Figure 97

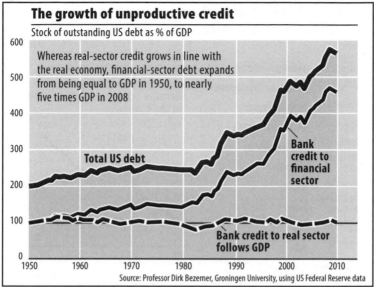

The growth of unproductive credit

Stock of outstanding US debt as % of GDP

Whereas real-sector credit grows in line with the real economy, financial-sector debt expands from being equal to GDP in 1950, to nearly five times GDP in 2008

Total US debt

Bank credit to financial sector

Bank credit to real sector follows GDP

Source: Professor Dirk Bezemer, Groningen University, using US Federal Reserve data

the conclusions I drew from Figure 1 at the start of the book, that the growth of the credit bubble led to GDP growth in excess of the real wealth creation taking place in the underlying economy.

We see the results of this disconnection of banks from the real economy in disasters such as the 1997 Asian crisis and the recent sub-prime fiasco. Claims that this financial speculation is somehow adding to the 'efficiency' of the markets (because it supposedly allocates capital more effectively) are obviously nonsense. What can possibly be efficient about sucking real wealth from the economy, destroying jobs and reducing real wages, while at the same time hiding wealth offshore and shifting the tax burden from the rich to the struggling middle classes?

Offshore money

In Figure 25 I showed the growth in offshore bank accounts, which according to Tax Justice Network now shelter between $20 trillion and $30 trillion, roughly 10% of all the world's wealth.

Figure 98

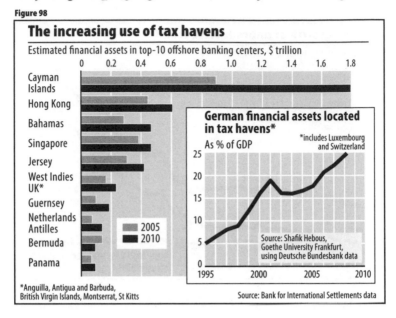

The increasing use of tax havens

Estimated financial assets in top-10 offshore banking centers, $ trillion

German financial assets located in tax havens*

As % of GDP

*includes Luxembourg and Switzerland

Source: Shafik Hebous, Goethe University Frankfurt, using Deutsche Bundesbank data

*Anguilla, Antigua and Barbuda, British Virgin Islands, Montserrat, St Kitts

Source: Bank for International Settlements data

The majority of large corporations, especially transnationals, make use of offshore jurisdictions to avoid paying certain taxes. An investigation by the British charity ActionAid in 2011 discovered that 98 of Britain's 100 biggest companies (the FTSE 100) had subsidiaries based in tax havens, including most of the big UK banks, which between them had over 1,600 companies registered in places like Jersey and the Cayman Islands. A 2009 report by the US Governmental Accountability Office, meanwhile, found that 83 of the 100 biggest US corporations had subsidiaries in tax havens. Although these offshore jurisdictions offer legitimate financial services, the main purpose of using them is to avoid the regulations and taxes applicable in the countries in which most of the business actually takes place.

The secretive nature of tax havens means there isn't much reliable data available regarding the scale of tax avoidance involved, but I came across a few independent sources that back up the figures provided by Tax Justice Network. Figure 98 shows the recent growth in assets located in the 10 most widely used offshore banking centers, while the inset graph shows the share of German financial assets located in tax havens, including countries such as Switzerland and Luxembourg, which are classed as tax havens under the broader definition of the term.

Christian Aid, using data obtained by the US Center for International Policy, estimates that around half of world trade, in accounting terms at least, goes through tax havens, and that the developing world is deprived of around $160 billion per year in corporate taxes because big corporations make use of unregulated tax havens instead of paying tax where they do the real trade.

Developing countries also lose out when negotiating deals with large global corporations, especially with regard to mineral extraction, which ought to be a major source of real wealth for many poorer nations, most of which are in resource-rich Africa. According to the IMF, most royalty rates on mineral resources paid by mining companies to the nation concerned – the effective 'owner' of the minerals – were in the region of 5% to 10% of the market value. Some were even lower. In addition, the companies often overstate their losses so as to minimize profits and therefore reduce the taxes paid.

Corporate tax evasion is just one part of the process, linked to globalization as well as to the accumulation of wealth in the financial sector, by which more and more of the world's wealth ends up with the very rich.

Wealth and work

There is in this world enough real wealth to go round, if only it can be distributed more evenly. This will require employment opportunities for everyone, so that people can earn their fair share of the world's natural wealth through work. It is only through work that we are able to connect with the earth, even if we no longer get our hands dirty; work represents our natural inclination to support ourselves and our families, and however mundane that work might be, it is the essential source of satisfaction and value in our lives.

It follows from this that no one person can really 'earn' a great deal more than another person – by this I mean hundreds or thousands of times more. We can all accept that some people work harder than others, might have better ideas than others, and should be rewarded accordingly. But when someone makes millions through financial speculation, for example, or even by being a competent business manager, there is no way they've 'earned' that money through genuine work. There is only so much real work one person can do in any given time.

In other words, there is a perfectly sound reason why the wealthy should pay higher taxes: their wealth came from the earth, but not because they dug it out themselves through sweat and toil. They have no particular right to it, as they might have if they had really worked for it. Even when a person has brilliant ideas and genuinely works hard, if he or she makes millions while others just as deserving make perhaps only thousands, then they are to a large extent simply lucky. Good fortune often plays a major part in any successful enterprise.

My point here is that it is ethically wrong for any one person to claim a disproportionate share of the world's natural wealth, which is what money ultimately represents. It therefore follows not only that the wealthy should expect to pay higher taxes, but also that successful corporations have a moral duty to create employment and generally to help spread wealth around, as industry did in the days before the financial sector took control and began creating credit instead of jobs.

In the final part of this book I will explore how our economic system might be improved in order to create a more equal society, one that also takes account of the environment and the depletion of the earth's resources. But first I think it is worth giving a brief résumé of the points made so far.

16 Ten reasons why the rich world is getting poorer

Summary, parts 1&2

To sum up the first two parts of this book, I have condensed my observations into 10 related reasons why the developed world must accept that the age of growth is over, each with a simplified graph (based on a previous chart, as indicated). In Part Three, I will look at some possible solutions to these challenges.

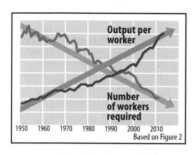

1 Excessive efficiency

The relentless drive for increasing productivity, accelerated by new technology and global competition, is now resulting in fewer jobs, not just in manufacturing, as in the past, but also in the service sector, which employs the majority of the workforce in developed countries.

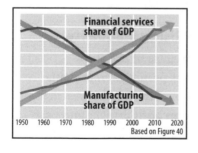

2 Making money instead of real stuff

The rise of the financial sector relative to real industry, a consequence of the accumulation of past industrial wealth, means less real wealth creation and more debt creation, as banks try to profit from this accumulated wealth.

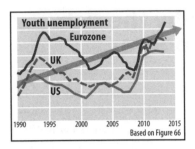

3 The vicious cycle of unemployment

Real jobs are disappearing, average incomes are falling, consumers are spending less, more jobs are lost, tax receipts fall, benefits are cut… In the past the cycle has ended with the revival of economic growth, but that was in the past. The future will be different.

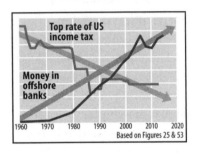

4 Globalization of wealth

The biggest problem with globalization is not the transfer of jobs from rich nations to poor, which on a global scale can be seen as a good thing, but the rising power of transnational corporations and the reduced influence of national governments, and therefore of democracy.

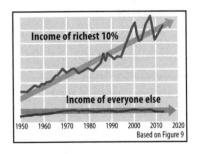

5 Rising inequality

Because of the above four points, an increasing proportion of the wealth from both present and past production is going to the very rich – the owners and financiers of big business – leaving less for everyone else. Fewer jobs in industry mean less of the earth's wealth is spread around and less value is added to the economy.

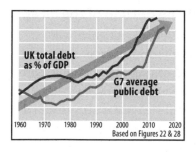

6 Debt repayment

Since the link between money and gold was broken, capitalism has become addicted to credit creation, which is dependent on economic growth. But, as real industry declines relative to financial services, the debt problem kills real growth. The system is bankrupt.

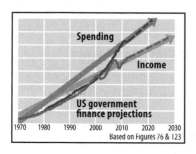

7 Budget imbalances

Not only are governments saddled with huge debt repayments, they are also committed to ever greater payouts for pensions and welfare obligations. But tax revenues are falling. The figures don't add up and, the way things are going, they never will.

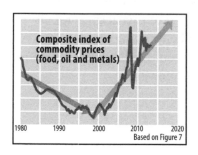

8 Rising prices

The trend towards cheaper goods is over. Everything from food to fuel will become more expensive as the supply situation adjusts to the fall in demand, which during the last boom had been boosted by debt-fuelled spending. Commodities have become undervalued; inflation is bound to catch up with all that money creation eventually.

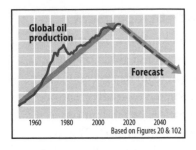

9 The decline of the oil age

Energy in particular will become more expensive, as oil and gas supplies become more difficult to extract. Reduced fossil-fuel use is also essential for environmental reasons, but because petroleum has been the biggest source of industrial wealth for more than half a century – accounting for over half of all wealth ever produced – its decline is bound to have far-reaching consequences for the global economy.

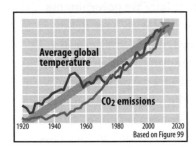

10 Climate change

Cutting down on carbon emissions, although essential, is bound to be bad for the economy. This is an unfortunate fact of life. So far in this book I have concentrated on the interconnected reasons why we face economic decline. Now it is time to acknowledge another aspect of this decline: for all the hardship and challenges that a contracting economy must inevitably bring, the end of growth could well be the only thing that will save humanity from destroying itself.

Part Three

Why We Should Be Glad

17 Economy or ecology?

More jobs, less fossil-fuel use

I have tried to give a convincing explanation, in the first two parts of this book, as to why the wealthier regions of the world, Europe and the US in particular, have reached a critical point in their economic development, and why the free-market capitalist system, which brought us half a century of genuine prosperity, is no longer working for most people.

I have also suggested that the self-destructive nature of free-market capitalism provides our best hope for the long-term survival of civilization because, even though it is quite obvious that an economic system that depends on continuous growth and debt creation is unsustainable, there will never be enough pressure to change the system as long as the majority are improving their lot and the leaders of the world feel safe in their positions of power. In other words, it is only in times of crisis that real change can be brought about.

Figure 99

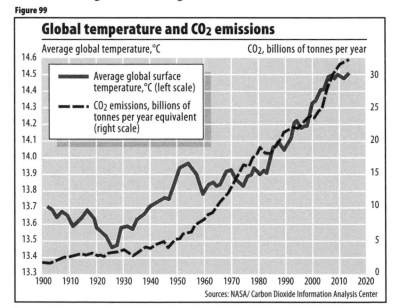

Sources: NASA/ Carbon Dioxide Information Analysis Center

But what kind of changes are we talking about? What should we do? I began this investigation because I thought I might have identified a way of illustrating the fundamental problems affecting the economies of the developed world, but I must make it clear at this point that I don't pretend to know the answers to those problems. I'm not even sure if there are any answers; not obvious answers, anyway. The arguments concerning the best political and economic systems have been discussed since the time of Plato and Aristotle, and we still can't agree on much. So the following ideas are just that: ideas to be considered as a basis for further discussion.

Degrees of devastation

Global warming; the environmental impacts of climate change; the degree to which human beings are responsible and what we should do about it: these are all major issues that occupy the minds of writers and academics far more qualified than me. So I will limit my own observations to the following point: the world is warming up, and scientific evidence suggests, beyond all reasonable doubt, that this warming is caused by increased concentrations of greenhouse gases, especially carbon dioxide (CO_2), in the atmosphere as a result of our burning fossil fuels.

There is general agreement amongst environmental scientists that we must cut CO_2 emissions drastically over the next few decades, or face serious consequences. A rise in temperature of 2°C above the 20th-century average is already unavoidable, according to the experts, bringing more extreme weather conditions and a 30-centimeter rise in sea levels due to thermal expansion. A further increase of 2-3°C by 2050, which is quite likely if we don't cut emissions very soon, could be catastrophic.

A rise of 2°C might not seem very much, but because of the uneven distribution of such an average, heating the poles more than the equator, it is enough to cause a significant proportion of the ice sheets that cover Greenland and Antarctica to melt over the next decades, raising sea levels by a meter or more by the end of this century, according to various estimates, as shown in

Figure 100

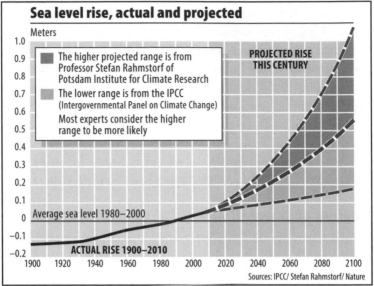

Figure 100.

The President of the World Bank, Jim Yong Kim, makes the following statement in the introduction to a scientific report on climate change: 'A 4°C warmer world can, and must be, avoided. We need to hold warming below 2°C.' He hopes that the report, commissioned in 2012 and titled *Turn Down the Heat*, and which concludes that a 4°C warmer world is not only likely but also that it would be 'devastating', will shock us into action. This is strong stuff, coming from an organization normally associated more with free-market principles such as economic growth and deregulation, rather than environmental protection.

So, according to even the most cautious scientific forecasts (meaning the least pessimistic), we are already on target for serious inundation of coastal areas very soon. To get an idea of what a rise of 4 or 5°C represents, it is worth noting that the last ice age was only 6°C cooler than the current average.

According to the Intergovernmental Panel on Climate Change (IPCC), we can expect more severe storms and droughts, inundation of low-lying coastal areas and greater coastal erosion.

We can also expect greater stresses on water resources as salt water migrates into freshwater aquifers, and as the mountain glaciers that supply rivers shrink – these supply one-sixth of the world's population with fresh water. And then there will be other problems related to more extreme weather, such as the reduction in farmland caused by the spread of deserts.

Yet, as we see in Figure 101, global efforts to curb the use of fossil fuels have so far been ineffective. Despite all the apparent concern from most (though not all) world leaders over the last decade, and the 'cap and trade' system of carbon credits (which brings market forces into play), emissions have continued to rise, and the rate of this rise is still increasing, as over two billion people in China and India, and also other developing nations, become wealthier.

We hear these reports and shrug our shoulders; we have more immediate concerns on our minds and, really, what can we do about it? Isn't it something for governments to sort out? There's a kind of mass denial going on, a general failure to accept the situation or even to give it any thought. But we need to start

Figure 101

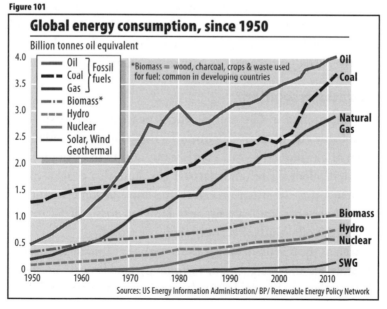

reducing carbon emissions right now, and that means cutting down on the use of fossil fuels for energy. The longer we leave it, the greater the reduction required, and the more difficult it therefore becomes.

One reason for this failure seriously to address the problem of climate change is the lack of a global body with any real powers. While this would require democracy to operate at a global level, with total transparency, it is an essential step in bringing about the necessary changes. For example, the United Nations has been trying to get agreement on environmental issues since the 'Rio Declaration' of 1992, when all 175 UN member states signed up to 27 worthy principles and goals aimed at improving sustainability. The conference was considered a great success at the time, but in the two decades since then very little has been achieved. The 1997 UN climate-change convention in Kyoto, in which targets were introduced for cutting emissions, was equally ineffective. Countries can simply decide not to implement the changes, as the US did at the time.

The UN has since declared the years 2005 to 2014 as the decade for 'Education for Sustainable Development'. Is anyone aware of this? Does it make any difference? The UN is a useful start as a global authority, but it needs more power to be more effective. I shall return to this contentious issue later.

No fracking solution?

As I mentioned in Chapter 8, our dependence on fossil fuels is probably the greatest dilemma facing civilization today. So much of our industry – and with it our ability to create wealth – is dependent on oil and natural gas, and also coal in many countries, that the situation can seem almost beyond resolution. Our whole economic system was built on fossil fuels, to the extent that oil wealth effectively rules the world.

Even as the debate heats up along with the climate, the search for more oil and gas goes on, technology enables new methods of extraction, such as hydraulic fracturing, or 'fracking', while at the same time, governments and energy corporations investigate ways of using more coal – the most abundant fossil fuel not just in China and the US but in the whole world – by supposedly making it cleaner to burn.

At the time of writing, the British government has just given the go-ahead for fracking in the shale rocks of Lancashire, amid claims that such technology can solve the UK's energy needs on the one hand and, on the other side, portents of disaster from the green lobby.

As usual with these things, the truth is likely to lie somewhere between these two extremes. Yes, there will probably be some economic benefit to Britain, though nothing like the scale of the North Sea oil boom (the revenues from which, incidentally, were frittered away on a combination of bubble-feeding tax cuts and higher public spending, unlike in Norway, where a sovereign wealth fund invests the oil money for future generations). And, yes, there is bound to be an environmental price to pay.

Britain's fracking debate reflects the much wider global issue. On the one hand, there is the quest for continued growth and development. On the other there is a recognition of the need for legislation to cut the use of fossil fuels – legislation that would obviously include a ban on fracking.

It's hard to see how the green lobby can win right now, with governments focusing, as always, on the short-term gains of economic growth, even as they try to sell us their own 'green' credentials. Looked at purely rationally, the answer seems obvious: we can't afford to put economic growth before the survival of the human race. Yet it's so easy to tell ourselves that the doomsayers are exaggerating or have plain got it wrong, that global warming is just a natural temperature variation and the world will carry on fine as it is, if we just recycle a bit more and drive a bit less.

But can we really afford to ignore the evidence? This might well be the greatest challenge that humankind has ever faced. Certainly it is the greatest challenge that civilization has faced while having so much knowledge of the facts, and the ability to do something about it. It's a great dilemma, as I said, but both the rational and the moral arguments point the same way, so in a sense the answer to the dilemma is clear: we must work towards a reduction in the use of fossil fuels, with as much urgency as possible.

At the same time, we must address a separate moral issue – separate in one sense, but deeply interwoven in another sense – that of spreading the earth's wealth more evenly by creating more jobs and reducing inequality.

Looked at independently, these two issues seem difficult enough to resolve. Looked at together, as they must be, they appear almost impossible to resolve, because to create more jobs and spread more wealth would normally, by traditional economic thinking, require more industrial activity to promote economic growth, and this would require the extraction and burning of more fossil fuels.

The problems are not insurmountable, however, though the solution will undoubtedly require a radical shake-up of our economic system. I have already shown that our current system of free-market capitalism is responsible for increasing inequality, both globally and within nations. It is also clear that the same system is adding to the problem of global warming, for the same reason – free-market capitalism depends on the profit motive and continuous growth, and cannot take account of long-term needs that aren't directly related to that profit and growth. An unregulated market system has no way of accounting for long-term sustainability or any other ethical issues, which is why modern civilization, having been effectively hijacked by the world's financiers and powerful transnational corporations, is currently in the process of destroying itself.

So we are left with one massive challenge: how do we transform our economic system into one that will ensure the well-being of as many people as possible, while at the same time cutting down on the use of fossil fuels?

I address these two related issues briefly in the next two chapters. I say 'briefly', because to address such important issues fully would require a book for each one. But this investigation would not be complete if I did not at least suggest where we might start looking for the answers to the above problems, and to give some indication of what those solutions might involve.

18 Life without oil

So what are the alternatives to fossil fuels?

I attempted to demonstrate, in Chapter 8, that over half the world's wealth has come from the reservoirs of oil and natural gas that lie beneath the earth's surface. My reason for making this claim is simple enough: all the world's wealth is derived from natural resources that have been transformed into something useful by industry, and somewhere in the region of 60% of those resources, in terms of the value added to the economy, started out as the carbon-and-hydrogen remnants of fossilized ocean life, which over millions of years formed the petroleum deposits that now power our lives.

To imagine a world without oil is almost impossible. Everything would have developed differently, with a lot less industry and transport taking place, and far less wealth being created. But our dependence on oil can't continue for much longer, not just because petroleum deposits are becoming harder to find and more costly to develop, but, more critically, because the scientific consensus suggests that burning fossil fuels is likely to lead, at some point in the near future – perhaps even this century – to an ecological catastrophe, one that might even bring an end to the human race. At the very least it will reduce the habitable area of the earth, as sea levels rise and inundate low-lying coasts, fertile lands are reduced by the spread of deserts, drought and floods become more frequent.

There are many conflicting views and accounts with regard to both our future supplies of oil and gas, and the consequences of continuing to burn them. But one thing we can be fairly sure about: fossil-fuel use is close to a peak right now, with reserves falling and production set to follow. The oil industry is good at making optimistic forecasts concerning potential new sources of oil and gas, such as the shales being exploited in North America and elsewhere, but according to a recent independent study by the German-based Energy Watch Group, global oil production will soon begin a gradual decline, while gas and coal supplies might peak a decade or so later, as shown in Figure 102.

So we are effectively already close to peak energy supplies, at least in terms of fossil fuels, which currently supply 80% of our energy requirements.

Earth, water, wind and fire

So what are the alternatives to fossil fuels? Nuclear energy is uneconomic and produces radioactive waste. Biofuels, meanwhile, barely provide net energy after the required industrial process; they also lead to deforestation or take up valuable farmland, pushing up food prices. This leaves us with the only genuinely 'green' forms of renewable energy: solar, wind, hydro (water power, either from rivers or ocean currents and tides) and geothermal (which uses heat from deep within the earth). These are all much more environmentally sound than fossil fuels or biofuels, leaving aside their impact on the landscape, about which, considering the lack of options, we cannot afford to be too concerned.

But these forms of renewable energy currently supply less than 5% of worldwide needs and, although their use is increasing, thanks to government subsidies in many developed countries, the rate of increase has slowed down due to the poor state of public finances since the 2008 crash. The free-market system is generally uninterested in renewable energy, primarily because capitalists don't see any profit in it. As I said, oil rules the world, even if that reign will soon be coming to an end.

The reality is that, because total energy consumption is still rising, renewables are not growing fast enough to keep pace, and fossil-fuel use is still increasing, as Figure 101 showed. We see in Figure 102 that the consumption of coal, which is the biggest source of carbon release, has increased considerably in recent years and is forecast to decline only slowly, after peaking around 2020. This is mainly because China and India have over a thousand coal-fired power stations between them – roughly half

Figure 102

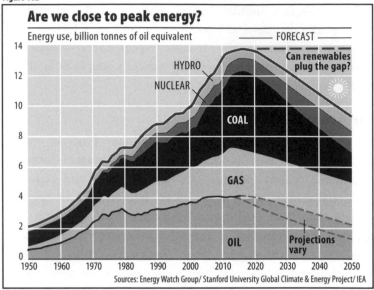

Are we close to peak energy?

Energy use, billion tonnes of oil equivalent ———— FORECAST ————

HYDRO

NUCLEAR

Can renewables plug the gap?

COAL

GAS

OIL

Projections vary

Sources: Energy Watch Group/ Stanford University Global Climate & Energy Project/ IEA

the world total – and are still building new ones, owing to the fact that coal is the cheapest fuel if one ignores the environmental costs, as the market always does.

The situation is not necessarily hopeless, however. There are several technologies that could help to cut fossil-fuel use by a significant amount. The obvious area for further development is renewable energy in the form of solar and wind power, which has only recently reached 1% of total energy production, plus geothermal for some heating applications. Of the other genuinely carbon-free forms of energy: hydroelectric has already been well developed in most regions of the world where there are suitable stretches of river; tidal and ocean-current power generation is limited by a lack of suitable locations and will probably remain small-scale; while nuclear power brings other environmental concerns into play, making it controversial, to say the least, (though it does have its supporters amongst environmental scientists, some of whom see nuclear energy as the only realistic alternative to fossil fuels, at least in the medium term[1]).

The goddess Sól

Those ancient worshippers of the sun weren't stupid: they knew where their bread came from. The sun is the source of nearly all energy on earth, including the wind (which is caused by regional variations in the heating of the atmosphere and the earth's surface), the rivers (dependent on precipitation, which is caused by evaporation) and ocean currents, again driven by the sun's heat. Fossil fuels are a store of past solar energy that was converted into carbon compounds by photosynthesis. The only other source of energy on earth is tidal (from the moon's gravity) and the geothermal heat and nuclear potential from the radioactive decay of certain minerals – the primordial nuclides – that came originally from supernova explosions before the formation of the solar system.

So sun worship makes a lot of sense. We should make the most of its bountiful rays, which provide enough energy in one hour to power the world for a year, if only we could capture it.

I mentioned at the end of Chapter 8 that one reason we can't just cover large tracts of desert in solar panels is that electricity needs to be generated reasonably close to where it is needed, otherwise too much energy is lost as heat through the resistance of the high-voltage transmission cables. But there is a potential technology whereby one can use solar power to generate electricity that can then be used to extract hydrogen from sea water. Hydrogen fuel cells can be used to power electric motors, and as such are one of the most promising technologies for the eventual replacement of the internal-combustion engine, a development that would go a long way towards reducing fossil-fuel use.

One reason fuel cells aren't already in general service is that the extraction of hydrogen from water, which is achieved through the process of electrolysis, uses as much electricity as the energy produced. There are also problems concerning the storage and delivery of hydrogen to points of use, such as filling stations. This latter problem will be overcome only when the first problem is solved and the whole process builds enough momentum to start a promising new industry.

So what is needed is more investment in the process of extracting hydrogen from water, in particular from sea water, because it is only in areas such as deserts that it makes sense to build huge solar power stations, and obviously deserts don't have much water. But there are a fair number of regions in the world where deserts lie alongside the coast, so these ought to be the ideal locations for such ventures.

What you end up with therefore is a process in which solar energy, which is most abundant in areas that don't need it, is converted into a fuel that can be stored and transported, and which can be used in power stations and vehicles thousands of kilometers from the source of the energy – much like oil, only without the environmental costs and the scarcity. It should also be possible to power ships directly from sea water in a similar process.

Such technology might represent our best hope for the future, but it will only happen if the right kind of businesses can be encouraged to invest heavily in such projects, knowing that the profits will be a long way down the line. This probably means state investment.

In the meantime, a lot more needs to be done to encourage people to use less energy. There have been attempts in Europe to bring market forces into play, by granting industrial corporations carbon credits, which they can trade on the open market, so that companies that use less than their allocation are able to profit by selling credits they don't use, and heavy users pay more because they have to buy more credits. The system has proved difficult to implement, however, being complex and only partially enforced.

The easiest way to change people's behavior is through taxation, but this is rarely tried to any significant degree because it is, not surprisingly, unpopular with voters. Nobody wants to pay more for fuel. But realistically, this is what is needed. Increasing the tax on fossil fuels is the most direct way to encourage people, and industry, to use less. We are all going to pay the price eventually anyway, and at least this motivates drivers to buy the most economical cars, and to use them less. Most people would cut out unnecessary journeys, walk or cycle more, use public transport, travel on trains rather than planes, if only the incentives were high enough.

We tend to think of driving or flying as a kind of entitlement these days, but really we don't have any particular right to do anything that harms others. If we can accept that driving a car is a privilege rather than a right, we might make more progress in reducing its impact. We have to accept that such privileges will become more expensive, and change our lives to suit the reality of the situation; the easy times are drawing to a close.

Human rights (and wrongs)

How much of a 'right' do we have to do any particular thing, whether it be driving a car, taking minerals from the earth, or simply doing what it takes to survive in this world?

According to Thomas Paine, in his book *Rights of Man* (published in 1791), human rights originate in nature and are therefore of a higher order than any government-ordained law. In the unwritten social contract that Locke and other Enlightenment philosophers wrote about, governments are brought into being by the people for the purpose of protecting those 'inherent and inalienable' rights.

One can make a perfectly valid argument that nature makes a lousy mother who cares not one bit about her children and is prone to random acts of violence; in other words, life is all a matter of chance and consequently such wishy-washy concepts as human rights don't really exist, that life is about getting what you can, while you can. But we are human, we have feelings, and one of those feelings is respect for life, which does therefore confer a kind of moral duty to consider the welfare of other people.

We have the right to exist; to freedom of belief and speech. We also have a right to liberty and the pursuit of happiness – but

Figure 103

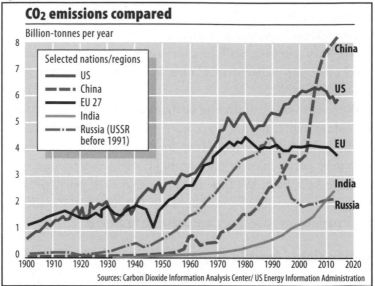

CO_2 emissions compared

Billion-tonnes per year

Selected nations/regions
- US
- China
- EU 27
- India
- Russia (USSR before 1991)

Sources: Carbon Dioxide Information Analysis Center/ US Energy Information Administration

only so far as our pursuit of happiness does not reduce the liberty and happiness of others. And this is where it gets tricky.

As the world becomes ever more crowded and interconnected, more of these so-called 'rights' come into question. More of our actions will impinge on the happiness of others. The whole concept of 'natural rights' becomes more difficult to isolate from the good of society, because society is forever growing, while nature's influence on our lives is shrinking, or at least it seems that way, as more and more of the earth disappears beneath concrete and asphalt. What happens when our right to exist as an individual starts to conflict with the rights of society in general?

The 'entitlement' to drive a car is a case in point. This is something that affects most people in the rich world and an increasing number in developing countries, and I think a lot of people in the West would claim to have a certain right in this regard, once they've paid the relevant taxes at least.

Without doubt, the livelihood of a great many people has become dependent on driving a car, both for work and for general survival, especially in rural areas. Whenever a government considers raising the tax on fuel or road use there's a media outcry: it will hit people hard, especially the poor. But at the same time, this is the most effective way in which governments can try to influence people's behavior in this regard. Using taxation to change the way we live makes sense, but obviously we don't like it, and in a democracy the government must take note of this.

We are back to the same conflict – the same dilemma between growth and prosperity on the one hand, and the environment on the other; between self-interest and society; between short-term profit and long-term survival. It isn't immediately obvious that driving or flying is harming others, but if we are to believe the consensus view of the experts, and we probably ought to, our burning of fossil fuels could eventually lead to the deaths of millions.

Again, it is this vagueness that is the problem here; it *might* happen at some indeterminate point in the future, but there again, it might not. But as I said in the previous chapter, with such strong scientific evidence pointing to the increasing risks of global warming, we have no choice but to work towards a reduction in the use of fossil fuels. The alternative is ethically unjustifiable: to continue living the way we live now is to put at risk the future of humanity, even if we can't quantify that risk. Life might resemble one great lottery in some respects, but this is surely a gamble we can't afford to take.

Should we put our faith in 'Progress'?

The 1950s optimism for the coming nuclear age, an age in which energy would be 'too cheap to meter', as predicted in 1954 by Lewis Strauss, head of the US Atomic Energy Commission, didn't last very long. The technology soon hit unforeseen limits, and his other predictions now seem equally fanciful: '...our children will know of great periodic regional famines in the world only as matters of history, will travel effortlessly over the seas and under them and through the air with a minimum of danger and at great speeds, and will experience a life span far longer than ours...'

The rapid increase in personal mobility that took place over the course of the 20th century can be seen as one of the defining features of the modern world and the machine age, along with electrification, mass production and cheap consumer goods. Following on from the development of the steam engine and the railways, the invention of the motor car heralded the age of speed. For several decades, refinement of engine technology resulted in faster and faster cars and aircraft, cutting journey times and encouraging ever more people to take to the growing network of roads and airports.

This brought about a revolutionary change in attitude, from a slow, local life to a fast, jetsetting one; a life in which, in the words of Le Corbusier, the most influential modern architect of the time, the street became 'a machine for traffic'. Architects embraced this exciting new world and planned new cities around this vision of an automated and mechanical future.

But even by the 1960s, before the dangers of global warming had become apparent, it was clear to some that this new car culture was taking over our lives completely, with fume-belching traffic jams and six-lane highways carving up communities, destroying the fabric of urban society.

And even outside the cities, long before the century was over, this oil-fuelled growth in mass mobility began to splutter. Despite continued advances in technology, travel speeds levelled off in the 1960s; journey times stopped falling and even began to rise again, as road and airport congestion increased. We can see now, after the failure of supersonic airliners and other such boom-era dreams, that there are more important priorities than flying round the world as quickly as possible in ever-greater numbers. In particular, we must try not to destroy the world.

Life in the slow lane

A realistic vision of the future – a new concept of progress, one might say – would surely be nothing like the 20th-century vision. Instead of speed and mobility, it will be necessary to accept a slower pace, to travel less and to live a more local existence; to make the most of a combination of local amenities and digital technology, which should continue to reduce the need for travel.

Such technology still has a long way to go towards reducing carbon emissions; by cutting the need for commuting, rush-hour traffic jams, unnecessary journeys to distant meetings and so on. Combined with a shorter working week, this should also help to reduce stress levels, lifting some of the burden from health services.

Although new technology now results in a lower level of wealth creation overall, for reasons I've already explained regarding the reduction in manufacturing and service jobs, it could be used to make the whole pattern of work more equal and more flexible, spreading what work there is around more fairly.

I made the point earlier that work is a vital part of our lives, and this is why unemployment is so bad for both individuals and for society, even if we can still produce enough wealth with fewer people working. So it follows that, if increasing productivity means there aren't going to be enough jobs to go round, we need to share what work there is more evenly. This will probably mean a reduction in working hours – reducing the average working week to 30 hours, for example.

Although there has been a trend in this direction, at least in Europe, global competition – a feeling that those harder-working nations would pull ahead in the global race for profit – has prevented such policies from gaining much ground.

It's not so much that we should be aiming to work less overall, more that we need to share work and wealth round more evenly, while at the same time reducing the pace of work for many people; getting out of the rat race, as it were, cutting down on consumption and putting more effort into family and community activities. Such a change would form an important component of our re-evaluation of values, and in particular our redefinition of prosperity.

Figure 104

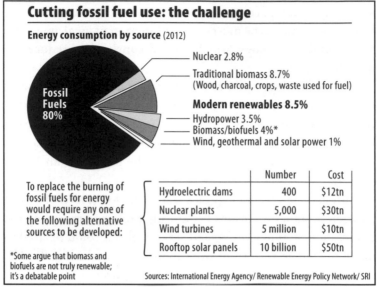

Cutting fossil fuel use: the challenge

Energy consumption by source (2012)

Fossil Fuels 80%

Nuclear 2.8%

Traditional biomass 8.7%
(Wood, charcoal, crops, waste used for fuel)

Modern renewables 8.5%
Hydropower 3.5%
Biomass/biofuels 4%*
Wind, geothermal and solar power 1%

To replace the burning of fossil fuels for energy would require any one of the following alternative sources to be developed:

	Number	Cost
Hydroelectric dams	400	$12tn
Nuclear plants	5,000	$30tn
Wind turbines	5 million	$10tn
Rooftop solar panels	10 billion	$50tn

*Some argue that biomass and biofuels are not truly renewable; it's a debatable point

Sources: International Energy Agency/ Renewable Energy Policy Network/ SRI

Muddling through

Under the current global economic system, dominated as it is by bankers and the corporate élite, it is unrealistic to expect anything more than a gradual reduction in fossil-fuel use, at best. Yet we can't just ignore the problem and hope it goes away, though this, I suspect, is the reaction of many people, if they give it any thought at all. In fact, this is probably the reaction of most of us, because even those of us who *do* give it some thought can feel overwhelmed by the sheer magnitude of the task that faces humanity.

'What will be, will be,' we might be tempted to say. Leave it to the gods, or fate, or whatever. The more optimistic still put their faith in technological solutions: 'Something will come along. We'll muddle through, like we always do.'

But technological progress brings a lot of false promises, as well as some genuine improvements to life. Landing men on the moon, for example, has proved a lot less useful to humanity than did the invention of the bicycle a hundred years earlier. Amid all the promise of modern technology, it is worth bearing in mind that the bicycle is still the most efficient way of getting around, despite the fact that it has barely changed in a century.

So my point here is that we shouldn't invest all our hopes in future technological solutions; we have to start changing the way we live, right now.

Although technology will surely play a part in the switch to renewable energy, it won't cut oil use as long as oil remains the easiest and cheapest option. Not under our present system, anyway. Even the President of the United States has trouble making progress on this most important of all issues – he is stuck in the same system as everyone else, and the system doesn't allow real progress on this matter, just as it doesn't care about jobs or any other social issues. It is clear that a world dominated by corporate capitalism and unregulated markets will never solve the problems now faced by humanity. Only some kind of united global initiative with real authority – a combination of national governments working together, backed by public mandate and funded primarily through state subsidies – will do the job.

Which brings us back to the first essential step in any possible solution: we must change the system. But how do we do that? What are the alternatives to free-market capitalism?

1 For example, the environmental scientist James Lovelock has written extensively on his reasons for supporting nuclear power, as have 'green' writers such as Mark Lynas and George Monbiot, all of whom make the point that nuclear-power plants, especially the latest generation (which can use recycled nuclear waste as fuel) are far less damaging to the earth than are fossil fuels.

19 Time to change the system

Re-evaluation of values; jobs first

We humans have always been good at adapting to whatever circumstances we find ourselves in – hence our domination of the world. Until recently, however, that adaptation has taken the form of trial and error, driven mostly by chance. We find ourselves born into this world, purely by chance, and we set about making the most of it, putting ourselves first, because that's what the survival instinct demands. Every one of the seven billion souls on this earth right now, except perhaps a tiny minority who have given up, is actively engaged (or passively engaged, for those who are sleeping) in trying to survive a bit longer.

This is what life is really about: survival. All the other stuff is secondary. We don't go around *thinking* about survival all the time of course, but that's only because we don't need to. Our instincts take care of that, which is why we think mostly about food and sex and making our lives richer, easier and generally as comfortable as possible.

Over the last million years the fittest survived, and over the last few centuries, humanity as a whole has prospered. In the last few decades, we prospered like never before, but in the last few years we appear to have hit some kind of limit.

I made the point that this limit is related to our economic system, which has a self-destructive nature and is therefore not good for the purpose of survival. I think also that the limit is related to our desire for an easy life. We made it our priority to become wealthy in material terms, and for a while we succeeded. But this desire for material wealth is responsible for the failure of the system, because it just isn't possible for more and more people to take more and more materials from the earth, creating more wealth and more goods, using more energy and generally expecting more of everything forever more. Everything has a limit.

So the big question is: what kind of economic system will do a better job of providing a sustainable and more equal future? We have already established the two main priorities: to create more real jobs and thus spread wealth more evenly, while at the same time cutting down on the use of fossil fuels. Difficult, certainly, but not necessarily impossible.

Life isn't fair

People have been arguing about politics and economics for thousands of years; there has never been any general agreement regarding the best system, and most likely there never will be. The core of the argument concerns the distribution of wealth. Why should some people have so much more than others? It doesn't seem right. It isn't fair. This simple response is true enough; life is an unfair business.

The wealth of this world has been distributed very unevenly over the centuries, and attempts to right this apparent wrong have not been particularly successful. Such arguments about wealth distribution inevitably lead us to the long-standing rivalry between capitalism and socialism; the free market versus the planned economy. To some extent this coincides with the right and left wings of politics, terms that date from the 1789 French National Assembly, when the loyalists sat to the right of the king and the revolutionaries sat to the left.

But to a large extent the old political arguments are no longer relevant: the problems we face today are different from those that resulted in the communist experiments of the 20th century, when the desire for economic growth was just as strong on the left as it was on the right. The ideological battles that resulted in the Cold War, and in the end were won by the free-market capitalist system that rules the world today, took place in a world that remained unaware of global warming and developed an addiction to fossil fuels without concern for the environment or for the welfare of future generations.

So it might seem reasonable to assume, after a century of trial and error in which every possible variety of political constitution must have been tried at some point, that the answer is not to be found in the divisive politics of the old right and left, of pure capitalism or pure socialism. Some form of compromise is inevitable. We need to retain the best aspects of capitalism, including some form of market mechanism for most goods and services (because recent history has shown that this is the only way we can have a functioning economy, as I explain on the following pages). But we need at the same time to restrain its worst aspects, to combat its inherent tendency towards greed, inequality and eventual self-destruction. Put simply, we need to take account of socialist ideals, but try to make them work within a regulated market economy.

Thanks to the free-market capitalist system, with a little help from democracy, humans have become very good at one thing in particular: producing as much stuff as possible at the lowest possible price in monetary terms. What it has not become good at, despite centuries of good advice and good intentions from a relatively small number of enlightened people, is the development of a fair and sustainable way of life.

The problem lies in the combination of human nature and the nature of democracy, which inevitably promotes perceived self-interest at the expense of the long-term interests of society as a whole. Human weakness – the understandable desire for a comfortable life – guides the majority to vote for the easy option. We want more stuff because it makes our lives easier and more comfortable (or so we are led to believe by the advertising and media in our consumer society). And, of course, we want it as cheaply as possible.

The long-term price of this short-term materialism might be very high indeed, but we don't look that far ahead, and most likely we'll be dead anyway. We live in a buy-now-pay-later world, but most people aren't even aware of the debts that are building up for future generations – the debts to nature, as well as the financial debts, both of which will make our grandchildren poorer. We don't tend to dwell on such things, but the time has come when we must take the future into account, for the sake of those future generations.

If it's broke, shouldn't we fix it?

So what are the alternatives to free-market capitalism? Over the course of the previous century, various interpretations of socialist and communist ideology have been tried, mostly based on the writings of Marx and Engels, in particular *The Communist Manifesto* of 1848. But although Marx's ideas provided the founding principles for most 20th-century experiments in communism, including the formation of the Soviet Union in 1922 (following the Russian Revolution of 1917) and China since 1949, few communist states kept to the spirit of Marx for long. Although the main aim of Marxism was a classless society in which the means of production would be in the hands of the people for the benefit of everyone equally, in reality this never came about. Human nature got in the way. In most cases the leaders soon became corrupted by power and forgot their original promises – as in the USSR, where Stalin became in many respects indistinguishable from the worst sort of fascist dictator, or from the despotic emperors that the revolution had supposedly banished to history.

China under Mao Zedong fared a little better perhaps, but it can't be denied (to condense a century of history into a few words) that communism has proved something of a failure on the whole, and this might be due, at least in part, to one fundamental failing in the Marxist concept of socialism.

In the early 1920s, at a time when socialism appeared to be gaining ground in Europe, the Austrian economist Ludwig von Mises attempted to demonstrate that pure socialism as envisioned by Marx was in fact an impossibility. His reasoning was that without the free market, there is no means of arriving at an agreed value for goods. I mentioned earlier how values are subjective, governed by individual needs and desires, but to participate in the marketplace these individuals must come to an agreement regarding the value of one thing relative to another thing.

Mises saw that this process had to begin with the market traders acting freely amongst themselves, making decisions with regard to their wants. Once you take away the freedom of the buyers and sellers to act as they please – by setting quotas and prices, for example – this process breaks down; the knowledge contained in those individual valuations is lost.

Although in a simple market situation it might be theoretically possible for a central authority to establish such values, based on the signals given by the actions of individuals, in reality, as the market grows in size and complexity, this becomes unworkable. The marketplace grows as the economy expands, and the number of traders grows with it, and therefore in a free market the ratio of information gatherers remains proportionate to the quantity of goods being traded, retaining a direct link through the traders to the processes of production, to the farmers and manufacturers. Disrupt this link, as happens when the government intervenes, and you lose the signals. So in a centrally planned economy, the people doing the planning have a shortage of information regarding the supply-and-demand situation. This is what led to the serious failings in the Soviet Union and in communist China (before it opened up to market forces): the inability to match production to demand.

Although in this book I've been critical of the way the market values everything according to supply and demand, it turns out that there is no other practical way of pricing goods. This is what economists mean when they talk about the 'efficiency' of the markets. My criticism concerns the inability of this system to take into account long-term factors such as sustainability and the environment, and this is an area that requires some kind of regulation to bring these vital factors into consideration.

To give a simple example, the free-market system as applied to the fishing industry led to a situation in which the oceans were

Figure 105

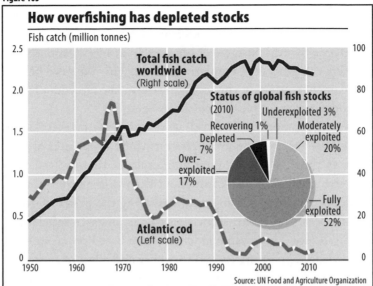

How overfishing has depleted stocks

Fish catch (million tonnes)

Total fish catch worldwide
(Right scale)

Status of global fish stocks
(2010)

Underexploited 3%

Recovering 1%

Depleted 7%

Moderately exploited 20%

Over-exploited 17%

Fully exploited 52%

Atlantic cod
(Left scale)

Source: UN Food and Agriculture Organization

practically depleted of the more popular species of fish, as shown in Figure 105. The industry became so 'efficient' at catching cod, for example, that it pretty much caught them all, almost destroying the whole cod-fishing business in the process. To try to save the fishing industry from this self-destruction, it has been necessary for governments to regulate the number of fish caught through quotas, but many individual market players – the people doing the fishing – object to this. They want to be free to plunder the oceans, even though it would eventually lead to the end of their livelihoods. This sums up the problem with the free-market system, and it can only be solved by greater regulation.

Having made this point, however, I think we have to accept that attempts to do away with market forces altogether always end in failure. Central planning doesn't work unless it is used in conjunction with market forces, as China has learned.

But surely planning is a good thing?

One of the difficulties of evaluating the importance of this social-market structure is that you can't really see it in operation.

Central planning makes sense in theory – a government ought to have a grand plan, and it rules from the center of things – but in practice the real business of life goes on at a local level, so this is where the process of regulation must begin. We need benign government strategy at the top, but we also need freedom on the ground to act as we please, within reason.

We can't comprehend the full workings of the marketplace in this global age, but the principles on which it operates are the same as those in the original marketplaces that evolved with the birth of civilization. Throughout the world, market traders are continuously evaluating and modifying the prices of goods and services, and it turns out that this is an essential element of any society. These value judgments are based on experience: a knowledge of past prices, and the cause and effect of actions.

If you remove incentives to individual action – reward for work, the right to private property, the freedom to choose between one action and another in satisfying our needs – the market system collapses, because the traders stop evaluating the cost of doing one thing rather than doing another thing, a concept in economics known as 'opportunity cost'. It sounds complicated, but in fact we are making such calculations all the time, simply by choosing between alternative actions, as when we buy produce in a street market, for example, and evaluate one stall relative to another stall.

Events in the Soviet Union during the decades after Mises pointed out the flaws in Marx's ideology proved him right. The communist system failed to match the supply of goods to demand, resulting in a serious shortage of basic commodities, especially food. It was only because the Soviets were able to buy grain on the world markets, using their oil revenues, that the system survived as long as it did.

So the marketplace is an essential element of any economic system, with the exception, perhaps, of a kind of universal communism in which prices become irrelevant, the state controls everything and freedom of action is severely limited. Having said that, once the market has set the initial prices of goods and services, there is no reason why government shouldn't use taxes to modify those prices – to impose a levy on fossil fuels, for example.

It is worth bearing in mind that Mises, while emphasizing the essential status of the free market, also stressed the importance of a sound and stable currency. He was in favor of the gold standard, and was writing long before financial speculation gained its current influence over the markets. Speculation distorts the process, especially when it comes to money itself. Money is supposed to be the medium that enables market exchanges to take place rather than a commodity to be traded. Being the reference unit for perceived value, it is obviously unhelpful if that unit itself keeps changing in value. How useful is a tape measure that doesn't keep a constant length?

So which 'ism' works best?

Perhaps the time has come to dispense with the failed ideologies of communism, socialism and capitalism. What we need is pragmatism, not idealism. We need to go with what works – to take the best from each system and create a new model that takes account of our new circumstances, our ever-evolving knowledge regarding the effects of development on the environment. If there's one area in which we have made real progress in recent times, it is surely the accumulation and dissemination of knowledge. It would therefore make sense to use that knowledge, rather than relying on primitive concepts such as 'the survival of the fittest'.

Free-market capitalism favors the individual. It rewards entrepreneurial spirit and hard work, but it also rewards greed and selfishness. Socialism, as its name suggests, puts the emphasis on society. It limits individual freedom, especially with regard to earnings, in a bid to spread wealth more evenly. Taken too far, it subdues the human spirit by removing incentives to work hard; it can stifle that entrepreneurial exuberance that is often cited as the reason for America's success.

It would seem reasonable, therefore, to look for the answer somewhere in between these two systems, or in a combination of both. The most successful nations of recent history – the US and much of Europe in the post-War 'golden age', for example; Japan and South Korea perhaps; Canada and Australia most recently, and maybe China too – have been those that borrowed from different ideologies while shunning the more extreme elements of right or left. Surely this makes sense: life is always a compromise, whether it be between self-interest and society, freedom and security, material and spiritual, mind and body, or reason and emotion. All of us have elements of these essential but opposing forces; we try to maintain a balance between the two extremes.

So the center, by definition, ought to represent the best compromise, just as long as the electorate, which in a sense decides where that center ground lies (in a true democracy at least), has a full understanding of what is at stake when they choose one party, or one system, over another.

If we acknowledge that the political middle ground is, by definition, what the majority has chosen, it doesn't mean that we can't try and move the general consensus one way or the other. One might argue that, in the boom times of the last century, capitalism became accepted as the norm, the best way to create wealth, and therefore the consensus drifted to the right, politically speaking. This was demonstrated in the UK by the way the Labour Party, under Tony Blair, moved away from its socialist roots and embraced much of the rightwing Conservative agenda, including privatization, deregulation and a belief in the mythical wonders of the financial sector. US Democrats also followed the non-interventionist line, and even in Europe this was seen by many leaders as the way to go; nobody wanted to alienate the finance lobby. In a sense, the majority were fooled into thinking that prosperity was almost guaranteed in the new finance-dominated global marketplace. That the whole thing was a mirage based on credit hadn't become clear at the time, at least not to those in power.

So the center moved to the right, as it were. The challenge now is to move it back in the other direction, though I would prefer to say that we need to move the consensus forward rather than leftward, because the situation is very different now than it was in the last century or, indeed, in all of history.

If our lives, and especially the lives of our children and grandchildren, are under threat from the way we live now, as appears to be the case, then obviously we have to make drastic changes to the current system, and many of these changes will be unpopular, unless people understand why they are necessary.

So if we want to keep society as democratic as possible while at the same time changing the way we live, it becomes essential to get the message across to the electorate, both current and future, in the hope that the majority will come to support the required changes.

The way things are at the moment, it appears that most people don't want to think about global warming, even as the evidence mounts up. They don't want to stop burning fossil fuels because it will involve sacrifices. But if people understood that it could well be a matter of survival, the situation would be very different; the majority would begin to accept the changes, in the way that people accepted sacrifices during the Second World War, for example. This is the challenge: to get the message across and move the center ground in the direction of environmental awareness and a more equal distribution of wealth; to put the needs of society before individual comfort and convenience; and, above all, to put the welfare of future generations before our current desire for luxury and ease.

The sacrifices don't have to be as painful as some might assume, especially if they are seen to be borne by everyone more or less equally, or, more to the point, if the wealthy, who cause a disproportionate share of environmental damage, pay a proportionately higher price. At the moment, the opposite happens: the rich use their wealth to escape any hardship, despite being responsible for most of the harm. And this applies on a global as well as a national scale.

Green at heart

So we need to move as rapidly as possible towards a situation in which to become environmentally aware, or 'green', becomes the norm, not some cranky exception. We need to get the message across that continuous growth and unbridled consumerism are not good for the earth, and certainly not for life – the planet will survive global warming in some form or other, but civilization, at least as we know it today, is unlikely to survive. As soon as more people begin to understand this and to accept it, then the middle-ground of politics can be shifted towards the green end of the spectrum, so to speak, and democracy can play its part.

But in terms of an economic system, what should this middle ground consist of? The answer must surely lie in a blend of the best of socialist principles with those elements of capitalism that really work. This would allow individuals to flourish in a more equal and sustainable society, one in which the animal spirits are tamed by a degree of regulation and wealth is spread more evenly.

Although socialism was envisioned by Marx as a kind of transition phase between capitalism and full-blown communism, it has in its milder forms, such as European social democracy, proved quite compatible with the kind of regulated market economy that worked for the US and Europe during the post-War years, in the days before the bankers took over.

Germany, France, the Scandinavian countries and others have tried capitalism diluted with a large dash of socialism, and it worked very well for the latter half of the last century, until the euro experiment and the boom in credit wrecked the system. The problem wasn't that market socialism didn't work, it was more that it wasn't suited to a highly competitive global marketplace ruled by finance-dominated *laissez-faire* capitalism. As with the post-war US system, in many respects it worked very well: unemployment levels were low, taxes were high but wealth was spread relatively evenly; there was general prosperity and few went hungry. There are few realistic alternatives when it comes to social organization on a large scale, as history has shown.

What do we mean by 'capitalism', anyway?

Winston Churchill famously declared that democracy was the worst form of government except for all the others, and I think this is true of capitalism too; it is far from perfect, but, for some aspects of the economy at least, there is no better alternative. We can, however, make it less divisive and less destructive when it comes to jobs and society as a whole.

And while I'm quoting great leaders of the past, it is worth remembering that Thomas Jefferson warned that a government '... founded on banking institutions and moneyed corporations will be the end of freedom and democracy.'

Perhaps at this point we need to clarify exactly what we're talking about here. I've been criticizing free-market capitalism throughout this book, and now I'm saying that capitalism has its good points. What does the word mean, anyway?

It was around the middle of the 19th century that the term 'capitalism' began to be used widely, in connection with the economic system that had evolved in Britain in the wake of the Industrial Revolution. Karl Marx referred to the 'capitalist mode of production', and by this he meant the private ownership of industry, with the profit going to the owners – the 'capitalists' – and the workers being paid a wage. This is still the main criterion for defining capitalism, along with the supremacy of the market as arbiter of prices, based on supply and demand.

I've already explained why the market is essential for the purpose of setting prices, and why central planning doesn't work. So what happens if we keep the marketplace and stick with wage labor (at least for those in employment); if we allow private ownership of at least some businesses (especially smaller ones) but we also introduce a mixture of co-operative and public (or state) ownership of some industry and banks; if we bring in a degree of regulation to keep the markets in check? Are we then still talking about capitalism? The answer is surely that we have a mixture of capitalism and socialism. Some call it market socialism, others a mixed economy. Perhaps we need to invent a new word. But does it really matter what we call it?

What I've really been criticizing is the current *laissez-faire* version of global capitalism: its lack of accountability, its emphasis on financial speculation, its hatred of taxes and regulation, its encouragement of greed and inequality, plus its total disregard for the environment.

The lesson here, then, is that the financial system has gained too much influence over our lives. It would be better for society if it were scaled back to a size that represents its real purpose in the economy as a service to industry and to households. Banks have grown far too big, which is one reason we've been hearing the argument that they had to be bailed out by the state because they were 'too big to fail'. But really it's absurd for governments – meaning taxpayers – to have to bail out private banks in what is supposedly a free-market economy. The whole point of the private sector is that market forces govern the behavior of individual traders. Here the system failed, unregulated free-market capitalism resulted in the financial crisis, and the state had to ride to the rescue.

By all means let's have a nationalized bank, owned by the state and guaranteed by the state. It makes a great deal of sense, and many countries (even some US states) do it. People can put their savings in the state bank in the knowledge that the money will be secure and will be used for productive investment rather than for speculation or to make the bankers rich. The rate of interest might be a bit lower in general (though it could hardly be lower than that which holds at the time of writing, as shown in Figure 106), but that is the price of security. Private banks will be free to offer better rates, but the risks will be greater. Such is the nature of market competition, supposedly.

Figure 106

The price of money

Interest rates, %

US Federal Reserve target rate

Bank of England official base rate

Sources: Bank of England/ US Federal Reserve

The state of the nation

Conventional wisdom, at least on the right, says that governments should leave business alone and let private enterprise get on with the job of running the economy. This is an extreme version of the argument Mises put forward, that the market knows best. But the market only knows best when it comes to the price of goods and services in the marketplace. It can't take into account the less obvious factors of long-term sustainability: the future consequences of ever-increasing productivity on jobs, or the influence of excessive wealth accumulation, debt creation and financial speculation. These things can only be factored in with the help of government regulation.

Even after the financial crash, the loudest voices on the right were still insisting that governments should tread lightly so as not to stifle the great innovative power of the capitalist system. In the US election campaign of 2012, the Republicans kept insisting that Barack Obama was a closet socialist, as if this was the worst thing that could be said about a president.

This hatred of anything remotely resembling socialism, which seems to be ingrained in the US business community, is based on a misconception; an irrational fear left over from the Cold War years. This fear appears to be instilled into many Americans during childhood: socialism is just another word for communism, and communists are the ultimate villains, out to kill the spirit of freedom.

It's all a part of the American way; that 'a-man's-gotta-do-what-a-man's-gotta-do' mentality. Survival of the fittest. It's an attitude I understand and even agree with in some respects. Like many boys growing up in the 1950s and 1960s, I was enthralled by the America we saw in the movies and would have given anything to be American: to drive around in a big fancy car between the towering skyscrapers and out along the gleaming ribbon of endless highway, into the wide open spaces of the brashest nation on earth. Why question it? Why think too much about the system when it's so obvious the American way is the best?

It's only when you grow up that you realize the American Dream, even for most Americans, was just that: a dream that only a lucky few could turn into reality. All that wealth, all that excess. Even now, as things get tougher for most of us in the developed world, the US is still the luckiest nation on earth. The tallest skyscrapers might be going up in China and Malaysia and the oil states of the Middle East these days, but neither China nor any other country is ever going to come close to the sheer abundance of the United States of America.

But really, are the ideals of socialism so bad? What's so terrible about using the power of government to restrain the excesses of individual greed; to redistribute wealth more fairly? Socialism doesn't have to mean drab concrete blocks and empty supermarket shelves. The truth is that US government policy included plenty of socialist principles during the post-War golden age, including high taxes on the wealthy and state aid for agriculture and business.

To suggest that national governments are no good at

running large corporations is tantamount to saying that the US government can't run NASA or its armed forces properly, which is absurd. If a government can manage a space program that puts men on the moon, or an enterprise as large and powerful as the US Air Force, it can surely manage anything that it puts its mind to.

Britain's National Health Service is another example – this is not perfect by any means (and is currently under threat from increasing corporate involvement) but, as Figure 107 shows, it is one of the biggest employers in the world, and gives far better value than the US health system and many others. And while we're looking at this chart of the world's biggest employers, it's worth noting that the US Department of Defense is said to employ more people than any other organization globally, and is proud of the fact. So where does that fit with the Republican Party's hatred of state-run enterprises?

The reality is that the state can run a large enterprise just as well as a private corporation can. There are plenty of examples of very successful businesses that come under state control, from

Figure 107

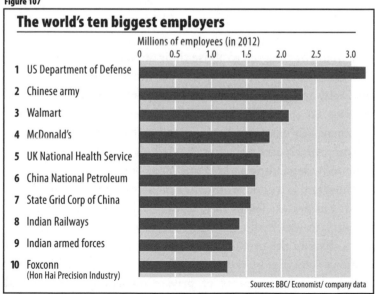

The world's ten biggest employers

Millions of employees (in 2012)

1 US Department of Defense	
2 Chinese army	
3 Walmart	
4 McDonald's	
5 UK National Health Service	
6 China National Petroleum	
7 State Grid Corp of China	
8 Indian Railways	
9 Indian armed forces	
10 Foxconn (Hon Hai Precision Industry)	

Sources: BBC/ Economist/ company data

Norway's Statoil to Singapore Airlines. And obviously there are numerous examples of private corporations that are (or were) run badly. It's all down to the way a business is managed.

A matter of size

The usual free-market arguments about incentive and the responsibilities that come with ownership – factors that play a big part in ensuring the success of small businesses – apply less as the size of an enterprise grows. The bigger the business, the less influence the owners have over the actual workforce, and therefore the more important the managers become. So what we find, as Japan and South Korea realized, and the Chinese have now discovered, is that the state can do a good job of running the heavy stuff such as mining, steel-making and shipbuilding (and in China's case oil extraction) just as long as it employs competent managers and keeps the politicians out of the business process.

The state can also run the railways and some utilities more efficiently than private enterprise can, because, as we have learned in Britain, there is nothing to be gained from privatizing what are natural-monopoly industries. All that happens is the state ends up overseeing the private companies, because otherwise they would be tempted to abuse their monopoly positions.

It also means that industries that are vital to the nation – electricity and gas supply, air-traffic control, highways and ports, railways etc – can be kept under government control. This argument can of course be extended to the mineral-extraction industry, which uses resources that belong either to everybody or to nobody, depending on how one looks at it.

There is also a good argument that some smaller-to-medium-sized businesses work best under co-operative ownership schemes, in which all the workers have a stake in the company and a share in the profits. Such ventures have worked very well in many countries of Europe, India and even in the US. They combine the best aspects of private ownership – individual motivation and the sense of responsibility that comes with being the owner – with the best aspects of state control – a more even distribution of wealth, a connection to the local community, and a sense of social responsibility.

Collective farming, or co-operative organization, also works well for smaller farms of the type that could go a long way to improving employment prospects and land use, as I explain in more detail in Chapter 21.

So my point really is that the best solution to the old arguments concerning state or private ownership is that a combination of both works best, depending on the nature and size of the industry. The state should concentrate on the big stuff and let private enterprise take care of small businesses, farming, retail and other services – individual initiatives operating in the local marketplace.

We are the state

In the boom years of the 1950s through to the 1970s, as the Cold War developed into a battle of military supremacy between the two superpowers, the US government invested as much public money on building its armed forces as did the communist leaders of the Soviet Union. There was never any suggestion that the defense industry should be left to market forces. It was obvious that an unsubsidized free-market capitalist system was incapable of supporting industries such as weapons and aircraft manufacture, which require massive investment on research and development and were therefore never going to make a profit in purely financial terms.

Even now, the big aircraft manufacturers can't survive without government support of some kind, though in these days of *laissez-faire* economics there has to be a pretense that such funding doesn't amount to state subsidy. But the simple truth is that many of the great technological feats of the last century, from putting men on the moon to the development of computers, satellites, the internet, cellphones and solar power – most great innovations of

Figure 108

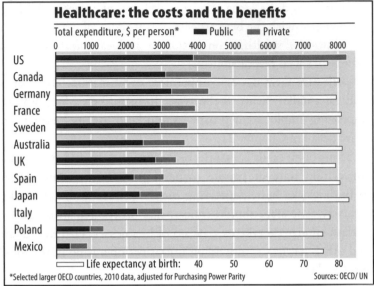

recent years, in fact – involved government support of one kind or another.

The health of nations

To return to the comparison between Britain's state-run National Health Service (NHS) and the US healthcare system, which is mostly run by the private sector, we find that the supposed inefficiency of the state system relative to private enterprise doesn't fit the facts.

Figure 108 shows the expenditure of various developed countries on healthcare, and it also shows the life expectancy in those countries, which gives some indication of the effectiveness of that healthcare spending. We see that the US system is by far the most expensive and inefficient, while many of the state-run health authorities, such as Britain's NHS, deliver far better value for money. The US gets no obvious benefit from its costly system, which is dominated by the interests of powerful private corporations, from the pharmaceutical giants to insurance companies and private hospitals, all of which make billions and spend millions trying to influence government policy. Mexico spends less than one-ninth the US amount per person on healthcare, yet, on average, Mexicans live almost as long as Americans.

I will return to the implications of healthcare spending in Chapter 21, in a slightly different context, but for now I think Figure 108 demonstrates quite clearly that not all aspects of the economy should be entrusted to the private sector.

We need to get away from this idea that there is something inherently wrong with state intervention. Just because the Soviet system failed and capitalism took over the world doesn't mean the former was totally bad and the latter vastly superior. Capitalism worked better because ultimately it created more wealth, and as long as the majority benefited, as they did in the boom years, most people were happy, even if the wealth was unevenly distributed. The wealth 'trickled down' from the factory owners to the workers. More people found well-paid work – tedious and strenuous work perhaps, but an improvement on previous employment conditions, be it in the mills or in the fields.

But capitalism only prevailed because of government support. Without all that state investment, the defense industry would never have produced the weapons technology that gave the US the lead in nuclear capability, the Cold War might have been won by the Soviets and recent history might have taken a very different turn.

What really beat the Soviet system was a combination of its own failings on the one hand – from corrupt leadership down to unmotivated workers – and on the other hand a powerful government making the best of a public/private partnership. The US government understood where it needed to use its wealth and power, and it also recognized where the strengths of the free-market system really lay: close to the ground, on the streets as it were, where individuals go freely about their business under the protection of the state.

Individuals make up the state; the 'public' consists of individual people. They are not separate entities, opposed to each other; we are all in this together, private people in a public world.

20 Redistributing wealth

Why the rich have too much

The movement away from state intervention has been paralleled and reinforced by the rise in influence of the bankers and corporate bosses who want to protect their own interests from government interference. Most of these people came by their money the easy way – the Wall Street or City of London way – rather than in the real industry that generated the wealth in the first place. They are, of course, doing what most of us would do if we were lucky enough to come into big money. Some of them might even believe that they have genuinely earned all that wealth. This mistaken view is understandable. It's not immediately obvious that finance is a zero-sum game, that however much money a banker makes for himself, it has to have come from elsewhere. You have to give it some thought before you realize that the money could only have been earned the hard way, that before it entered the banking system, some real industry must have taken place out on the ground somewhere, perhaps halfway around the world.

I mentioned in Chapter 2 that the economy is divided into three broad sectors. The first two sectors take the raw materials of the earth and add value by transforming that natural wealth into something useful. This is the industrial process, and it is this industry that produces the real wealth of the economy. I also mentioned that the work that goes into this industry – the energy, both mental and physical – is the source of all value. The earth's natural wealth has no great value, in economic terms, until we apply effort to turn it into something useful. At the lowest end of the scale, this might simply be to pick an apple from a tree. At the other extreme, it is to build a ship or a skyscraper.

One could argue that the earth's natural wealth must have a kind of intrinsic value whether we use it or not, but that's beside the point for us humans. The concept of value, like that of wealth or any other 'concept', is a human invention. As I pointed out in Chapter 4, value is a function of the needs or 'wants' of individuals in relationship to the scarcity or abundance of the goods or services in question.

Services make up the third sector of the economy and, although it doesn't create wealth, the service sector performs two essential functions. First, services help the producers in various ways – selling their goods, delivering their mail, preparing their meals, lending them money to build new factories and buy machinery, educating their children – allowing them to devote more time to the business of wealth creation. Second, services are the chief means by which the wealth of industry is distributed among the general population, thus boosting industrial demand in a 'virtuous' cycle. In this role, services also add value to the economy through labor, although this extra value is dependent on the initial wealth-creation process, just as the value added by industry is dependent on the natural wealth of the earth. You can only add value to something that already exists.

In recent years, following the breaking of the link between the dollar and gold and the subsequent deregulation of the banks, there has been a new development, a fourth layer of activity. The financial sector, which in the past concentrated on lending money as a service to others, has moved into a new realm, one that adds no value of any kind, and in fact, in attempting to make money from other people's money without doing any real work, reduces the value of existing wealth.

This might sound harsh, but although one can see some value in most services – even things like advertising help to spread a bit of wealth around – I just cannot see that society derives any benefit from a sector that attempts to profit from speculating on everything from the relative movement of currencies to the future prices of commodities, and even on things as intangible as the risk of other people not paying their debts.

The source of all value lies in real work, as I have tried to show, and this unproductive financial activity involves no real work and actually destroys value by transferring wealth from the majority of workers to a wealthy minority. Such activity is harmful to the economy, not just because the rich have no need for the wealth and will distribute less of it around, but also because wealth that accumulates in bank accounts and hedge funds will be devalued through the credit-creation process.

Wealth is most useful to the economy when it is spread as evenly as possible, instigating a virtuous cycle of job creation and a moderate degree of consumer spending based on real earnings, adding value to society. In the hands of the financiers, however, excess wealth leads to a vicious cycle of debt creation, asset bubbles and the subsequent devaluation of existing wealth and future earnings, as shown in Figure 109.

It follows, therefore, that part of the global recovery process must involve a reduction in the influence of the financial sector over the economy and a return to the original purpose of banking, which is the productive investment of other people's savings. Financiers generally have become greedy parasites on the economy, their only aim being to profit from the wealth of

Figure 109

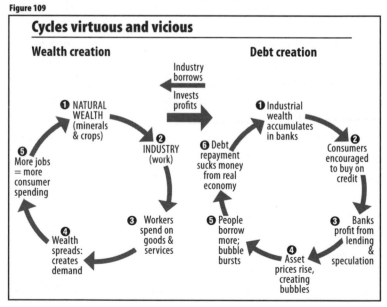

others. Bankers need to re-enter the real world and provide a decent service to their customers. Perhaps then they can start to rebuild their tattered reputations, and even to earn a reasonable wage, though not, of course, the inflated earnings they seem to expect, and which they have never truly earned.

As for the glut of accumulated wealth that led to the rise of the banking sector, that should be put to better use than speculation and unsustainable debt creation. But how? What should be done with all this accumulated wealth, the profits of industry past? The logical answer, bearing in mind that the wealth originated in the earth, where it obviously didn't 'belong' to anyone, is that it should be used for the benefit of as many people as possible.

A question of efficiency

If we accept that the state represents the people, as it supposedly does in a democracy at least, then perhaps it would make sense for the state to oversee the distribution of natural resources, rather than letting the strongest or the richest grab the most, as tends to happen with a system based on survival-of-the-fittest principles. Large corporations, be they oil companies, mining conglomerates, food giants or whatever, tend to become dominant in their field through acquisition and economies of scale. But large corporations are becoming increasingly global in reach. They tend to be based offshore and therefore to be less regulated, less accountable to any government and less connected to the communities in which they operate. Less responsible, one might say.

There is surely a conflict between the freedom of the individual and the power of big business. The transnational corporation is much closer in reality, if not in concept, to the autocratic state: all-powerful and unrepresentative of the people. It therefore makes no sense to equate modern free-market capitalism with individual freedom. When corporations reach a certain size, it is usually bad for the people. When one self-interested group becomes too powerful, be it a military clique, an autocratic government or a large corporation, it tends to ignore individual rights.

The hidden influence of corporations over the political process, be it through financial contributions or crony capitalism (self-serving friendships between corporate executives and politicians), is distorting democracy. This is especially true in the US, where large sums of corporate money flow into party coffers, and where the leaders of politics and the leaders of business (banking executives in particular) often swap places. Unless it is kept separate from politics, which it rarely is, big business can be the enemy of true democracy. Which is better for the individual: to have the consumer's choice between two or three transnational companies, all of which are basically the same and interested only in profit, or to have a say in who runs the whole show, from the national power company to the local co-operative bank?

Surely it must be in the interests of individuals, and be more democratic, for large-scale industry and banks to be in the hands of the state, which ought to equate to being in the hands of the people? I have already given examples to show that nationalized industry is not inherently less efficient than private industry; it is far more a question of good or bad management, which can apply whatever the ownership structure.

I would also argue that there are different aspects to efficiency; it might be better for the sake of society overall not to cut the workforce just to make an industry more 'productive', especially with regard to primary industry, which involves the process of adding value to the natural wealth of the earth through labor. In other words, rather than concentrating on efficiencies of scale, we should think instead about the efficiency of society as a whole. Having reached the point where increasing industrial productivity merely adds to the unemployment lines, there might be more value added to the wider economy if we made it a policy to employ more workers, rather than continuously replacing workers with machines, especially in areas that don't cause significant or lasting ecological damage.

I'm not suggesting that we fill the factories with useless workers – rather that we think twice before taking the most productive track. To give two examples, I mentioned in Chapter 11 that we might expect, in the near future, to have farm tractors harvesting the crops without a farmer in the cab, or robots making the dinner and cleaning the home or the office.

Farmers, assuming they own their businesses, would presumably welcome such innovation, as it would free their time for other jobs on the farm. But if the farm workers who become redundant as a result of such technological innovation can't find other work, then what is the point of this improvement in productivity, besides making food even cheaper? As I said earlier, it might be better to pay more for the goods and have everyone employed, and at the same time we can produce food of a higher quality, because more workers can add more value, for reasons I explain in the next chapter.

The same applies to our office-cleaning robots: what will happen to the former cleaners that end up on the dole? Either this new army of unemployed workers reduces its wage demands to the point where they cost less than the robots, or they will be forever without work, to the detriment of their own self-esteem and to society generally.

I think we have reached a critical phase in the evolution of economic development, one in which we have to re-evaluate the whole concept of ever-increasing productivity.

A taxing problem

That the developed world has become less equal in recent decades is surely beyond dispute. The arguments begin when discussing possible solutions to the problem of inequality. The traditional capitalist answer is to create as much wealth as possible through growth and hope that 'the rising tide raises all boats'. This worked quite well in the 'golden age' of the second half of the 20th century, but we have seen how, with the subsequent rise of the financial sector, the emphasis has shifted from job creation to credit creation.

Technology has made industry so productive that it employs

fewer and fewer workers, and the service sector can no longer expand to take up the slack because there's not enough wealth feeding through from industry for that very reason: the unemployed and poorly paid can't afford to spend money on services that only evolved in the first place due to the excess wealth of an advanced society.

The traditional socialist solution to inequality is to raise taxes on the wealthy and distribute some of that wealth to the poor through welfare payments of various kinds: unemployment benefit, tax credits for the low-paid and so on. This works to some extent, but there are two big problems that need to be addressed concerning the distribution of wealth through taxation. One is that it doesn't always result in more revenue to the state, because in this increasingly globalized market the wealthy have become very good at avoiding higher taxes by various means, such as registering companies in tax havens and banking the profits there.

The second problem, which I think is ultimately more important, is that inequality cannot be solved in the long term purely through the redistribution of wealth that has already been created by past industry. Even if we accept a lower level of wealth creation than we had in the boom years, we still have to keep creating new wealth, especially since we've already spent some of the proceeds of future industry by building up massive debts. The world cannot prosper on old wealth alone because the value of that wealth will soon be eroded by rising prices and a shortage of employment – the vicious cycle of declining prosperity that has already begun, in Europe at least.

Work as a right

The real solution, as I have tried to show, must involve the creation of more jobs, because it is only through work that real value is added to the earth's natural wealth, and it is only through work that everyone can be given the opportunity to achieve a truly satisfying life. This is a fundamental quality of

Figure 110

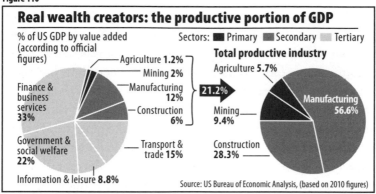

Real wealth creators: the productive portion of GDP

% of US GDP by value added (according to official figures)

Sectors: ■ Primary ■ Secondary ▨ Tertiary

Agriculture **1.2%**
Mining **2%**
Manufacturing **12%**
Construction **6%**

Finance & business services **33%**

Government & social welfare **22%**

Information & leisure **8.8%**

Transport & trade **15%**

21.2% ▶

Total productive industry

Agriculture **5.7%**

Mining **9.4%**

Construction **28.3%**

Manufacturing **56.6%**

Source: US Bureau of Economic Analysis, (based on 2010 figures)

human existence, related to our need to provide for ourselves and our families, as I attempted to demonstrate in Chapter 13. It is not something one can prove with a scientific equation, because it goes much deeper than empirical evidence – into the human soul, as it were. Our right to wealth is linked to our need to work. We must all be given the opportunity to earn a living.

This being the case, and with the current economic system failing to provide enough employment, it becomes necessary to examine ways in which the state can create real jobs. I have already shown why only real industry – the primary and secondary sectors of the economy – can create real wealth. It therefore follows that the state needs to become more involved in the industrial sector, going beyond its usual connection (in most capitalist countries anyway) with services such as defense, education and healthcare.

Figure 110 shows the proportion of the US economy, in terms of GDP, that represents productive industry. The second pie chart gives a breakdown of the primary and secondary sectors, which make up 21% of US output in terms of GDP, but which form the basis of all America's real wealth creation (and the situation is broadly similar in much of Europe). Without these sectors, none of the other 79% could exist. So it might make sense to try to reverse the trend towards declining employment in these vital industries.

The manufacturing sector presents a problem, however, because we can't just fill the factories with more workers to counter the recent improvements in productivity. More manufacturing jobs would be a good thing, certainly, but there isn't really any logical way for the state to bring this about, other than investing in renewable-energy and recycling technology and other 'green' initiatives. We already make more things than we really need and, because we have to cut down on energy use anyway, it doesn't make much sense to increase the overall size of the manufacturing sector, however desirable this might be from the employment and wealth-creation perspectives.

So that leaves us with three productive industries that I think offer more promise with regard to job creation: construction, utilities and agriculture, all of which have important roles to play with regard to reducing fossil-fuel consumption. I shall return to this in the next chapter, after we've completed our tax returns.

Can anyone really 'own' the earth?

As I mentioned earlier with regard to the boom years that followed the Second World War, most people accepted that they should pay taxes; it was part of the social contract. How else could a nation fund defense and security, education and infrastructure?

For centuries, wealthy landowners had also accepted, for the most part, that they should pay taxes. As long as the tax rates were seen to be reasonable, there was little reason for complaint. They knew that their wealth had come from the earth, from the land and from the raw materials of the earth, because in those days it was obvious. They understood that this wealth wasn't theirs alone, just because they owned the farms and the forests and the mines, and later the factories.

But with the rise of the service sector, particularly the financial sector – the owners and executives of global investment funds and banks, who take so much of the wealth these days – the link between their money and the land is less obvious. Ask a hedge-fund manager or a currency trader how they made their money, and they'll likely tell you they used their expertise to make some wise investment decisions; they are unlikely to admit that they won it from someone else with a lucky bet.

The truth is that, whatever the investment fund might be called, and however much it might have been shifted around in the meantime, the wealth in those funds came originally from real industrial activity, using the raw-material wealth of the earth. As I said earlier, it belonged originally to nobody or to everybody, depending on how one interprets ideas regarding natural rights. The people who might have a legitimate claim to that wealth are the workers whose sweat transformed those raw materials into something useful, but they are rarely the ones to profit much from it.

This brings us to the concept of land ownership. How much land can any one person legitimately claim as his or her own? The traditional answer to that question is as much land as one person can work. In other words, one stakes a claim to a piece of land through one's labor, as in the 'homesteader' principle. The Enlightenment philosopher John Locke, whom I mentioned in Chapter 15 with regard to social-contract theory, wrote that anyone who 'hath mixed his labour' with the land, thereby through his work can turn nature, or common land, into his own property, 'at least where there is enough, and as good, left in common for others.'[1]

One of the distinctions between capitalism and socialism is in the concept of private property. To the capitalist, the right to one's own property is a fundamental part of the system, linked to the idea of individual freedom and personal wealth. At the other extreme, communism considers all property, apart from immediate personal possessions such as clothing, as belonging to the state (meaning, theoretically at least, to everyone equally).

As with politics generally, I would suggest the answer lies somewhere between these two extremes. It seems quite reasonable to me that people should be able to own their own homes, and even the plot of land on which that home is built. It seems reasonable also that a farmer should be able to claim as his own the land that he works. Locke's argument that we can 'earn' a plot of land through our labor seems fair enough, though obviously there isn't much unclaimed or 'common' land left in the world these days, at least not land that can be farmed. In the modern sense, this would equate to how much land one might be able to buy with money that has been earned through honest labor.

Where I would begin to question the right to ownership is in relation to the earth itself, and obviously there must be some distinction made here between the soil as worked by the farmer, and the earth in a deeper sense (both literally and figuratively).

It comes down to a matter of definition. The concept of 'ownership' is meaningless beyond the legal framework; it can only refer to agreements between people. Nature lies outside this concept of ownership: we can't 'own' the environment or the earth, so it follows that we can't really own the land. We might claim a piece of it while we're alive, but nature will ignore our claims anyway, especially if we stop working that land. We refer to the 'wilderness' for this reason; an acknowledgment that nature is beyond our control.

So when we talk about farmers' ownership of their land, it is simply a legal acceptance that nobody can come along and kick them off that land as long as they are farming it. In human terms, farmers have a right to their fields, and this right is earned through their labor.

But what happens when oil is discovered beneath a farmer's land? The farmer can't really 'own' the oil, though they might claim some right to it. At one extreme, as in some US states, the owner of the land is granted the right to the minerals beneath that land while, at the other extreme, in a communist state, there is no issue because the land and everything else is owned by the state. In reality most countries fall somewhere between these two extremes, with the state claiming the actual mineral wealth and issuing licenses for mineral extraction, usually with the agreement of the landowner, who is often entitled to a percentage of the profit. Legally, it can become very complicated, but that's not the issue here. My point is simply that, once we get to mineral rights or areas of land greater than a person can work by himself, the whole concept of ownership seems rather limited and questionable.

The right to private property is one of the pillars of capitalism because it is linked to the idea of personal freedom. If we farm the land and build our own house then we can claim the right to that land and that house, assuming we harm nobody else, because we earned that right through our labor. And because of that right, people become responsible for their own property and take good care of it. This was one of the problems of communism: people had no incentive to make the most of the land because they had no personal claim to it. The idea of 'the state' doesn't carry enough of a personal connotation for most of us, so we aren't inclined to feel any responsibility for its upkeep.

Citizens might feel a certain loyalty to this so-called state, or nation, but there again they might not. They might not feel that they really belong to any state, or that the state should have any claim over them. This is why the notion of the individual is more powerful than the concept of the state. The failure of communism wasn't the failure of an ideal, it was a failure of human nature. The idea that we are all equal is very noble in principle, but in practice it fails because that supposed equality doesn't translate into equal ability, and human nature is such that the more able don't feel inclined to support the less able, especially if they have no obvious responsibility to do so.

We are more inclined to look after our own interests, which is why we look after private property better than we look after public property. We work harder when motivated, and we are motivated by reward. Taken to an extreme, this looks like greed, but most of the time the concept of private property, at the scale of the individual or family at least, works well, giving the property owner a stake in the local community. And this sense of 'belonging' to the community can be of benefit to everyone, including those who might not own their own homes.

When it come to the earth, however, it becomes an entirely different proposition. No one person can realistically claim large tracts of farmland or forest, just as we can't own the oceans or the water flowing in the rivers, and by extension the coal or oil in the ground beneath us.

Most of us can accept that if a person finds a nugget of gold in a river, to take my previous example, then it becomes theirs. But that doesn't mean they have a claim to all the gold in that river, though they might be free to grab as much as they can before others arrive on the scene.

It becomes a matter of degree. What seems reasonable on one scale – the scale of one person's labor – becomes clearly unacceptable at some larger scale, say if a person tries to claim a whole forest. So where do we draw the line? What happens when an individual or a corporation buys up huge tracts of farmland, forest or mineral wealth? Or when a small number of wealthy or well-connected people benefit from the privatization of state assets, including its mineral wealth, as happened in Russia following the collapse of the Soviet Union?

In practice this depends on the laws of the land, but from an ethical point of view I think we have to stick with Locke's original argument that we 'earn' property through our labor, and even if this no longer means literally working the land, the concept can still apply through the amount of money one can realistically claim to have 'earned', which through this fundamental principle is still related to working the land, or processing the produce of the land through industry. This brings us back to the ethical arguments regarding taxation.

How much can one person 'earn'?

Money is ultimately a representation of our labor, the amount of physical and/or mental effort that we have put into our work, adding value to whatever materials we might have used, if any. All exchanges in the marketplace are therefore, in effect, an exchange of one person's labor for another, just as a wage is payment for work. In the modern economy, this point is far from obvious, but, once we accept that it must be so, we can appreciate the impossibility of any one person's labor being worth thousands or even millions of times that of another person. This surely must mean that the wealthy minority of the world can't possibly have earned that wealth in any moral or even literal sense. It just isn't possible for any one person to have put enough effort into one life to justify a claim to millions. The wealthy owe their fortune to just that – to good fortune, luck, chance. It might be a case of being in the right place at the right time, being born into privilege or knowing the right people, but it must have involved a lucky break of one sort or another. And once you have money, it's not so hard to make more.

That the wealthy should pay more tax seems clear enough. Arguments to the contrary usually run along the following lines: high taxes reduce the incentives for entrepreneurs to work hard; the opportunity to 'earn' great wealth is an essential element in the wealth-creation process; exceptionally gifted people will take their amazing abilities, along with their money, elsewhere – to another planet perhaps – and everyone will be worse off because we'll lose that 'trickle-down' element. The tide won't rise, so all the boats will remain mired in the silt of the harbor.

Do these arguments really make sense? Surely there is a much more logical basis for the opposite viewpoint, that anyone who has made lots of money through financial speculation of any sort, be it from banking, a property empire or any other rent-seeking activity, is a parasite, sucking the wealth from the real economy, where it might have created real jobs, and using it instead for their own gain.

While it is undeniably true that investment in productive industry is a good thing – an essential thing, even – most financial investment these days doesn't result in productive investment, as we saw in Figure 97. And most shareholders are far more concerned about profiting in the short term than they are about creating long-term employment.

However much the financial sector claims to be helping the economy through investment, it is a simple fact that investors are hoping to make money for themselves and are not doing it for the good of society. Unless the money they make is a share of the profits of productive industry – industry that is actually creating new jobs thanks to that investment, which as we've seen is rarely the case these days – then their investment is not helping the economy. It is more likely that their profit has come at the expense of job creation, because money in a Cayman Islands hedge fund will most likely be adding to the debt problem.

As I have tried to show, the majority of investment income these days is simply money that has been taken from someone else, from wealth already created elsewhere. It follows, therefore, that the rise of the financial sector results in a situation whereby the real economy is shrinking relative to GDP. There isn't as much real wealth creation going on relative to the overall size of the economy, so as the rich get richer, the rest of society must be getting poorer, as several of my charts have shown to be the case. We end up with asset and credit bubbles, rather than genuine wealth and job creation.

Put simply, the rise of finance has served mainly to create apparent 'wealth' out of nothing but credit; in other words, by borrowing from future production. It has made society poorer.

As a postscript to this point, another reason finance has been bad for society is by luring talented people away from areas in which they could have been more useful. The promise of rich pickings in banking has attracted many of the best graduates in the past three decades or so, people who might otherwise have gone into real industry or even politics, to the benefit of society as a whole.

As we aim towards a more equal society based on sustainable industry rather than on greed and credit, as we must do, we will need to attract a higher caliber of person into politics, and although by definition such people shouldn't be the greedy types, it will still be easier to do this if the excessive pay levels of the corporate world are reduced.

The solution to the problem, as we have already established, is to create more jobs in the wealth-creating sectors of the economy. We need to invest the accumulated wealth of past industry in future industry, and in the services that support that industry, rather than using it for speculation and individual gain.

But if the financial sector can't be trusted with all this accumulated wealth, who can? Assuming that we will have to leave most of this old wealth in the hands of the rich for now, apart from some transfer by taxation (because I'm not actually advocating a revolution here, at least not a violent revolution) the solution for the future should be to keep more of the wealth produced by industry in the hands of the state, which is, after all, the closest one can get to keeping it in the hands of the people generally. The important thing is for the state to be both well run and truly answerable to the people.

1 Locke's *Second Treatise of Government*, published in 1690.

21 Jobs without growth

Why we need global regulation

Having read reports and books by researchers and authors writing for organizations such as the World Bank and the United Nations in which there is much use of the word 'decoupling' – which refers to the economy somehow growing while at the same time using fewer resources per unit of growth – I feel I must spoil the party.

This well-meaning and optimistic viewpoint is unfortunately unrealistic, as I have made clear. We cannot create material wealth without using raw materials. The only possible way in which we can create more wealth with fewer resources is to cut down on waste by using those resources more efficiently. But although we can and should continue to recycle more materials, reduce waste and improve energy efficiency in transport and factories and homes and so on, there is a limit to how far this process can go in the medium term, bearing in mind our current dependence on oil for energy.

The only realistic solution to the problem of global warming is to reduce our consumption of fossil fuels – something we have to do anyway, as oil becomes more difficult to extract – and this can be achieved by switching to renewable energy sources. But we have to accept that this will constrain economic growth. We have to accept that continuous growth is impossible, that we have reached the point, in the West at least, where we shouldn't even be trying to expand the economy further.

It has become clear in recent years that the developed world has passed its peak of prosperity, at least when measured in terms of material wealth. The era in which we gauge success by the size of our houses and cars is drawing to a close. It is also clear that the developing world, while still having room to grow in terms of average personal wealth, will never attain anything close to the material prosperity that we have come to expect in the West. It would actually be impossible, even if it were desirable, which

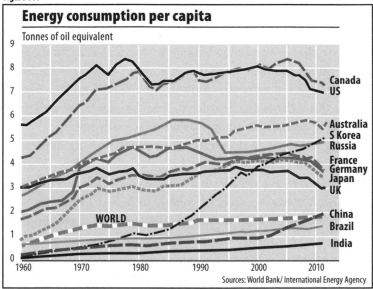

Figure 111

Energy consumption per capita

Tonnes of oil equivalent

Canada
US
Australia
S Korea
Russia
France
Germany
Japan
UK
China
Brazil
India

WORLD

Sources: World Bank/ International Energy Agency

from an environmental perspective it is not.

I say this because, if one thinks of the average wealth of Americans, who with 4% of the world's population consume 24% of global resources (especially energy, as Figure 111 shows), then for the whole world to live like that would require six times the raw materials currently produced each year.

Obviously this will never happen, not just because there aren't enough resources, but also because the world is a very different place now than it was when the US and then Europe grew so wealthy in the 'golden era'. We will never again experience that combination of demand, optimism, opportunity and abundance of cheap oil. So the balancing out of wealth, in global terms, will have to include a reduction in material wealth in the West, a process that appears to have begun already in some countries (albeit involuntarily) for the reasons I've already explained.

But really we should be glad that the rich world is getting poorer: from an environmental point of view, which is the one that matters most when it comes to the survival of humanity, we don't want more rich people anyway.

Accepting the new reality

What is needed now, by politicians and economists and everyone else, is an acknowledgment that this is in fact a good thing, rather than the same old talk about how we must boost the economy and return to growth. The end of growth doesn't have to mean the end of prosperity, not if we spread wealth more evenly and re-evaluate what prosperity actually means.

The good news is that happiness is not directly dependent on material wealth, as my following two charts show. Various surveys over recent decades have come to the same conclusion, that once we attain a level of wealth sufficient to live on, with enough money to keep us out of poverty, then increasing our income further doesn't necessarily increase our happiness. In fact, as Figure 112 shows, happiness can actually fall as income rises. This is because our expectations increase along with our wealth: the more we earn, the more we want, and the less easily we are satisfied. And as we try to maintain the high income to which we become accustomed, the higher our stress levels rise.

Most studies of the relationship between income and

Figure 112

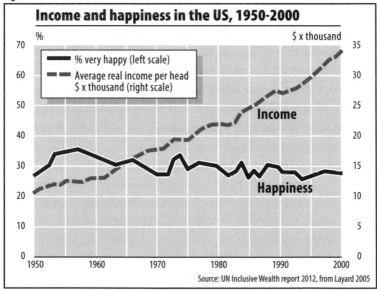

Income and happiness in the US, 1950-2000

Source: UN Inclusive Wealth report 2012, from Layard 2005

Figure 113

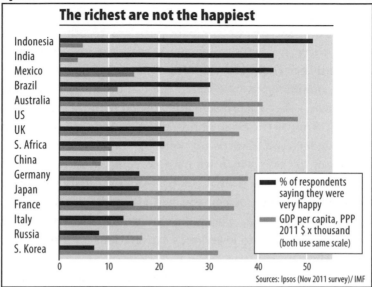

The richest are not the happiest

happiness, or wealth and well-being, have shown little correlation between these two important aspects of life, but they have shown a significant correlation between income equality and happiness.[1]

As Figure 113 shows, some of the poorest countries have some of the happiest people, just as long as the wealth is spread reasonably fairly. Obviously there are other factors one must take into consideration, such as climate and culture and the way people respond to such surveys, but the important point as far as this investigation is concerned is that a reduction in average incomes doesn't have to mean a decline in well-being, and if such a reduction can be accompanied by greater equality, could even lead to greater happiness.

The key is how reality conforms to people's expectations, and expectations increase with wealth, often more than the actual standard of living. Once certain basic necessities are provided for, greater income leads to greater aspirations, and these aspirations often become unrealistic; our satisfaction relative to spending decreases. It is likely also that the kinds of people who aspire to have more are also those who are less easily satisfied.

As we become wealthier, we become more concerned with our place in society: we compare ourselves to others, and of course there is always someone around the corner who is apparently better off than us. We resent the rich flaunting their wealth, reminding us how unfair life can be. But we shouldn't envy them – they are probably dissatisfied with their own lives anyway. And, as the Stoic philosophers of ancient Greece and Rome understood, there is no point in worrying about all the aspects of life over which we have no control. Better to heed the advice of Seneca: if what you have doesn't satisfy you, then, however much you possess, you will always be miserable. Or, better still, Epictetus, who pointed out that the best way to achieve happiness is to lower one's expectations until they meet with reality.

Cause and effect are not obvious when it comes to such a vague concept as happiness, but the evidence suggests that equality is much more important than outright wealth, at least in monetary terms. Prosperity is linked to other things besides money – health, relationships, environment, work – while unemployment is, not surprisingly, one of the biggest causes of unhappiness.

Another advantage to redefining prosperity is that all the arguments against higher taxes and greater regulation of finance – that we will discourage free enterprise by limiting the motivation of entrepreneurs to create great wealth – lose what little credibility they might have had, once we accept that growth is no longer desirable and that we need to cut our consumption of resources anyway. The big question now is how to improve our living standards in more subtle ways than simply consuming more and more of the world's finite resources and warming up the world, threatening to wipe out humanity in the process.

While it will still be desirable and even essential to encourage investment in real industry, and also to encourage entrepreneurs to find solutions to problems through technology, we shouldn't have to rely on the motives of self-interest and greed.

Wrong values

At some point during the second half of the 20th century, there crept into US corporate culture (and spread from there across the Atlantic and around the globe) the idea that senior managers and executives generally, whether industrial or financial or whatever, should be rewarded highly for their 'success', assuming the company did well and profits were high (and sometimes even if they did badly). Never mind that they were already well paid and that their only real achievement was to do their job properly, that there were many factors involved in the success of the company, not all of them due to brilliant management.

These people had decided amongst themselves, in boardrooms across America, that they deserved bonuses for doing a good job, that it was important to have these 'incentives' to keep them motivated and to prevent them from being lured away by a rival company.

Why was this? Surely the kind of person who has no loyalty to anything other than money is just the kind of person you don't want in charge of something as important as a large corporation employing thousands of people. Can we not see now, after the excesses of the last boom and the resulting bank failures and scandals, that these were never the right people anyway, that values had somehow become distorted by a culture in which the only things of importance were sales, profit, status and material riches? There was no consideration for society as a whole, for the environment or how sustainable such a lifestyle might be.

And all the while the real workers were left behind as the wealth gap widened, and none of this had anything to do with merit or justice. It is essential for the well-being of future generations that we abandon this whole culture of excessive reward that can never truly have been earned. It is time to consider what really matters in life, to look at the long-term benefits to society and humanity, rather than the short-term profit.

If we can encourage a new outlook in which talented people work for the good of society rather than an inflated wage, we will discover rewards far beyond material wealth. Far more satisfaction can be gained from solving some of the world's problems than from 'earning' a high income.

Employment before productivity

I made the point earlier that there's enough wealth being produced in this world if only it can be spread around more evenly. We can cut down on consumption without sending the world into greater poverty, but to achieve this objective we need to reverse the trend towards inequality, and there are only two ways to do this.

The first is the obvious one involving taxation, as noted in the previous chapter; a revision of tax policies in favor of a more even distribution of earnings. But although this makes sense and is perfectly justifiable, there are structural limitations with regard to the redistribution of wealth this way. It would be far better to distribute the wealth more evenly in the first place.

The solution lies in making sure everyone has work, while at the same time accepting a lower average wage in rich countries, with the average being brought down from the top. Rather than having a small number of very high earners and a large number struggling along on low pay or no pay at all, we need to get to the heart of the problem and reverse the trend towards higher productivity that has led to the current situation. All this competition for market share, and for profit, has gone too far.

As I said in Chapter 14, the only benefit to higher productivity, when viewed on a global scale, is cheap goods. There are benefits initially for the nations that produce the goods for the least cost, but in the end we all lose out because there aren't enough jobs to go round. So perhaps the answer is to stop trying to make everything as cheaply as possible.

What does it matter if we employ more people than is strictly necessary? The traditional answer is that it's 'inefficient', and this is bad because we live in a competitive world. Going back further, it was the increases in productivity that enabled workers to move from agriculture to the textile mills and create more wealth for society as a whole. That is what industrial development was all about. But as I've already explained, this process has gone beyond the point where it creates more wealth for everyone, because continuous advances in technology mean there aren't enough jobs any more.

If we were to reduce the competitive element and put job creation before productivity, as I argued in Chapter 20 – putting the efficiency of society before the efficiency of any one company or industry or even nation – then the market price of goods would rise to some extent; this is inevitable. But this shouldn't be a problem as long as everyone has work, especially if the cost of housing is reduced at the same time, which should be easy enough to bring about by increasing the stock of public housing and thus reducing the pressure of demand.

In much of England, for example, especially London and the southeast, rising housing costs mean that most people spend ever more of their income on either rent or mortgage payments, as shown in Figure 114, and this money goes to the financiers,

Figure 114

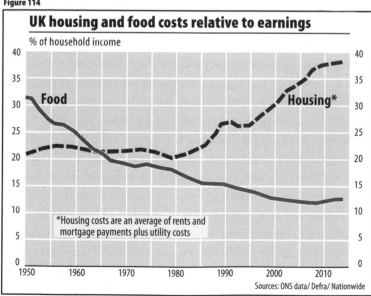

UK housing and food costs relative to earnings

% of household income

*Housing costs are an average of rents and mortgage payments plus utility costs

Food

Housing*

Sources: ONS data/ Defra/ Nationwide

where it benefits the wealthy few, rather than into the general economy. High housing costs relative to wages are a major factor in the rising inequality that is wrecking society. The real producers – the agricultural and industrial workers – and also most service workers, receive an ever-diminishing share of society's wealth as their real earnings fall, while the bankers gain from rising asset prices.

Reasons to be cheerful

So what we find is that several of the problems we've identified – problems linked to the decline in real jobs and the rise of the financial sector – can be tackled by reducing the ratio of finance to real industry. This gives us some hope, because governments can do something about this through policy initiatives, beyond the obvious actions regarding the tightening of bank regulation. For example, by directing investment towards public housing and therefore reducing rental and mortgage costs, the government can help to free up more lower- and middle-class earnings for other purposes, while at the same time reviving the construction industry, which is less affected by productivity improvements than most industries, and is therefore likely to become more important as an employer.

Despite the fact that recent policy in some developed countries, the UK especially, has taken the opposite direction, there is no good reason why the government shouldn't be involved in the business of ensuring that everyone has a place to live. It actually makes a lot of sense for the state to provide affordable housing, as many European nations do and as Britain did before the rise of the monetarists and the financiers. It is hardly coincidental that house prices have risen so much in the UK while the stock of local-authority housing has fallen, as shown in Figure 115.

Such state involvement doesn't have to be heavy handed or bureaucratic; the public sector can oversee the process at a regional or local-government level, while contracting out the actual building work to the private sector. The cost of housing

Figure 115

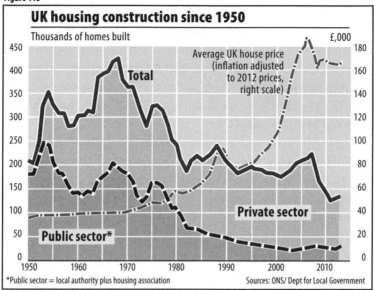

UK housing construction since 1950

Thousands of homes built — £,000

Average UK house price (inflation adjusted to 2012 prices, right scale)

Total

Private sector

Public sector*

*Public sector = local authority plus housing association   Sources: ONS/ Dept for Local Government

can be brought down and lower-paid workers will have more of their income to spend on other things. At the same time, construction jobs will be created, and because construction is a productive industry that is not too dependent on oil and uses resources that are not in danger of depletion,[2] this is an area – along with the related business of providing public utilities such as power, water supplies and more efficient transport networks – where it is particularly helpful to create employment.

We can also tie this policy in with our other major initiative besides job creation, because the government can ensure that the new housing is built to the latest energy-efficiency requirements, with higher standards of insulation, solar panels on the roof, geothermal heating, efficient appliances and so on. It can also be built on land that has no other use, such as old industrial sites or other 'brownfield' areas, within urban boundaries that are served by extensive public transport. In addition to this new construction, local authorities could instigate a program for the upgrading of existing buildings to the latest standards.

The construction boom of the post-War era, as illustrated by

Figure 115 (for Britain, but which also occurred in the rest of Europe, the US and elsewhere), was not just a result of rising wealth but was also a key component of that wealth – part of the virtuous cycle, cause as well as effect. Construction creates real jobs and real wealth, so as long as there is a need for the buildings (unlike in Ireland and Spain during the last boom, for example) it should be encouraged.

There are many such improvements that could be made to the infrastructure generally with more imagination and more commitment from governments, which should show genuine leadership and be unafraid to upset the establishment by directing investment to something useful and productive in the long term, rather than printing money to give to the bankers. The state sector could make use of its 'reserve army' of unemployed workers to do much of the work, without worrying so much about the cost, and this brings me to another idea regarding employment policy.

Army of the employed

I suggested in Chapter 13 that the priority of governments in Europe should be jobs. But it is not just Europe that will have this problem. The priority of governments everywhere should be to ensure that there are enough jobs to go round, especially for younger adults, who are now bearing the brunt of the reduction in real work opportunities. To this end, we might need to think about some form of voluntary recruitment of the unemployed into a civil workforce.

Instead of being paid unemployment benefit for doing nothing while looking for a job that most likely doesn't exist, perhaps young people could be encouraged to join an 'army' of workers and be paid a basic wage to work on government projects. This basic wage would obviously be significantly higher than the unemployment benefit that they would otherwise receive, and where necessary, accommodation and food could be provided, as with a real army.

Such projects would be geared in particular towards rebuilding the infrastructure, but could also include work such as policing, civil defense, looking after the elderly and the needy; anything that could benefit society and provide useful training. These jobs would be like apprenticeships, and would surely be more valuable to most young people than expensive but almost worthless college degrees (perhaps these apprentices could do one of those free internet-based university courses in their spare time!).

Surely it makes more sense to use revenue from taxes to teach useful trades and skills, rather than to pay unemployment benefit for no productive purpose. The kind of construction work involved in rebuilding the infrastructure has a double benefit to the economy, because as well as training and making use of Marx's army of unemployed, it obviously benefits society to improve the roads, railways and sewers, for example, to build new social housing, renovate schools and hospitals, turn industrial wastelands into parks and even perhaps into urban farms. Such productive investment is money well spent, even if the cost has to come from borrowing. Productive debt is useful debt, and if it results in real economic activity, shouldn't add to inflation.

Two other areas in which it should be worthwhile for the state to invest are renewable energy and recycling, as I mentioned earlier. Although the private sector should be encouraged to develop these industries, there are sound arguments for some form of government involvement in such activities, which are becoming vital but are not necessarily profitable in the short term, and which therefore might not attract private investment.

Recycling might seem like just another service along the same lines as waste collection and disposal, which it is often linked with, in the sense that the nature of the work appears similar. But not only is recycling beneficial because it means industry can re-use scarce resources (rather than dumping them in landfill sites, as we've been doing for decades now) it is also becoming an important industry in itself, comparable in nature to the extraction of raw materials from the earth.

The actual work involved might not seem to carry the same 'heavy' connotations as mining, but the resulting provision of raw materials for industry means that recycling should be considered as a primary-sector business, and as such a creator of real wealth. In other words, it should be developed as far as possible, even if this requires state investment. Although the proportion of materials being recycled has grown considerably in recent years – half of all metals used in industry now come from recycling, for example – there is plenty of room for further improvement, as shown in Figure 116.

The same applies to the renewable-energy industry and the infrastructure that will be required for its development. The overwhelming dominance of the oil industry makes it difficult for renewable energy to compete on equal terms with oil and gas, so state intervention of some kind is essential, if only to encourage the private sector to get more involved in what ought to become perhaps the major growth industry of the future.

Although there have been state subsidies for the installation of solar panels in the UK and elsewhere during the last decade, with successful results for the most part, many such initiatives died after the financial crisis, as politicians diverted funding towards propping up the banks, rather than supporting worthwhile ventures that might in the longer term lead to a revival of employment in the real economy.

In addition to higher prices, what other drawbacks might there be to employing more workers than are strictly necessary in purely economic terms? Wages will be kept down, certainly, but that is already happening under the current system, and we can still maintain a reasonable minimum wage. Profits will be reduced, but as we need to revise our conception of wealth anyway, we shouldn't worry too much about profit. Our priority should be to get everyone working, or as many as are able to work at least, so that everyone has the opportunity to create the value that comes only through work.

More wealth will be created by having more people working

Figure 116

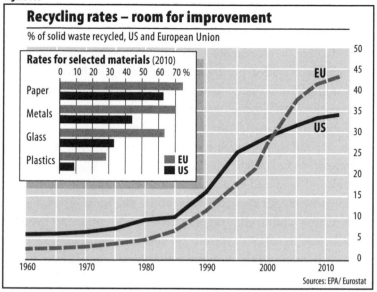

Recycling rates – room for improvement

% of solid waste recycled, US and European Union

Rates for selected materials (2010)

Sources: EPA/ Eurostat

in real jobs, even if that wealth can't necessarily be measured in monetary terms. And as there will be fewer very poor people, society will benefit from having the wealth spread more evenly around the local economy, rather than going into offshore investment funds and adding to the debt problem.

Obviously there's a limit to how 'inefficient' we can make industry before it becomes ridiculous. I'm not suggesting that we fill the factories with however many workers happen to be loitering outside the gates. Everyone should have a definite job to do. All I'm suggesting is that, just because you can replace 10 workers with one machine, it does not mean you should do so. It might not be the most efficient solution for society as a whole. If we examine certain aspects of agriculture, for example, we get some idea of the implications of such policies on productivity.

Back to the land

Agriculture was the first major industry and, for most of the last 9,000 years, following the planting of the first crops by early civilizations, it remained the most important. Right until the very end of the 20th century, farming employed the majority of the world's workers. And despite the fact that, according to GDP figures, it represents only one or two per cent of most developed economies, one could argue that agriculture is still the most important industry. If we don't eat, we don't do anything.

I mentioned in Chapter 4 that the US is the biggest agricultural producer in the world, or the third biggest after China and India, depending on which measure we use. The reason for this vagueness in the statistics is that, although the US has the most agricultural land and the highest crop yields in the world, and therefore we might expect it to produce the most crops, figures from China and India suggest that both countries produce considerably more food overall. Such data is not always accurate or directly comparable, but the interesting point is that China and India, while being much less 'efficient' than the US, in that they require far more farm workers to produce the same amount of food, actually manage to feed a lot more people, despite having less farmland.

This is of course partly because, on average, each Chinese or

Figure 117

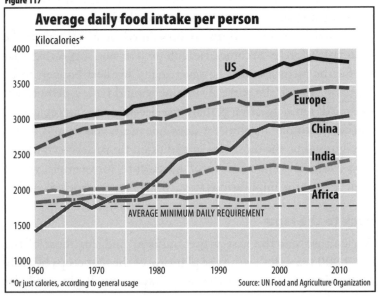

Indian eats less than the average American (as shown in Figure 117), but in reality there's a lot more to it than that.

The US has a highly mechanized farming culture, the most productive in the world in that respect. China and India use much more traditional farming methods, much less advanced in terms of mechanization. Comparing the US with China, we encounter some interesting statistics. First, the two countries are very close in geographical size, China having a bit more land area, while the US is listed as being slightly larger only when territorial waters are included. They also grow about the same amount of produce, at least in terms of crops (China grows more vegetables).

There the similarities end, however, because the US has a lot more arable land on which to grow this produce, while China has around a hundred times as many farm workers. So which is the most productive? The nation that grows 500 million tonnes of crops a year with only 3 million workers, or the nation that produces the same amount of food from half the agricultural land, using 300 million workers?

China obviously makes more efficient use of its land, if not of its workers. By most estimates, it produces considerably more food than the US, because many of those farming families keep pigs and hens and work small plots of land very intensively. Nobody really knows exactly how much pork or how many eggs

Agriculture: top producers compared

	Total grain & oilseed production, million tonnes	Arable land, million hectares	Agricultural land total*, million hectares	Average farm size, hectares	Head of cattle, million	Total agricultural workers (thousands)
US	498	140	370	167	96	3,300
China	495	90	160	1	120	300,000
India	255	100	140	1.5	280	250,000
Brazil	150	60	190	70	200	17,000
Russia	100	120	200	50	22	10,000
France	72	19	28	54	20	900

*Including pasture, range etc, not necessarily in permanent use

Figures are for 2010/11   Sources: US Department of Agriculture/ Eurostat/ FAO

they produce, or how many vegetables they grow in their gardens. What matters is that China feeds four times as many people and employs a hundred times as many farm workers, while having only half as much good farmland. And while it is now a net importer of food, whereas the US is a net exporter, China was largely self-sufficient until its people became wealthier and began to eat more.

What would those 300 million workers be doing if they weren't farming the land? As Figure 92 showed, manufacturing in China, having drawn 100 million workers from the fields to the factories, has already stopped expanding in terms of employment, as it follows the development pathway to ever-increasing productivity. The technology giant Foxconn, which makes parts for big global brands such as Apple and Sony, is in the process of building two new fully automated factories in China and has stopped recruiting workers altogether in some areas.

Chinese agriculture has its failings – linked to misguided government policies in the past, when the motivation factor was killed by central planners, and overuse of chemical fertilizers in the present – but in many respects it must count as an extremely successful industry, one that will remain vital to the employment of the majority of Chinese workers long into the future, until perhaps the population dwindles to half its current size.

Surely it is better to have lots of people working on the land, at least managing to feed themselves, rather than having them migrate to the cities, only to find that all those jobs they'd heard about have already disappeared because the factories have become more productive.

Fields of opportunity

If the US, or any other developed nation, were to reverse the trend towards mechanization and industrialization to some degree, and to utilize some of the more labor-intensive farming methods that work for countries such as China and India, while still making the most of modern techniques, it could improve

Figure 118

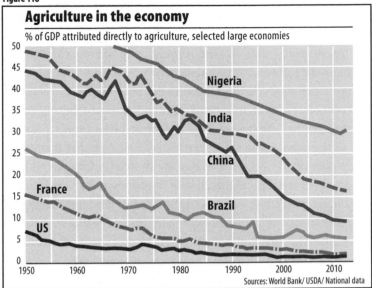

Agriculture in the economy

% of GDP attributed directly to agriculture, selected large economies

Nigeria

India

China

France

Brazil

US

Sources: World Bank/ USDA/ National data

soil conditions and sustainability, and produce higher-quality food while maintaining high yields.[3] At the same time this would create several million real jobs – jobs that would be extremely beneficial to a new generation of workers who would learn about good farming practice, and to society as a whole, especially the rural areas that have suffered in recent years from depopulation.

So the question is: does it matter that the Chinese and Indian farm laborers are less efficient than American farmers in terms of output per worker? Land is in short supply, and becoming ever more so, while workers are more abundant than ever. So if employing more workers means better use of the land, it surely makes sense to use them.

The traditional economic argument is that once the economy becomes more developed and workers move from agriculture to industry, they will produce more wealth. This is what 'development' means, in the economic context. But, as I have pointed out, this can only apply if new jobs are created in new industries, as happened in the West and Japan over the last two centuries, and over the last decades in China and other emerging nations.

But there won't be millions of new jobs created in new industries if the factories of the world are all going to become ever more productive, so we should stop trying to increase productivity and concentrate instead on creating useful jobs.

Figure 118 shows how agriculture has been falling, as a share of total economic output, in various large countries at differing stages of development. We can see how in China it now represents only 10% of the economy in GDP terms, even though it still employs nearly 40% of all workers. I've already shown (in Chapter 4) how this apparent trend for the declining importance of farming to the economy is misleading, because of the way GDP figures exaggerate the contribution of services, especially finance. I think we need to acknowledge this failing in the figures that most governments rely upon, and appreciate the importance of agriculture and the critical role it will play in a sustainable economy (assuming, of course, that we still want to eat real food).

A move away from the large-scale industrial farming methods that are common in North America and Britain and other parts of northern Europe, back to a more family-oriented scale, as seen in much of southern Europe as well as Asia and Africa, would be generally beneficial. It might include the kind of co-operative structuring that can bring economies of scale without taking mechanization and productivity so far that they destroy jobs and reduce the long-term productivity of the soil, as tends to happen with farming methods that rely heavily on chemical fertilization. There would be many benefits to such a shift and only one cost, which would be a rise in food prices. But paying a bit more for better food is not such a bad thing if it improves the environment and creates real jobs. In the end, society – meaning all of us – will be better off.

Figure 119 illustrates three different aspects of total world grain production since 1950. In particular, it shows how the yield – the amount of grain produced per given unit of land – has been rising at about twice the rate of overall production as a result of improved farming methods. But this trend towards higher yields

Figure 119

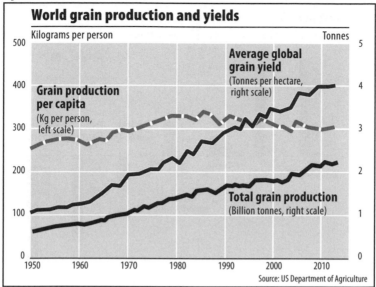

World grain production and yields

Kilograms per person — Tonnes

Average global grain yield (Tonnes per hectare, right scale)

Grain production per capita (Kg per person, left scale)

Total grain production (Billion tonnes, right scale)

Source: US Department of Agriculture

has levelled off in the last few years, and food production per head of population has fallen slightly since 1980.

Pessimists have been predicting that population growth would lead to food shortages and mass starvation since the late 18th century, when Thomas Malthus became famous for expounding such ideas, and although since then there have been terrible famines in various regions of the world, they have been the exception rather than the rule. On the whole, agricultural improvements have continued to deliver plenty of food, though not always to the parts of the world that really need it (as seen in Figure 120).

From the firm to the farm

There must be a limit to how much food we can grow, however, especially if the amount of fertile land is reduced by climatic changes, so it makes sense to look at more labor-intensive farming methods for the developed world, if it will lead to higher yields, as it obviously does in parts of Asia.

As it happens, this idea of creating more jobs in agriculture is actually taking place in the struggling nations of southern

Figure 120

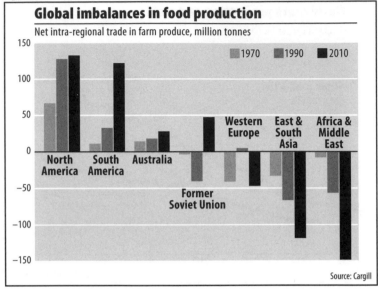

Global imbalances in food production

Net intra-regional trade in farm produce, million tonnes

Source: Cargill

Europe. With so many young people unable to find work in Spain, for example, many are returning to family farms to help out in an unofficial capacity (meaning they are still registered as foot-soldiers in the ever-growing army of the unemployed), even if they aren't strictly needed and are paid little. To be doing something in the countryside is better than doing nothing in the city. The same thing is happening in Greece, especially with the young, but also with middle-aged people who have given up on the urban struggle and gone back to the land. We are instinctively drawn towards the land, those of us who haven't entirely lost that primordial connection.

Even in China there has recently been a reversal of the trend for migration from rural areas to the new cities. Already people are going back to their family farms, having endured the monotonous work and cramped living conditions for long enough.

To live in a city is to live among humanity and all its manifestations, which has its own appeal. But to live away from the city, to be surrounded by the sky and the land, the hills and the forests and the fields, is to understand that humanity is only a tiny part of the environment, that we are entirely dependent on the land, on nature. You can't see that in the city. And as more and more people move from the rural heartlands to the city, so more and more people lose this feeling for the land. Yet this connection with the land must not be lost, because the earth is our only source of wealth.

We will continue to live a predominantly urban existence – there is no practical alternative as populations grow, and city life has certain advantages in that it can be made more energy-efficient than rural life – but we must not forget or ignore our link to the land. The answer must lie in education: a more sustainable lifestyle is something that can be taught. Once people begin to understand what is at stake, it will become much easier to bring about the necessary changes.

A part of every child's education should therefore be about this dependence on the earth that lies beneath the concrete and the asphalt that forms and engulfs our cities. Cities are just islands of humanity in the vast oceans of land (and the real oceans) that are the source of all our wealth. The skyscrapers of the city represent that wealth, have risen from the earth, even if the earth can no longer be seen around them.

Because of its inability to account for anything outside the marketplace, capitalism fails to include the true value of nature in its pricing structure. The capitalists, meaning the owners and the financiers, run blindly along on a 'treadmill of production', to quote Marx, caring only about the next sale. The future beyond the next deal doesn't enter into the equation, and neither does the natural wealth of the earth, which is there only to be exploited, regardless of the long-term cost.

This failure of our current system to include nature in the picture has set us on the path to self-destruction. To see nature as separate from the economy, from life, is obviously absurd, yet that's the way most of us go about our business.

This remoteness from the land, this 'separateness' from nature, leads us to forget that we are entirely dependent on nature, leads us to take no account of the fact that all our wealth, everything we have, has come from the earth, and must always come from the earth. We can't create new wealth from old money, simply by recycling and leveraging the accumulated capital of past industry. The result of trying to do so is the devaluation of that past wealth and the end of real work. Trying to make money from money can lead only to poverty and the devaluation of life itself.

1 These surveys include: Easterlin (1995) – individual happiness appears to be the same across poor and rich countries; Oswald (1997) – extra income is not contributing dramatically to the quality of people's lives; Diener and Seligman (2012) – income growth in developed countries over recent decades has led to no significant increases in subjective well-being.

2 Most of the raw materials used in construction are in plentiful supply and relatively easy to extract without great damage to the environment, with the exception of the growing use of plastics in some countries. In the UK, for example, there has been a trend towards the use of PVC window and door frames, which ought to be reversed in favour of timber from sustainable forests. Plastic is a poor material from an ecological point of view, and from every other viewpoint except convenience. The spread of PVC window frames represents another example of the reduction in overall quality that results from trying to make things easier; less work equals lower value.

3 There is no reason why sustainable agriculture – organic, a variety of crops in smaller fields, crop rotation with fallow periods, biological pest control – shouldn't produce just as much or even more food than industrial-scale monoculture. Genuinely organic farms in California have shown yield levels for corn, wheat and soya in the region of 95% to 100% of the most productive farms in the US. And in many parts of the world, the organic SRI (System of Rice Intensification) method has consistently produced higher yields than conventional methods, according to the Cornell International Institute for Food, Agriculture and Development.

22 Where next?

Likely trends; why the US will stay on top

It seems inevitable that the process of globalization will continue its relentless march until the world becomes one giant free-trade zone, affecting all our lives in ways both good and bad, while sidelining the individual nations that try to hold out against it. National borders are, for the most part, artificial and arbitrary, and, even when they aren't, such as the seas surrounding Britain, they hardly contain a unified and separate people. We are all citizens of the world now, whether we like it or not.

So how is this continuation of globalization likely to affect us, and how does it relate to the problems I've been writing about?

We have seen how the market, basing prices on the immediate supply-and-demand situation, but ignoring less obvious factors, such as sustainability, often fails to value things correctly. I cited the example of some financial traders earning huge sums from betting on the currency markets, even though such 'work' lacks real value and is actually detrimental to society.

Building on Marx's theory that labor is the source of all economic value, I have tried to show how every transaction in the global marketplace represents an exchange of labor, and that money ultimately represents the value of that labor, or at least it should do. But the distortion of values by the free-market mechanism – that inability to account for factors beyond the immediate supply-and-demand situation – means that prices often fail to reflect the true value of labor, just as they fail to reflect the true value of the limited resources, or the hidden cost of environmental destruction. We have a situation in the world today in which we can buy a complex piece of technology such as a digital camera, to take a simple example, for as little as $50. This camera might be bought by a doctor or a lawyer in the West who earns $200 per hour. This is obviously not a fair exchange: the global marketplace has failed to establish the correct relationship between the two forms of labor, overvaluing the Western professional while undervaluing both the Chinese worker and the cost of materials.

This is a function of a particular stage in the development of globalization, one in which unfair competition, brought about by unequal opportunities regarding the flow of money relative to the flow of labor, has distorted values. This is likely to change, however, because already there are doctors and lawyers in countries such as India and Romania who are able to offer their services globally at a much lower rate, and this trend will grow as the English language spreads into classrooms everywhere. And, as I mentioned earlier with regard to university courses, services such as law and accountancy, and even medicine to some extent, will become increasingly vulnerable to competition from sophisticated computer software.

Breaking down the barriers

This expansion of the global marketplace is a natural progression of the desire to trade goods that began thousands of years ago, when the early civilizations of Mesopotamia, Egypt and the Indus Valley dispatched merchants in search of spices, cloth, dyes and precious metals, creating the incense routes of southern Arabia, the Silk Road to China and the coastal shipping routes that led eventually to mighty empires and the interconnected world of today. Civilization was built on trade.

Barriers to trade, and periods of nationalistic isolation generally, might be seen as a relatively recent phase of human history, and even if such sentiments still lurk in the dark extremes of politics, they're becoming less common and will surely fade away as less isolated generations – those growing up with the internet – take over. Such protectionism, and the nationalism that goes with it, has of course been a major cause of wars, as the French economist Frédéric Bastiat noted in the mid-19th century: 'If goods don't cross borders, armies will.'

It was partly for this reason that what is now the European

Union was formed in 1951, as the European Coal and Steel Community – a common market with a 'supranational' level of authority, designed specifically by the French to end forever the possibility of war with Germany, 'to make war unthinkable', as its founder Robert Schuman proposed. And despite the Eurozone's current difficulties, and much huffing and puffing by conservative politicians, the European Union has been a great success. War in Europe really is unthinkable now. The nations of Europe have also benefited from an ever-expanding open market, and from having a united voice that can still be heard in the bustle of the global marketplace.

But this continued march of globalization brings with it the need for a higher level of democratic representation, otherwise democracy will be weakened further by the rise of the powerful transnational corporations, the biggest beneficiaries of this lack of regulation. As some of the less open societies are finding now, the free flow of information and ideas around the globe is difficult to control in these days of instantly accessible data and communication. Although most of us might have nothing to fear from the universal spread of information and ideas, we should at least be concerned about the lack of regulation when it comes to the free transfer of money out of the realms of national jurisdiction – money that supposedly represents the wealth of the people.

There is an inconsistency – a source of potential conflict – between a global marketplace on the one hand, and sovereign states on the other, with their politics governed by national interests, seemingly in competition with other nations. We need to reduce this competitive element and work together as members of one great civilization, with certain rules set by some form of global governing body. This might sound horribly totalitarian, but it doesn't have to be; the democratic process can still function at this level, aided perhaps by modern technology.

But who is going to bring about this necessary change? Who has the power to rule beyond national borders? We hear much talk about the 'international community', but in reality this is a rather meaningless and self-contradictory term. Yes, we are all citizens of the world, but, as for community, that is a local thing: we can't be expected to involve ourselves in the affairs of people on the other side of the globe. For this reason, we need democracy to work at several levels: local or regional, national and international. But we also want less bureaucracy and pointless regulation.

The two goals are not as incompatible as they might seem, but they require more transparency, greater accountability and simpler rules that are fairly enforced. At the moment we have complex layers of ineffective bureaucracy, especially above the national level. The United Nations, for example, has far less authority on the world stage as an organization than the more influential of its member countries have individually. Nothing is going to change without the backing of the nations that really rule the world. But change is essential: we have to figure out the best way for local communities to function democratically within a global economy. In the end, it all comes down to the people.

I shall return to this subject later in the chapter, but first we should take note of a few other global trends that seem bound to affect all our lives in one way or another.

The taming of the dragon

Much has been said about the likelihood of China overtaking the US to become the world's largest economy in the next decade or so, as I showed in Figure 94. But although China might become the world's biggest economy in terms of industrial output, it is highly unlikely that nations such as China and India will ever approach the levels of wealth seen in the US and Europe. Ignoring the fact that an increase in consumption on such a massive scale – the two nations account for 2.5 billion people, compared to 800 million for the US and Europe combined – would surely be disastrous for the environment, the economic growth required to boost

Figure 121

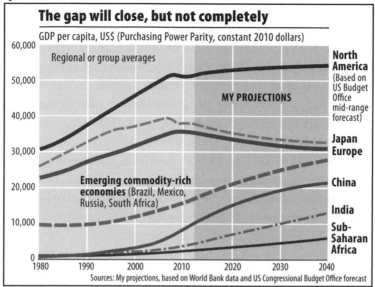

The gap will close, but not completely

GDP per capita, US$ (Purchasing Power Parity, constant 2010 dollars)

Regional or group averages

MY PROJECTIONS

North America (Based on US Budget Office mid-range forecast)

Japan Europe

Emerging commodity-rich economies (Brazil, Mexico, Russia, South Africa)

China

India

Sub-Saharan Africa

Sources: My projections, based on World Bank data and US Congressional Budget Office forecast

individual wealth to such levels cannot be sustained for more than a few years without the economy overheating. China's rapid growth is already slowing down, as wages and productivity rise along with prices, and demand eases off both within China and throughout the world.

It seems far more likely, and far more desirable from an ecological viewpoint, that the developing nations will gradually close the gap on the rich world through a combination of continuing moderate growth on their part, accompanied by a decline in overall wealth levels in much of the rich world.

In Figure 121 I have plotted, with a little help from the US Congressional Budget Office, what I think is a likely scenario for this adjustment in relative wealth.

While it seems inevitable that Europe and Japan will see a permanent decline in wealth, the prospects for the Americas generally, and North America in particular, seem less bleak. This is due mainly to the ratio of natural resources to the number of people. There has always been a direct relationship between natural resources and wealth, but whereas in the

317

past Europe grew rich by plundering the natural wealth of colonized lands, these days it has to pay the going rate for the raw materials of industry, most of which it must import, and this rate is bound to keep rising as resources become scarcer. So it follows that those bigger nations with abundant natural wealth and not too many people will most likely benefit, as we have already seen to varying degrees in Canada, Australia, Brazil and Russia.

The US has two big advantages over Europe. As well as having a much greater abundance of land and mineral wealth, it also has demographic advantages related to a younger population, and both of these factors will give it greater flexibility when it comes to budget balances and debt repayment.

There is a big question mark here, however, because the US debt burden could get a lot worse over coming decades, depending on what action the government takes. My next two charts come from recent reports by the US Congressional Budget Office, which analyze the long-term outlook and come to some rather startling conclusions.

Obligations that won't be met

Figure 122 shows how US debt is set to explode unless the government can cut spending and raise taxes (which as I write it is trying to do, but the rival politicians can't agree on much). In the worst-case scenario envisaged by the Budget Office, which means carrying on the way things have been going over the last few years: 'The reduction in GNP would lie in a broad range around 4% in 2027 and in a broad range around 13% in 2037.'

In other words, the economy is set to contract significantly because of the debt burden, entering a vicious spiral of job losses, falling incomes, inflation and rising interest rates, all of which will make the problem far worse. The report concludes:

'The ageing of the US population and the rising costs for healthcare mean that the combination of budget policies that

Figure 122

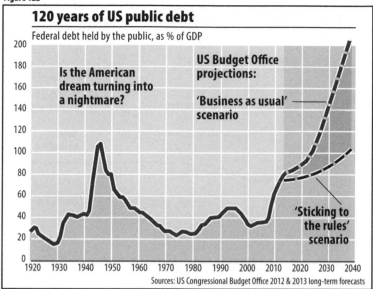

120 years of US public debt

Federal debt held by the public, as % of GDP

Is the American dream turning into a nightmare?

US Budget Office projections:

'Business as usual' scenario

'Sticking to the rules' scenario

Sources: US Congressional Budget Office 2012 & 2013 long-term forecasts

worked in the past cannot be maintained in the future. To keep deficits and debt from climbing to unsustainable levels, as they will if the set of current policies is continued, policymakers will need to increase revenues substantially above historical levels as a percentage of GDP, decrease spending significantly from projected levels, or adopt some combination of those two approaches.'

This is quite a dramatic admission from a government office, one that is also applicable to some European nations, though they are less inclined to state the issue so clearly. The report is making the point, quite simply, that the West is going to get poorer. Without going so deeply into the fundamentals, the authors are confirming many of the points I have been making in this book. We have been borrowing substantially from future earnings, and one way or another we will have to repay those loans.

So the US is faced with currently unsustainable social-welfare obligations: it cannot meet future pension and healthcare promises, as Figure 123 shows. Much of Europe is in the same

Figure 123

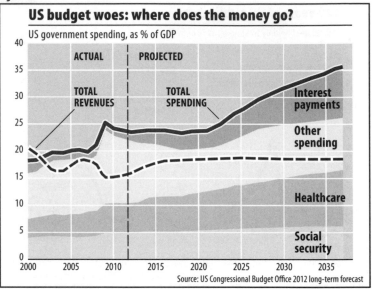

US budget woes: where does the money go?

US government spending, as % of GDP

ACTUAL | PROJECTED

TOTAL REVENUES

TOTAL SPENDING

Interest payments

Other spending

Healthcare

Social security

Source: US Congressional Budget Office 2012 long-term forecast

position. These promises will be broken.

The US, however, has better prospects for solving this problem, partly because its economy could still show spurts of growth, helped by new oil and natural gas reserves made possible by its development of 'fracking' technology. The resulting cheap natural gas is already attracting businesses from other nations, as the US becomes once again a competitive place to make things. In addition, China will lose its cost advantages as wages rise there; the balance is likely to swing back in America's favor, especially if US wages continue to fall in real terms.

Despite environmental concerns, fracking is the only real boom industry on the horizon right now, and the US will most likely be the biggest beneficiary, thanks to its technological lead in the field. From an ecological viewpoint this is not good news, but as far as the US economy goes, it probably is.

On top of this advantage on the revenue side, the US has greater leeway than Europe in making the required spending cuts, especially with regard to healthcare, an area in which the US is spending twice as much as most other developed nations, while getting extremely poor value for that spending, as I showed in Figure 108. If the government can get its act together and drastically cut health spending, all is not lost.

In fact healthcare in all developed economies is an increasing burden on budgets, and the returns on this spending are declining. The evidence suggests that we have gone too far along this route into costly medical care. I mentioned in the previous chapter how the US spends nine times as much per person on healthcare as its southern neighbor Mexico, yet Americans on average live only a year or two longer than Mexicans.

Something is obviously not right here. Even compared to Britain, the US is getting very poor value for its health spending, as Figure 124 shows.

Modern technology has led to impressive advances in medicine, but often these are extremely expensive, which is why health services can be such a huge drain on the wealth of individuals and states alike. It is, of course, understandable that most people think it worth spending large sums of money to extend life expectancy, to gain a few years having been diagnosed with cancer, for example. But from a wider perspective, if a rather inhuman one, such costs do not represent good value.

Even the wealthiest nations can no longer afford to spend vast sums on healthcare, and must target their money to obtain the best value. We have to accept that resources are limited and difficult decisions have to be made. We have to accept that we can't live forever.

Survival of the fattest

We inhabitants of the rich West have become unsuited to a poorer world. We have been sheltered too long from the brutality of life on the edge. The survival-of-the-fittest rule might still apply in the marketplace, but it no longer applies to the mollycoddled, overweight, car-dependent, air-conditioned citizens of much of the developed world. Instead of being lean and fit, we survive only with the help of gargantuan healthcare systems that now

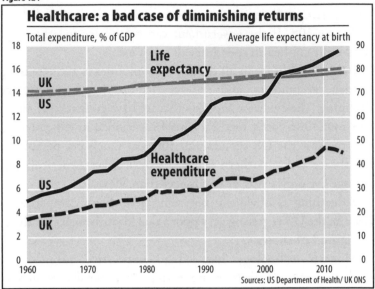

Healthcare: a bad case of diminishing returns

threaten, along with other 'essential' life-support systems, to bankrupt us all.

The reality is that ultra-expensive healthcare services are a luxury we can barely afford. We attach so much value to treating every ailment, forever seeking the miracle cure to cancer and anything else that might prevent us squeezing a few more years out of our precious lives, that we have created a huge non-productive 'industry' that, like its close cousin finance, sucks an ever greater share of the wealth created by real industry. Is it worth it?

Not only is there a law of diminishing returns involved with regard to health spending, but it is quite possible that if the drain on national budgets reduces the spending power of the people, as it ultimately must do, it could actually have a negative impact on health, because it increases unemployment and poverty and thus causes greater stress on those affected. Could some of this wealth not be put to better use in ensuring that young people have jobs and places to live, instead of in attempting to raise the average lifespan by another year or two?

Perhaps the time has come to face a few hard truths. We can't escape the Grim Reaper, and spending billions of dollars on healthcare doesn't really change that fact. Keeping people going beyond their natural time is economically unproductive, and in the overall scheme of things there is no value in it. We must make the most of our youth, try to live our lives to the full – we must go for quality rather than quantity. This is where the real value of life lies, not in gaining a few more years when we are already past it.

It might even be that we have ended up with an economic system that panders to our desire for an easy life because the evolutionary process itself has been disrupted by our success. Having become accustomed to comfort – to the idea that the good life doesn't have to require much real work or physical effort, that we can find solutions to everything through technology, even to old age and the ill-health that results from this addiction to ease – we have ended up with a society that is too far removed from nature to function properly.

In one sense, the drain of health spending represents the cost of disrupting the laws of natural selection, and the more we interfere, the more we must pay. We have become too lazy, and the system reflects this. We have become too dependent on our cars and computers and cellphones and all our other labor-saving gadgets. The wealthy of the world might have thrived in a material sense, but physically and mentally this desire for comfort – this laziness – has made us vulnerable to any failure of the system, a system that has become too complex to control or even to be fully understood. If life gets tougher on the streets, the survivors won't be the wealthy of the world. The survivors will be those who have already adapted to life on the margins and have mastered the art of survival.

As the developed world becomes less wealthy, attitudes will most likely return to the more realistic approach that we find in poorer regions of the world, or even some reasonably wealthy ones such as Mexico and other Latin American nations, where everyone accepts that some people die before their time, and really there's not a great deal we can do about it, however much money we might spend on overpaid doctors and state-of-the-art equipment. Whatever the reason, whether it be pragmatism or poverty, we are going to spend less on healthcare in the future, simply because the money won't be available.

But as my charts on health and happiness showed, this doesn't necessarily mean a decline in quality of life, or even in lifespans, merely an end to the unrealistic and rather pointless quest to live beyond our naturally allotted time on this earth.

East or west?

Despite its huge build-up of debt, and assuming the government can do more to reduce inequality and focus on job creation, the US is likely to retain a level of prosperity above all but a few less populous nations that have oil wealth or other minerals, such as Norway, Australia, Canada and some Persian Gulf states. Inflation will reduce the debt burden one way or another, as I explained earlier, and the price of raw materials will rise to reflect this devaluation of money and the scarcity of resources.

All of these factors will be highly significant regarding America's future prospects relative to China or any other potential rival to its current world dominance. China will close the gap, but it seems unlikely that it will get anywhere near to US levels of wealth per person. The US might have woken from its 20th-century dream to find reality a bit less alluring, but it remains the world's only real superpower, and the situation is unlikely to change in the foreseeable future, partly because of its overwhelming military superiority, as shown in Figure 125.

Such a huge defense budget obviously presents the US government with another area in which it could significantly reduce public spending. But it seems unlikely that this will happen to a degree that will affect America's pre-eminent position, which is closely linked to this military superiority, not just because of its overwhelming firepower, but also because the US lead in

Figure 125

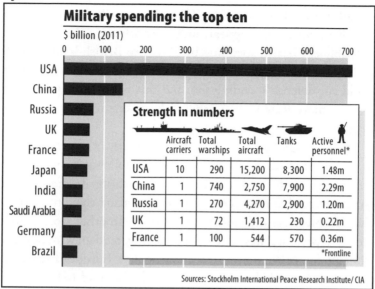

Military spending: the top ten

$ billion (2011)

Strength in numbers

	Aircraft carriers	Total warships	Total aircraft	Tanks	Active personnel*
USA	10	290	15,200	8,300	1.48m
China	1	740	2,750	7,900	2.29m
Russia	1	270	4,270	2,900	1.20m
UK	1	72	1,412	230	0.22m
France	1	100	544	570	0.36m

*Frontline

Sources: Stockholm International Peace Research Institute/ CIA

technology generally is a direct result of government spending on research and development, as I mentioned in Chapter 19. America's huge defense budget also has hidden benefits related to the employment of millions of people, not just in the armed forces but also in aerospace and other industries – industries that manufacture things, and therefore create real wealth.

One could perhaps make the same argument regarding healthcare spending, and it is true that some of that money goes into making medical equipment. But there are big differences. Much of US health spending goes to insurance and drug companies and to highly paid doctors, where it adds to the inequality that is wrecking society. The military, on the other hand, is relatively egalitarian, with a top general's pay reaching only around 10 times that of the lowest-ranked private, compared to the hundred times or more found in the private sector, including healthcare.

One can argue about the moral aspects of such a huge military budget, and the fact that doctors are surely more useful to modern society than are soldiers, but, from an economic perspective, defense spending is not necessarily the huge drain that it might at first appear, unlike healthcare. The US could probably cut health spending by 50% – to British levels – with little loss to society and with long-term gains to the economy. It could cut defense spending too, and this is my main point: the US has more leeway than other rich nations when it comes to debt reduction.

It is also significant, with regard to America's continuing role as the only real superpower, that the US dollar and the English language have become the *de facto* international standards, a situation that has both resulted from, and also helped to sustain, that US business and cultural dominance. In other words, such global supremacy has a self-perpetuating tendency, making it difficult for other nations to challenge, as Europe discovered when it launched the euro, partly in the hope of reducing the influence of the US dollar. This has not happened, as Figure 126 shows. The dominance of the dollar is not good for the world, which feels compelled to put much of its savings into US dollars, even though the ability of the US to service its debts is declining, as the chart shows.

There is a potential solution to this problem, however.

Time for a global currency?

I suggested earlier that a process of excessive credit creation over the last two decades or so has resulted in the inflation of the money supply relative to the real process of wealth creation in the underlying economy, so that money is now overvalued by around a third in relation to the real wealth of industry, meaning that commodities are currently undervalued. As with many aspects of economics, this is difficult to prove, but it is generally accepted that our monetary system is far from perfect, and is one of the primary causes of the present crisis.

The Austrian economist Ludwig von Mises, whom I mentioned in Chapter 19 with regard to the necessity of a free market, also stressed the importance of the gold standard in keeping the

Figure 126

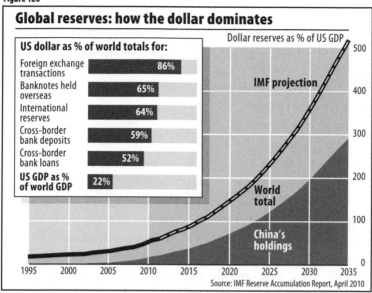

Global reserves: how the dollar dominates

Dollar reserves as % of US GDP

US dollar as % of world totals for:	
Foreign exchange transactions	86%
Banknotes held overseas	65%
International reserves	64%
Cross-border bank deposits	59%
Cross-border bank loans	52%
US GDP as % of world GDP	22%

IMF projection

World total

China's holdings

1995 2000 2005 2010 2015 2020 2025 2030 2035

Source: IMF Reserve Accumulation Report, April 2010

money supply independent of politics and in protecting against spendthrift governments.

The British economist John Maynard Keynes, whom I've also referred to several times, held very different views than Mises in many respects, being more inclined towards government intervention to help economies through lean times. Both men were in agreement, however, when it came to the importance of sound money.

Keynes was in favor of a global currency, as he made clear when helping to implement the Bretton Woods monetary system that reintroduced a form of gold standard after the Second World War. His idea of a global currency was overruled by the US, and ever since that time the US dollar has served as the unofficial international currency, its value linked initially to gold, until the Bretton Woods agreement was abandoned in 1971.

Mises considered gold to be the global currency, in effect, whereas Keynes had doubts about the suitability of gold for such a purpose, partly because of its ever-diminishing supply relative to the growth of the global economy, and the resulting inability of central banks to buy enough gold to back their currencies. Keynes was also concerned by the situation whereby a few nations could dig gold out of the ground, giving them greater influence over supplies, and therefore an advantage over those countries – the vast majority these days – that don't possess productive gold mines.

Global imbalances in currency reserves, such as the one between China and the US (in which the US effectively owes China over one trillion dollars, as explained in Chapter 12) constitute a major threat to global stability. One problem is that the value of US dollar reserves held globally as assets, being roughly equivalent to the total annual output of the US economy, far exceeds America's ability to meet those obligations.

Further devaluation of the dollar, which is very likely under these circumstances, and the subsequent reduction in the value of all dollar holdings, could lead to a rapid switch out of dollar assets and a subsequent rise in interest rates (because the risk of US default will rise). This in turn could lead to a global financial crisis far greater than the one in 2007-8, potentially wiping out a third of the world's supposed wealth, as the dollar, and all money generally, falls to its true value when measured against genuine economic wealth, as I have attempted to demonstrate in previous chapters.

A return to gold?

So the situation whereby one nation issues the *de facto* global currency, in this case the US dollar, is not good for the stability of the global economy. National priorities don't necessarily coincide with international priorities. In addition to this point, and linked to it, there has been a rapid expansion of the world's financial markets since the demise of the Bretton Woods gold standard, based on the creation of excess credit through the unchecked leveraging of accumulated wealth. The combination of these two related developments has resulted in unproductive debt creation, excessive currency speculation and volatile capital flows, leading in turn to recurring financial crises, as we have seen.

The only solution to this value-of-money problem is to restore the link between money and the underlying wealth creation of the real economy. Does this mean a return to the gold standard? I would suggest not, for the reasons cited by Keynes. Better to introduce a global currency tied in some way to the global output of genuine industry – similar in principle to the gold standard, but more generally representative of overall wealth creation rather than being linked to the value of one particular commodity.

In theory, this ought to be quite straightforward. The global currency would be issued by a global central bank, created perhaps by combining and reforming existing institutions such as the IMF, World Bank and/or the Bank for International Settlements, and would circulate in parallel with national currencies, replacing the dominant role of the US dollar.[1]

The global currency would be a stable measure of value linked to real industrial production, rather than to sovereign credit creation. This link could be provided by an index of global commodity extraction, something that would have been difficult to establish in Keynes' day, but with modern technology should be quite simple. Commodities (mineral resources, grain, timber and so on), being the raw materials of industry, are the origin of all wealth, as I have already explained. It follows that the quantity of raw materials mined or harvested bears a direct relationship to industrial production, and therefore to genuine wealth creation.

A global currency linked to such an index would represent this wealth, and as such it should become accepted as the one truly reliable store of value, unaffected by market speculation (unlike gold). National currencies would be free to float, but it would be in national interests to try to keep within a close band of the global currency. Responsible central banks would be encouraged to peg national currencies to it; less responsible governments would pay the price, as printing too much money would soon show up as inflation. Excessive and unsustainable credit creation would therefore be discouraged. Some restructuring of current debts – including at least partial default – would be required, but this will become necessary anyway.

There would obviously be many obstacles to overcome with regard to national acceptance of such a scheme, but that doesn't mean it shouldn't be aimed for. One problem would be that a global central bank would require some form of global government, and this would still have to represent national interests in some respects, while retaining independence from national political parties. Perhaps this could be some kind of council linked to the United Nations, with national or regional representatives, elected democratically at a regional level.

None of this is likely to happen without much closer co-operation between nations, of course, and the way things are at the moment, such international agreement seems unlikely, to say the least. But that doesn't alter the fact that a global marketplace requires some form of global regulation.

Globalization has already led to a reduction in the influence of national governments, not only with regard to currencies and interest rates, but also regarding taxation policies, as nations compete to attract business and unregulated transnational corporations gain ever more power.

The current situation where we have a global market for trade and finance but not for policy and regulation is, as I said earlier, inconsistent and ultimately unworkable. It was this same separation of markets from national-government policy that resulted in the failure of the Eurozone economic system. It is no good letting the global marketplace govern major aspects of our lives, when there is no global regulation of those markets.

But the answer is not to retreat from globalization, as some politicians advocate, but to embrace it fully and make it work to the advantage of the whole world, while at the same time strengthening local democracy to compensate for the reduced power of national governments.

The time has come to treat the world as one civilization, one great society. Surely this is where we've been heading these past 10,000 years or so? In this globalized world, we are all affected by events everywhere, by economic decisions taken in any region of the world. A global authority could put an end to tax havens and ensure a fairer distribution of wealth. It could also ensure that environmental issues are addressed by everyone; a process that can be reinforced at a regional or local-community level, where the real business of life takes place, and where real economic and ecological reform must begin. And, as has happened with the European Union, such a global authority could reduce the likelihood of war.

If we take away the pointless competition between nations and reduce the power and size of transnational corporations, we can ensure that there is enough work to go round, with realistic prices for scarce commodities. The key point is that regulation is kept simple and enforced effectively and fairly, and that the process is conducted democratically and openly, both locally – where democracy works best, and where it must begin – and globally. Then perhaps people will begin to feel that they can trust politicians. Because however much we dislike governments, taxation and regulation, there is no way that civilization can exist without such things.

Population trends

I mentioned earlier that one reason why the US is likely to remain the world's dominant power is because its population will retain a better balance than many nations, in terms of geographical density and the proportion of younger to older people. The US is likely to see a continued slow expansion of its population, both through natural increase and selective immigration, whereas the situation in much of the rest of the world, where populations are either set to fall (Europe, Russia, Japan) or to continue rising beyond the abilities of economies to alleviate poverty (much of Africa and parts of Asia) is less favorable.

While falling populations are a good thing with regard to

Figure 127

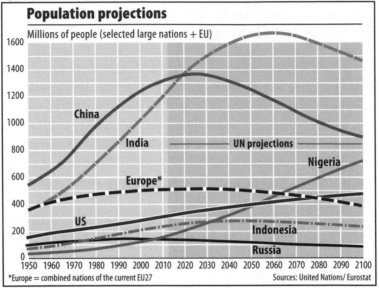

Population projections

Millions of people (selected large nations + EU)

China

India — UN projections —

Nigeria

Europe*

US

Indonesia

Russia

1950 1960 1970 1980 1990 2000 2010 2020 2030 2040 2050 2060 2070 2080 2090 2100

*Europe = combined nations of the current EU27   Sources: United Nations/ Eurostat

ecology and future sustainability, such shrinking economies face increasing problems when it comes to the ratio of tax revenues to government spending, as the proportion of wage-earning workers falls relative to the numbers that require state support in an ageing society. This is going to be a very serious problem for Europe and Japan in particular, and a big factor in their declining prosperity, as I pointed out in Chapter 13. It will, of course, help to alleviate unemployment, but at the same time it will mean having to raise the retirement age significantly so as to boost the ratio of workers to dependants. We might expect to see some revisions in immigration policies, with the more productive economies, such as Germany and Japan, welcoming younger workers from elsewhere.

As Figures 127 and 128 show, China's demographics are also less favorable than America's, as it faces the prospect of a rapid decline in fertility, brought about by its one-child policy, which, because of selective abortion, has led to a situation in which there were 118 boys born for every 100 girls in 2010, for example. For the planet as a whole, fewer people is obviously a good thing, but for China it will slow economic growth and cause other problems related to the gender imbalance.

For some nations in the poorest parts of the world, the problem is likely to be the opposite, as populations continue to expand while economies struggle to keep pace. The only consolation is that the population growth rates of the less developed regions are falling, as the effects of better education, the decline of subsistence agriculture, a growing middle class, increasing urbanization and changing priorities among the younger generations all lead to a preference for smaller families. As Figure 128 illustrates, fertility rates have been declining for several decades now.

At the same time, decreasing prosperity in the more developed regions also makes people less inclined to have large families. Economic factors can have a big influence on family-planning decisions; there is recent evidence from both Europe and the US showing a further decline in fertility rates, caused by the severity of the downturn and the fall in confidence regarding employment opportunities and future prospects generally.

But even with declining fertility rates, the global population

Figure 128

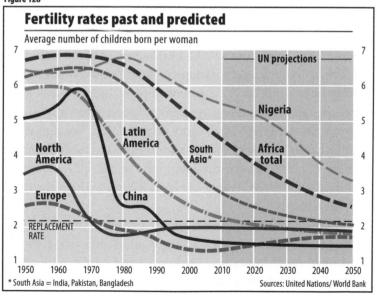

333

Figure 129

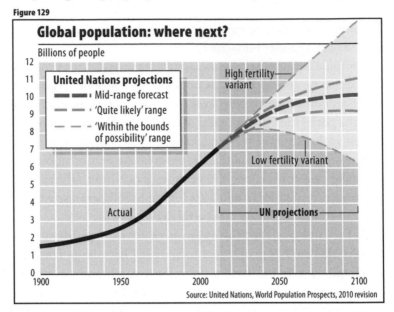

Global population: where next?

Billions of people

United Nations projections
- ■■■■ Mid-range forecast
- — — ' 'Quite likely' range
- — — - 'Within the bounds of possibility' range

High fertility variant

Low fertility variant

Actual

UN projections

Source: United Nations, World Population Prospects, 2010 revision

is set to rise further for many years to come, hitting around 10 billion before it levels off, as shown in Figure 129. This is because in the less developed regions of the world, sub-Saharan Africa especially, the rate is still well above replacement level, and also it takes at least two generations of sub-replacement birthrates before the total population begins to decline.[2]

Most of the increase would be in poor African countries and some Middle Eastern nations such as Yemen, where recent fertility rates would suggest potential population explosions to come, though some experts on demographics think the higher range of the UN forecast is unrealistic, simply because there won't be enough water or food in those regions to feed that many mouths. For this reason, the lower line of the UN projection (within the 'quite likely' range in Figure 129) is perhaps the more likely scenario.

From a global perspective, there are huge imbalances in population trends, and some of them point the wrong way in terms of where the resources are located and how the climate is likely to change if global warming continues. For example, it is conceivable that the climates of Canada and Russia might become more favorable for agriculture as temperatures rise. Combine this with the fact that these two countries are very sparsely populated while also being rich in mineral wealth, and one begins to wonder if there might not be a case for some kind of northward migration in future decades. If this sounds rather fanciful, it is worth bearing in mind that Russia faces a severe fall in population in years to come, a process that is already well under way.

Partly as a result of this trend, Russia is the only nation with large areas of underdeveloped agricultural land, brought about by a shortage of workers and lack of investment (though Brazil perhaps has more *potential* farmland[3]). After the Soviet Union collapsed, and the communist system with it, many of the collective farms and remote villages lost their state support. Farms were simply abandoned, and although these farms weren't particularly efficient by Western standards and were vulnerable to extreme weather conditions, they often produced good harvests of wheat, cotton, flax and other crops, on some of the best alluvial soils in the world.

It seems probable, and also sensible, that, as the hotter regions of the world lose fertile lands to desert, while at the same time populations in Africa and parts of Asia continue to expand, all that Russian farmland will need to be developed. We are likely to see a situation where these imbalances between resources and populations, made worse by climate change, will have to be addressed.

Perhaps a program of resettlement will be required in which farm workers from southern Asia or Africa head northwards to the wide open steppes of Russia, building new communities that can help to feed the world. Although this might seem rather unlikely the way things are at the moment, we will need to find radical solutions to the global problems that are building up right now, and making better use of the land, in terms both of sustainable agriculture and gainful employment, could well become a priority.

Revolution from the top

I have made some fairly contentious claims concerning the world's economic problems, and outlined what might appear to be radical suggestions with regard to potential solutions. If such solutions seem a little far-fetched, we should bear in mind that the system is going to change anyway, one way or another, because even if we don't end up with mass rebellion, there is likely to be a revolution of sorts as the problems become harder to ignore.

Perhaps it will come from the top. After all, it is those with the money and the power that have the most to lose when inflation hits and the value of money falls; when interest rates and loan defaults rise and stock markets plummet; when the reserve army of the unemployed gathers in the streets and the whiff of revolt drifts into the wealthy suburbs; or when more hurricanes strike wealthy coastal cities or droughts cripple more US farms.

It might seem odd to put much faith in the very people who have been cutting the workforce and investing the profits offshore, but we shouldn't blame the captains of industry for acting like selfish human beings. Most of us would probably have done the same, given half a chance.

Capitalism might be a system in decline, at least in its current form, but if combined with greater social and ecological awareness, helped by the right kind of regulation, there's no reason why the market shouldn't still form the basis of our economy. We'll still be reliant on our animal spirits, and on the entrepreneurs of this world. We should try every avenue *en route* to a more sustainable future, and that includes appealing to the better natures of the corporate élite, the real powerbrokers of this world.

Even as most US conservatives deny and ignore the evidence of global warming, others push ahead with significant environmental regulations that do actually make some difference – though nowhere near enough. If more can be done in this way, the US can still show the world the kind of useful leadership qualities it demonstrated after the Second World War, which reminds me of another Churchill quotation: 'You can always count on Americans to do the right thing – after they've tried everything else.'

Let's hope he was right, because no global initiative will work without the co-operation of the world's superpower, as we've seen in recent years with various failed attempts to tackle climate change.

We must be realistic and appeal to the baser human instincts; we must take our moral philosophy from the camp that believes we do everything out of self-interest – Hume rather than Kant, one might say. So what if we give to charity because it makes us feel better, just so long as we give? Such is human nature.

The rewards will be there for the right people. Not mere financial rewards, but something much greater: the opportunity to make a difference and gain respect. But really it is not potential leaders that we are short of in this world; rather, it is the spirit that seems to be lacking: the motivation to change the system from one in which short-term gains always come before long-term survival prospects. In the end, if future generations are to be given a chance, it will require action from all sides: a stronger message from the people, combined with a desire among those with the money and the power to do the right thing.

1 The IMF and World Bank, legacies of the Bretton Woods agreement of 1944 (as mentioned in Chapter 5), appear to be in need of reform anyway, having been much criticized in recent decades, in particular for their US-dominated, neo-liberal bias (enforcing policies of privatization and deregulation as conditions for receiving loans, for example) and their failure to understand the requirements of the poorer nations that they are supposed to be helping. Replacing them both with a single organization, more representative of the world as a whole, would make a lot of sense.
2 The replacement-level birthrate is 2.1 children per mother in developed countries and 2.3 children per mother in developing countries, the 'extra' children in the latter being required to offset infant mortality.
3 Brazil has been gradually increasing its agricultural lands by transforming vast areas of the cerrado (natural savannah-type grasslands) into pasture or arable farms, but although this has been successful in economic terms, it is less beneficial from an environmental perspective.

23 Is there a better way?

Conclusions

We appear to have reached a critical stage in the development of civilization. Having invented the internal combustion engine and the traffic jam, we have unwittingly set in motion the process of global warming, and now we must break our addiction to fossil fuels or risk the unforeseen and unpredictable consequences.

In addition to this, we have already spent some of the profits of future industry in a futile attempt at making our lives even easier, and must now make repayments out of reduced earnings, thus becoming poorer. We thought we could prosper without effort, make money from money, get something for nothing. Not surprisingly, perhaps, this turned out to be an illusion.

So now we face the daunting task of reducing our dependence on oil while at the same time distributing the world's natural wealth more evenly. Linked to this goal, we have to reverse the destructive trend towards greater financialization and the increasing concentration of power in the hands of a few dominant global corporations, which has led to a decline in real industry and to rising inequality. This will involve greater and more effective regulation, the development of renewable energy supplies and the creation of more real jobs. By this, I mean jobs in the primary and secondary sectors of the economy in particular, because, as I attempt to illustrate with my final chart (Figure 130), the root cause of the developed world's problems is that not enough people are doing the right kind of work any more.

We have to face up to this simple fact: the easy days are over. We will never again be able to achieve such a rise in material prosperity as occurred in the second half of the last century. It would be a physical impossibility to create so much wealth for so many people, even if it were desirable, which from an ecological point of view it obviously is not. The more people there are on

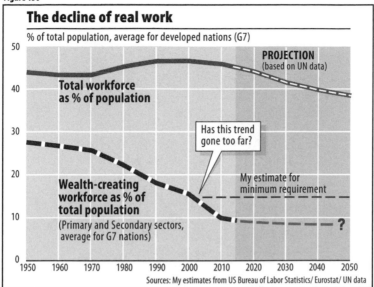

Figure 130

The decline of real work

% of total population, average for developed nations (G7)

Total workforce as % of population

PROJECTION
(based on UN data)

Has this trend gone too far?

My estimate for minimum requirement

Wealth-creating workforce as % of total population
(Primary and Secondary sectors, average for G7 nations)

?

Sources: My estimates from US Bureau of Labor Statistics/ Eurostat/ UN data

this earth, the smaller each person's allocation of the earth's natural wealth must be, especially if the rich minority continues to grab an ever bigger slice. However difficult it might seem, we have no option but to change the system.

There is the possibility of a better world than the one we are living in now – a more equal world – but it will require a change of priorities away from productivity and growth towards jobs and sustainability. It will also involve an acknowledgment that the well-being of our grandchildren is more important than immediate self-gratification, and that happiness and prosperity are not dependent on the continuous accumulation of material wealth, but rather are totally dependent on the natural wealth of the earth.

That better world will also require more co-operation between nations and a greater degree of supranational regulation – a recognition that, despite our separation of the world into developed and emerging economies, rich and poor, west and east or north and south, there is really only one world, and we are all in it together.

Ten steps towards a better world

In an attempt to balance the 10 gloomy points with which I ended Part Two, I will finish with 10 observations that at least hint at possible solutions.

1 Share the wealth more fairly

We should recognize that all wealth comes from the earth. Bearing this in mind, the most ethically sound policy, in theory at least, would be to share that wealth as evenly as possible amongst the world's population. While accepting that true equality is not possible in the real world, we should at least aim towards a fairer distribution of the world's wealth, both globally and within nations. This would obviously involve a move away from the extreme form of free-market capitalism that now dominates most advanced economies and towards what one might call market-oriented socialism, combining egalitarian principles with capitalist drive.

2 Resurrect the goal of full employment

The best way to reverse the trend to inequality is through the creation of jobs. Although some redistribution of wealth through taxation should be a part of the process, the main aim should be full employment, or as close to such a thing as possible. Work is the source of all value; it is only through work that the natural wealth of the earth can be transformed into real wealth for the people. It is only through work that we gain the opportunity to 'earn' our share of the world's wealth. We must therefore shift the focus of the economic system away from profit for the few towards jobs for the many; away from productivity and cheap goods towards sustainability and the well-being of future generations.

3 Reduce competition between nations

For free-market capitalism to work in a truly global marketplace, workers would have to be free to move to where the work is. This is of course impractical, which is one of the reasons why capitalism isn't working any more. We need to reduce the competitive element between nations so that the focus can be on creating jobs everywhere, and not just where labor is cheap and unregulated.

4 Create a global authority

Globalization is here to stay – there is no going back to nationalism and isolation. National borders are an artificial concept that should be seen as an administrative convenience rather than dividing lines between different peoples; the destiny of the human race is surely a matter for everyone. So it follows that the global marketplace requires a global authority to oversee policy and regulation, especially concerning the environment.

5 End tax havens and offshore accounting

Such a global authority could go some way to solving current problems associated with the rise of global corporations. We have seen how large transnational banks and other businesses are able to avoid national jurisdiction with regard to regulation and taxes. If world leaders can agree on certain rules regarding trade and taxation, it will be much easier to end the current practice of registering businesses in tax havens and hiding the wealth of nations in offshore bank accounts.

6 Introduce a global currency

This same global authority could also introduce and oversee a global central bank that issues a global currency – a currency that would be linked to genuine wealth creation through a commodities index, a successor to the gold standard. This would restore true value to money and remove the distortions arising from the dollar's dual role as a national and international currency. Such a global central bank could oversee a process of debt forgiveness and restructuring, while a global currency should end most of the problems associated with currency speculation.

7 Restore responsible finance

Finance should be scaled back down to a level that reflects its status as just one of several useful services; there should be less speculation and more public banks and credit unions, with real bank managers who have a stake in the local community and can get to know their customers. We can dispense with the gambling culture of the shadow banking sector, as it serves no useful purpose and is part of the problem.

8 Keep tax systems simple

While recognizing that a greater degree of regulation is necessary, it is vital to keep those rules as simple as possible. The same goes for tax systems. Complexity is bad for everyone, except perhaps lawyers and accountants. It is mostly because of excessive complexity that lawyers and accountants find ways to avoid taxes and regulations.

9 Strengthen transparency and democracy

It is essential for all government and business to be completely open and transparent, to banish all undue influence and corruption. This would require an end to the common practice in some countries of political parties being funded by private individuals and corporations, a process that favors the wealthy and encourages crony capitalism. It also means that the democratic process, as well as moving beyond national borders to encompass a global authority, should also be strengthened at a local or regional level – in the real communities, where people can make their voices heard, and where true democracy has its roots.

10 Invest in renewables, sustainable agriculture and construction

Finally, we must return to the real values of real industry by giving greater priority to the wealth-creating sectors, while at the same time recognizing the need to move away from fossil fuels and finite resources towards those raw materials that are sustainable and less damaging. By directing more of the accumulated wealth of past industry towards genuine investment in research and job creation, especially in the fields of renewable energy, organic agriculture and ecologically sound construction, and away from the current obsession with making money from money – which is ultimately impossible anyway – we will increase our chances of solving the world's problems.

•

A few words about the author (by the author)

Several people have asked me a variation of the question: 'Why should we take any notice of anything you say?'

The point being, I suppose, that I'm not distinguished in any particular field; not as a writer, not as an economist – not even as a journalist, though I've worked in journalism for over 30 years.

But the reader of course wants to know what qualifies the author to break what might appear to be new ground in such an old subject as economics. All I can say is that I stumbled across something which set me off on a line of thinking that most economists might consider too simplistic.

I studied economics in the days before it developed into a complex pseudo-science, dominated by computer models that, as we have recently seen, don't work. They don't work because economics is concerned primarily with human behavior, and we don't always do the logical thing. We don't always react in a predictable way to events: circumstances change, we learn and adapt, the world evolves. But there again, there are some fundamental principles that never change, which is of course one of the main points of my book.

My area of expertise, or the closest I come to such a thing, is the interpretation of data and the illustration of such information in graphic form, accompanied by words that preferably make some kind of sense. And for three decades this ability earned me a good wage at various British newspapers, from the *Daily Telegraph* and *The Independent* to The *Economist* and the *Financial Times,* the last during the boom years leading up to the crash.

When the continued decline of the newspaper industry led to my third redundancy, I quit the business altogether and moved with my family to rural France, where I renovated our farmhouse and attempted, without much success, to make a living from painting. It helped, I think, to get away from the city, to live amongst the farmers and get a feel for a kind of life that most people don't really see any more – the kind of life where people go quietly about their business, oblivious to the roar of the rat race and the madness of the media. The kind of life, in fact, that most of the world lived, until recently.

But it doesn't really matter what I've done in my life. What matters to the reader is this book. Does it make sense? And, even if it does make sense, will it make a difference?

Sources and inspiration

I've read a great deal over the years that must have contributed to this book in some way; far too much to list or even to remember. A couple of classics come to mind, however: *The Affluent Society* by JK Galbraith, and the somewhat more radical *Small is Beautiful* by EF Schumacher.

I have made much use of the online databases of various organizations, from the American Bureau of Labor Statistics to the World Bank: all source material used for this book is as quoted in the text, or on the charts. I have done my best to verify data and be as accurate as possible, but it must be accepted that not all statistics are particularly true. Some might even be damned lies.

INDEX